Environmental Advertising in China and the USA

T0330833

Since the late 1980s, green consumerism has been hailed in the West as an efficient solution to environmental problems. However, Chinese consumers have been slow to warm up to eco-friendly products. Consumers prefer SUVs to hybrid cars, health supplements and snake oil medicines to organic foods, and eco-fashion is still secluded in high-end designer studios. These choices contradict the findings of many sustainable lifestyle surveys that claim to register a rising desire for green products among the Chinese.

This book examines the psycho-cultural differences that disrupt the translation of "eco-friendly" appeals to China by analyzing environmental advertising. It explores the different notions of "green", the structures of desire that underlies the advertisements, and how they are shaped by ideological, cultural, and historical differences. Rather than arguing the superiority of the American or Chinese version of green consumerism, the book interrogates the role of advertising in the global spread of Western ideologies and explores the possibilities for consumers to resist transnational corporate hegemony in the green movement.

This book fills an important gap in the critical scholarship on green marketing and should be of interest to students and scholars of environment studies, green advertising and marketing, environmental communication and media studies, China studies and environmental sociology, ethics and cultural studies.

Xinghua Li is Assistant Professor of Media Studies at Babson College, Massachusetts, USA. She writes about the global spread of consumer capitalism through the perspectives of psychoanalysis, environmental communication, and critical media theory.

Routledge Studies in Environmental Communication and Media

Environmental Advertising in China and the USA

The desire to go green

Xinghua Li

LONDON AND NEW YORK

First published 2016
by Routledge

2 Park Square, Milton Park, Abingdon, Oxfordshire OX14 4RN
711 Third Avenue, New York, NY 10017

Routledge is an imprint of the Taylor & Francis Group, an informa business

First issued in paperback 2018

British Library Cataloguing in Publication Data
A catalogue record for this book is available from the British Library

Library of Congress Cataloging in Publication Data
Names: Li, Xinghua (College teacher)
Title: Environmental advertising in China and the USA : desire to go green /
Xinghua Li.
Description: New York, NY : Routledge, 2016. | Series: Routledge studies in
environmental communication and media | Includes bibliographical
references.
Identifiers: LCCN 2015020521| ISBN 9780415744133 (hb) |
ISBN 9781315797373 (e-book)
Subjects: LCSH: Green marketing--United States. | Green marketing--
China. | Green products--United States. | Green products--China. |
Advertising--United States. | Advertising--China.
Classification: LCC HF5413 .L5 2016 | DDC 659.13/1--dc23
LC record available at http://lccn.loc.gov/2015020521

ISBN: 978-0-415-74413-3 (hbk)
ISBN: 978-0-367-02682-0 (pbk)

Typeset in Times New Roman
by Taylor & Francis Books

To My Parents,
Who inspired this book in more ways than one

Contents

Acknowledgements

This acknowledgement is a perfect testament to the limitation of human memory. Only a small portion of the people who have helped me is mentioned here. If you cannot find your name here, please remember: the unconscious never forgets and the support you offered me has become a part of me and will remain indelible in my mind, forever.

First, Chapter 1 and 2 of this book are derived from my doctoral dissertation *Communicating the "Incommunicable Green:" A Comparative Study of the Structures of Desire in Environmental Advertising in the United States and China* (2010). I would like to thank my dissertation committee from the University of Iowa: Professors John Durham Peters, David Hingstman, Kembrew McLeod, Judy Polumbaum, and David Wittenberg. Under the supervision of these brilliant professors—especially Professor John Durham Peters, my fabulous dissertation advisor and advisor for life—I completed the first 55,000-word marathon of my academic career.

I would like to thank Babson College's BFRF (Babson Faculty Research Fund) for funding my three archival research trips to China between 2011 and 2014. Without the continued support from BFRF, this book would not be here now.

My editor and friend, Lucas Freeman, deserves huge thanks for editing all six chapters of this book and providing me with structuring advice and ideas. Thank you for "unstuck" me during moments of thought congestion. You are my "thought plumber."

My old and new friends—Dan Vandersommers, Jody Hepperly, Carol Gignoux, Dana Riechman, and Sarah Birgé—thank you for letting me pick your brains during the different stages of the book and offering me insightful suggestions.

My gratitude also goes toward my colleagues at Babson College: Professors Fritz Fleischmann, Steve Collins, James Hoopes, and Kevin Bruyneel, thank you for your timely help with the book's proposal and contract acquisition; Professors Blake Pattridge, Mary Godwyn, Kandice Hauf, and Kathleen Kelly, you were wonderful for providing feedback for my BFRF grant proposals; and Professors Melissa Manwaring and Cheryl Kirschner, your professional opinions about the copyright issue regarding the use of images in this book were highly valuable.

My appreciation also goes to the editors and editorial assistants at Routledge-Earthscan. Your professionalism, commitment, and patience for bearing with me during my family emergency and my rookie practices allowed me to do my best.

Finally, Ryan Meyer and Natalie Allen Benson, I cannot overstate how important you are to me. You are my family in the United States. Thank you for giving me love and support during the past years and the many years to come.

And my parents—Li Jian and Sun Ximei—thank you for creating me and, particularly, for helping me create this book. Although you do not speak English, you inspired me numerous times with your stories, worldviews, and deliciously cooked food. They made me think about the relationship between desire, environment, consumption, and history, which became the themes of this book. During the last two years of my writing process, Mother suffered a stroke but luckily survived. She is now slowly recovering day by day and is diligently learning English (perhaps in hopes of being able to read this book in the near future). Congratulations, Mother and Father, for bouncing back from this hardship. Your experience convinces me that, as long as time is given, we can always adapt to the environment—no matter how hostile it is—and re-find the path to a good life.

How to Access Advertisements in this Book

Due to copyright concerns, advertisements analyzed in this book are published not alongside the text, but on the author's private blog: "Environmental Advertising in China and the USA." Please visit this book's official publisher website (http://www.routledge.com/books/details/9780415744133/) to obtain the URL address for this private blog. Or, a simple web search of the blog title can help the reader locate the address.

This private blog belongs to the author alone and does not connect to Routledge-Earthscan. It contains over eighty images for the print, television, and online ads analyzed in this book. The author strongly recommends the reader to view these images, which will provide more vivid understanding of the following analysis.

1 Introduction

Advertising, Desire, and the Environment

In 2006, when I was still a graduate student in the US, I watched Al Gore's *An Inconvenient Truth*. It predicted that imminent global warming disasters would put many cities, including my hometown Shanghai, in danger of complete inundation. Terrified, I called my parents in China, urging them to move. Seemingly unfazed, my father responded: "Don't worry, we live on the 11th floor, we'll survive." My mother chimed in: "It's great that your uncle lives on the 10th floor in the next building. We can just buy a boat to visit him!" My parents' mocking angered me. What upset me more, however, was that I sensed something profoundly incommunicable in the apocalyptic anxiety I was experiencing. Having lived in the US for several years, I was familiar with the Western apocalyptic narrative in science fiction novels and disaster movies, and thus had no difficulty imagining a global-scale environmental catastrophe. But since the apocalypse genre is absent from Chinese traditional belief systems and narrative traditions, it was difficult for my parents, who rarely watched Hollywood movies, to imagine the world ending. Moreover, my warning came at perhaps the worst time in their lives for them to take it seriously: after half a lifetime of poverty and political repression, my parents finally achieved their long overdue "good life" and bought their first property. For my father, the 11th floor condo was his pride and joy and it elevated them away from the problems of ground-level flooding below. On what grounds could I demand that they give up their hard-earned "right" because of a distant risk that they could not envision?

This particular gap in my parents' imagination – a prevalent gap among the Chinese – gave me serious pause for thought. What would motivate Chinese consumers to be concerned about the environment? How do they imagine the environmental crisis differently from Americans and, to what extent do these differences owe to the cultural, ideological, and historical conditions of these two countries? What role do media and communication play in shaping these consumers' desire for environmental change? As consumerism spreads globally, is there an ethical way to resolve the conflict between the desire to consume and the urgency to preserve the environment? These are the questions that motivated this book, questions that interrogate the relationship between media, desire, and consumerism in the face of the global environmental crisis.

In a nutshell, this book conducts a cross-cultural comparison of environmental advertising in China and the US. I target advertising for its ubiquity in the public sphere and as an institution that notoriously manufactures consumer desire. Named by Raymond Williams (1980) as the "magic system," advertising manifests the fantasies and dreams of a society and produces interesting artifacts for examining the relationship between media discourse, social imagination, and collective desire. Similarly, environmental advertising functions as an object for revealing a society's collective imagination vis-à-vis environmental threats and remediation. The term "environmental advertising," when defined broadly, refers to advertising that contains environmental messages or promotes pro-environmental attitudes and behaviors. This includes a wide variety of public discourses, such as NGO public service announcements, governmental propaganda, corporate image campaigns, and green product advertising, among others. This book defines the term narrowly as commercial advertising that promotes eco-friendly products and services to consumers. Also known as "green" advertising, it aims to propagate green consumerism – the market solution to mitigate humans' environmental impact by having them purchase ecofriendly products and services. Originated in the US (and Europe) in the late 1980s, green consumerism has been widely hailed by Western marketers as an effective solution to environmental problems. In the new millennium, it has evolved into an international phenomenon and has gained global hegemonic status as a corporate-led, commerce-driven environmental movement. Environmental advertising, as an important aspect of this movement, both shapes and bears witness to how consumer culture responds to environmental crises.

The US and China are the world's two largest consumer economies and top greenhouse gas contributors. By bringing these two countries into a dialogue, I seek to understand the driving forces of these important consumer cultures and explore the political, ideological, and historical differences that underlie their environmental endeavors (or lack thereof). As previously stated, Western environmental media often use apocalyptic appeals to motivate the audience, but China's civil religion lacks an imaginary anticipation of the End of the World. Can an environmental apocalypse occur in a country that does not believe in the "apocalypse"? As my research later reveals, Chinese-American cultural differences also exist on other significant fronts, including individual identity, family structures, social and class relations, historical attitudes, religious traditions, educational philosophies, and so on. These differences have contributed to the profound disjunction in the understanding of "green" between these respective national audiences and could disrupt the cross-national translation of environmental messages. Many of these differences can be readily observed, as I intend to demonstrate, in environmental advertising.

In Western academic literature and mass media, green advertising and green marketing has been a heated topic of discussion. The main debate takes place between marketing scholars (e.g. McIntosh 1991, Hailes 1998, Prothero 2000, Scott & Peñaloza 2006), who believe that green marketing is a progressive movement that raises the public's environmental consciousness, and cultural critics (e.g. Smith 1998, Monbiot 2002, Meister & Brown 2006, Williams 2007), who see it as a profitable but dubious effort to "greenwash" the public and perpetuate wasteful consumer behaviors. However, both sides of the debate share a commonality: they are mainly concerned with the "external" effects of green advertising on consciousness raising or behavior changing and tend to ignore the "internal" questions of desire, subjectivity, and ethics. This book employs a critical interpretive method informed by psychoanalysis to supplement this lack. Psychoanalysis is known for its conceptualization of desire through the notion of the *unconscious*. As I will later elaborate, the unconscious problematizes the assumption of a rational, sovereign subject that will take rightful actions after its consciousness is raised; it also challenges the assumption of a passive, controllable subject that will alter its conduct after the right "behavior buttons" are pushed. Psychoanalysis speaks of the *subject of the unconscious*, who is radically divided from consciousness and its immanent social conditions. This division, inflicted by human symbolic actions, is what constitutes desire, the psychic force that propels our actions. It is also, for psycho-analysis, the very foundation of ethics. The job of the critic in my position, therefore, is to read the structure of desire embedded in symbolic texts (i.e. envir-onmental advertising) and identify the pathologies manifested as "irrational" interruptions in the preordained "consciousness-behavior" formula. During the past two decades, psychoanalysis has been increasingly applied to the analysis of environmental problems. Critics (e.g. Killingsworth & Palmer 1995; Giblett 1997; 2008; 2009; 2011; Lertzman 2008; Dodds 2011) identify an inextricable link between desire – a fundamental psychic lack – and the social and ecological imbalance that plagues the modern world. Insisting on the continuity between mind, society, and ecology, my book extends the psychoanalytic framework via a cross-cultural comparative study and explores the pathologies of desire manifested in and through Chinese and American "green" advertising.

China's Consumerist Boom and Environmental Crisis

To explore the relationship between desire, consumerism, and environment, one cannot overlook contemporary, urbanizing China. With a population of 1.4 billion, China is the world's fastest-growing major economy, with an average growth rate of 10 percent over the past thirty years (IMF 2013). Since the 1990s, the country has jumped-started its growth by applying low-cost labor and abundant resources to the manufacturing of exported goods. As its economy grows, the "world factory" is turning into the "world market." Nationwide, more and more people experienced an unprecedented income rise and started to use their newfound wealth to fulfill the long-standing desire for consumer goods. Smith (1997) enumerated the most wanted household commodities in China, which had evolved from "a wrist-watch, a radio set, a bicycle and a sewing machine" in the 1960s and 1970s, to "a color television, refrigerators, tape recorders and automatic washing machines" in the mid-1980s and 1990s, and to "air-conditioners, video recorders, motorcycles, and [even] the ultimate status symbols – a private car and a house" towards the new millennium (4). Among the different social strata, the most prominent group of consumers is the urban middle class. Estimated to be around 300 million in 2012, and to rise to 700 or 800 million by 2022, these new economic elites function as the pillar of China's consumer economy (Barton 2013). Many have the buying power to emulate affluent Western lifestyles, and have developed a voracious appetite for real estate and various types of modern consumer goods, including cars, electronics, fashion, food, luxury, vacation, etc. (Doctoroff 2013).

The rapid rise in domestic consumer demands, driven by a longing for a Westernized and modernized "good life," has taken a heavy toll on China's environment. Everywhere, forests and farmland are being converted into luxury condos and shopping malls; the rise in automobile ownership installs the perennial and noxious smog in the city atmosphere; rivers and streams are replete with wastewaters from factories that churn out thousands of pieces of new clothing daily; the soil is chockfull of pesticides and growth stimulants from excessive industrial farming. China's consumer revolution also has global implications. In Africa and South America, Chinese industries are expanding their extraction of energy resources and raw materials; its polluted air and waters have reportedly flowed to its Asian-Pacific neighbors and its trash has washed up as far away as the California coast; but more importantly, in 2008, China surpassed the US to become the world's current largest carbon dioxide emitter. Its obstinate use of coal does not show any sign of slowing down and neither, therefore, does the process of global warming. Elizabeth Economy (1999) calls it China's "Faustian bargain:" while the country opted for economic growth and improved living standards, it had also agreed to trade away its own environment and that of the world.

However, it seems unfair to be blaming merely the Chinese for pursuing their age-old aspirations. Having long been deprived of material wealth, the Chinese have historically yearned for the affluent lifestyles of the West and recently of its economically developed Asian neighbors. Zhao (1997) calls it the "window effect," where developed nations display their high living standards in front of the developing countries and generate their desire to emulate. This "window effect" did not occur in China accidentally. In large part, it owed to the orchestrated efforts of cross-cultural marketing and advertising that dates back to the nineteenth century. According to O'Barr (2007), Western advertising had entered China after the Opium War of 1842 when large coastal cities were forced to foreign trade. "Western products in shops attracted both the curious just to gawk and the wealthy to purchase some modern item" (Laing 2004, 2, quoted in O'Barr 2007). Along with Western products came advertising in the form of "signboards, posters, black-and-white newspaper ads, and colorful advertising calendars" (O'Barr 2007). Prospering in major coastal cities during the early twentieth century, foreign advertising planted the seeds of desire for Western products in Chinese minds. After China's economic reform at the end of 1970s, these desires were rekindled. In 1980s and 1990s, multinational advertising agencies set offices in large cities such as Shanghai and Guangzhou and successfully promoted new waves of Western goods (fast food, gum, sneakers, cars, etc.) to the Chinese (O'Barr 2007). To a large extent, it was international trade and marketing – initiated by developed nations – that had taught the Chinese to desire and consume like the First World.

But it might be too late to point fingers. The predicament of climate change is too pressing. What would happen if the 1.4 billion Chinese all started to live high-consumption lifestyles? This is the question that captured a group of Western authors who became deeply concerned about China's raging consumerism. In *When A Billion Chinese Jump* (2010), Jonathan Watts fears that the demands of a billion Chinese bent on becoming prosperous consumers could "knock the world off its axis." Although the West had invented industrialization, Watts writes, its negative environmental impact was confined to a handful of small countries and was relatively local. When China takes up the unsustainable model of the West, it induces a global game-changer as it amplifies the potential environmental disaster by both scale and speed. Karl Gerth, in his similarly provocative *As China Goes, So Goes the World* (2010), points out that China's booming consumerism will certainly accelerate the opportunities for multinationals such as GM, McDonald's, and Starbucks, but it will also initiate a new tidal waves of global challenges, especially to the environment.

Hence the question: How to motivate the Chinese to be concerned about the environment and change their current patterns of consumption? Many invest their hope in green consumerism – "the use of individual consumer preference to promote less environmentally damaging products and services" (Irvine 1989, 2). The commerce-driven solution places advertising and marketing right at the center of the green revolution. Ironically, advertising, the stimulator of consumer desire and the potential contributor to the environmental crisis, now has taken up a new role and become the primary means of disseminating environmental messages. According to cultural critic Sut Jhally (2000), modern advertising emerged alongside industrial capitalism, with the goal to stimulate market demand. As industrialization quickened the speed of production, massive quantities of goods were churned out and far exceeded what societies could previous consume. To ensure that commodities speedily "go through the circuit of distribution, exchange and consumption," the advertising industry attaches fantasies and wish fulfillment to material objects, which effectively disintegrates after purchase (Jhally 2000, 185). This practice keeps consumers permanently under-satisfied and desiring, which fuels the capitalistic economy of mass production and mass consumption. The ecological impact of this system is grave: it has led to worldwide environmental degradation, resource shortage, and especially, climate change. In the documentary *Advertising and The End of the World* (1997), Jhally suggests that consumer society look into the future of the human race and start shifting its direction before it is too late. But he adds that, the current commander of consumer culture – advertising – is incapable of stimulating this social change. "The time-frame of advertising is very short-term," writes Jhally (2000), "it does not encourage us to think beyond the immediacy of present sensual experience [and the] value of a collective social future does not, and will not, find expression within our commercially dominated culture." However, the rise of green marketing seems to undermine Jhally's point. Since the end of the 1980s, the Western advertising industry has started to withdraw from its hedonistic discourse and began to promote "long-term," "collective" interests. Environmental sustainability became one among many "ethical" values that corporations now tout in their annual reports and PR campaigns. So, has Jhally been proven wrong? Or should we not celebrate this advertising's "prodigal return" too quickly?

The Rise of Green Marketing in the US

The scheme of green marketing has been brewing since the heyday of the American environmental movement. In 1975, the American Marketing Association (AMA) held the first workshop on "ecological Marketing." In 1988, the first green consumer guide was published in the US, signaling to many the rise of green consumerism. *Advertising Age*, the flagship magazine of the American advertising industry, began to hold annual Green Marketing Summits since 1991. Since the end of 1980s, "eco-friendly" claims started to appear on product packages. Over the next three decades, green marketing has evolved into a multi-layered promotional culture, including product advertisements, corporate image campaigns, public service announcements, and lifestyle journalism. It resorts to a wide range of appeals, such as ecological harmony, social equality, civic responsibility, individual wellbeing, among others. In commercial media and business literatures, green marketing has received many accolades. Supporters not only valorize it for fostering eco-friendly consumption habits, but also praise its track record in raising the public's environmental awareness. For example, Hailes (1998) argues that green advertising uses the corporations' international prestige to "green the consciousness" of the Americans. Calfee (1998) suggests that advertising is a good medium for environmental communicators to outreach to the public, as "its mastery of the art of brevity, its ability to command attention, and its use of television" touch the population that scientific communities or governmental agencies are desperate to reach. Prothero (2000) compares green advertising and environmental news and argues that the latter always "polarize and simplify the ongoing debate concerning sustainability" and that the former "can be used just as successfully by those seeking to achieve environmental enlightenment as it can for those who aspire to ecological martyrdom" (46).

From a traditionally hedonistic medium to an allegedly responsible one, the apparent renaissance of advertising did not take place in a historical vacuum. Its emergence and popularization can be traced to three social movements occurring in the US since the 1960s and 1970s: the environmental movement in the political realm, the neoliberal movement in the economic realm, and the New Age movement in the religious and cultural realm. First of all, green marketing rose out of the context of American environmentalism. Emerging from nineteenth century transcendentalism and early twentieth century preservationism and conservationism, the environmental movement took center stage in national politics in the 60s and 70s (Cox 2012). The publication of landmark books such as *Silent Spring* (Carson 1962), *The Population Bomb* (Ehrlich 1968), and *The Limits to Growth* (Club of Rome 1974) drew attention to the impact of industrialization on the environment and, as a result of vigorous political struggles, led to legislative breakthroughs such as the Clean Water Act, Clean Air Act, Endangered Species Act, and the National Environmental Policy Act. Having watched a few decades of news about ozone-layer depletion, oil spills, and overflowing landfills, the nation developed a "general fear of an ecological crisis and a public willingness to act" (Smith 1998, 97). This widespread fear and anxiety paved the way for green marketing, which promised to restore the ecological and social harmony compromised by modern technology and industrial capitalism.

The second condition for the emergence of green marketing was the global spread of neoliberalism. During the 1980s, waves of economic liberalization swept around the world. Nation after nation saw the privatization of state enterprises, deregulation of private businesses, and reduction of governmental welfare programs (Herman and McChesney 1997). These changes contributed to the cross-border expansion of multinational corporations and the rise of a highly integrated global economy. What informed this shift in political economy was the free-market ideology, which believes that "the market allocates resources efficiently and provides the means of organizing economic (and perhaps all human) life" (Herman and McChesney 35). Guided by this ideology, corporations gave birth to a series of new business strategies, ranging from the corporate social responsibility movement (a form of corporate self-regulation to preempt governmental intervention), social marketing (commercial marketing that claims to promote public good), and a whole business ethics industry from "corporate ethics programs, university and college centers, socially responsible investment, [to] the consulting industry" (Neimark 1995, 84). Environmental issues consistently remain among the top agenda of business ethics, which also include public health and social development (Andreasen 1995).

The third spring for green marketing was the so-called New Age spiritual movement. This movement drew from an eclectic mix of older world religions such as Buddhism, Chinese folk religions, Hinduism, and Native American spirituality (Melton 1989). Taking form during the American counterculture movements, the New Age philosophy opposes Cartesian dualism and promotes connectivity. It emphasizes the sanctity of the Earth and Nature while upholding the importance of spirituality and magic (Scott and Peñaloza 2006). Neo-Paganism, one of New Age's most important components, challenges the Christian mandate to "dominate and subdue" nature and the "instrumental, cause-and-effect ways of capitalism and Newtonian science" (60). On multiple levels, New Age philosophy echoes the morals of the environmental movement and is often adopted as a spiritual remedy for the traumas inflicted by modern industrialization. Many of its terms – e.g. harmony, balance, connectivity, health, and wellbeing – were appropriated by green marketing and became popular lingo in commercial publications. In short, green marketing built up its discursive elements by assimilating catchphrases and popular imaginaries from various strands of discourse like environmentalism (e.g. "nature," "environment," "ecology"), neoliberalism (e.g. "business ethics," "corporate social responsibility"), and New Age philosophy (e.g. "harmony," "balance," "spirituality"). However, the symbolic structures with which these words and images are organized, as I will later show, often diverge from their original contexts.[1]

The Introduction of Green Marketing in China

Green marketing received a warm welcome upon its introduction in China. In 1992, marketing scholars from Mainland China attended an international conference in Hong Kong and learned about the term for the first time. They strongly recommended this Western novelty to the government and entrepreneurs and published ample literature on the subject. Over the next two decades, the concept of green marketing seeped from academic theory into governmental propaganda and business practices. Li Rongqing (2006) divides the process into three stages: the inception (1993–1994), when the importance of green marketing was first put forward for academic and governmental discussion; the growth stage (1995–1997), when academic discussions focused on the international "green trade barriers" and the negative effect it had on China's export trade; and the maturation stage (1998–2006), when the discussion broadened to the whole field of green economy (including consumption, distribution, and marketing) and green business practices began receiving more governmental support (96).

The Chinese government readily adopted the idea of green marketing as it promised to solve the country's urgent conflict between economic growth and environmental protection. Since the economic reform at the end of 1970s, numerous environmental complaints had risen from residents of the urbanized coastal zones (Dasgupta & Wheeler 1996). During the early 1990s, the first nationwide environmental controversy unfolded around the construction of the Three Gorges Dam, a controversial hydroelectric project with massive environmental and human cost (Jing 1997). Meanwhile, social conflicts intensified along with environmental degradation. Following Deng's slogan "let a group of people get rich first," economic growth had ended the previously flat social structure – a heritage of Mao's egalitarianism – and created a gap between the "new winners" (e.g. entrepreneurs, educated professionals, and technocrats) and the "new losers" (e.g. the urban unemployed, underemployed state-owned factory workers, and peasants displaced by mammoth hydroelectric projects) (Lu and Simons 2006). Environmental deterioration deepened social inequality, as many of the direct environmental victims were rural residents, whose homes often became the dumping grounds for industrial waste, or the workers, who were at the front lines of toxic chemical exposure before the consumers.

In 2005, President Hu Jingtao put forward a new political slogan at the National People's Congress: "Building a Harmonious Society." The phrase aimed to direct China away from single-minded economical development towards an overall societal and environmental balance. In 2006, the Party incorporated the goal of "sustainable development" into the Eleventh Five-Year Plan. It proclaimed its aims were to "save resources, develop circular economies, protect ecological environments and speed up the building of a resource-saving, environmentally-friendly society" ("Sustainable Development," China.com.cn, 2006). The political milieu was highly conducive to the promotion of green marketing. Aligning with the governmental rhetoric of "harmonious society" and "sustainable development," Wei Mingxia and Si Lingsheng (2001) define green marketing as:

> Under the demand of sustainable development, bearing the goal of assuming social responsibilities, protecting the environment, efficient use of resources, and long term development, entrepreneurs take corresponding measures in the whole process of product design, production, sales, after-sale service, in order to ensure the three-way balance among consumer's sustainable consumption, industry's sustainable production, and society's sustainable development.

Since its inception, green marketing was promoted as a part of the official sustainability discourse as a hegemonic strategy to appease social and environmental conflicts.

Compared to the speedy endorsement from the government, Chinese businesses were however slow to adopt green marketing. Writing in the beginning of the millennium, Si (2002) observed a very underdeveloped and unbalanced green market. Most businesses had not learned about this latest marketing strategy, and the ones that had learned feared the high risk and cost of developing new products. Many still adopted backwards production and distribution methods that were far from meeting the government's environmental standards. But more importantly, according to Ren Zhixiang (2007), businesses lacked the motivation to "go green" because of a basic lack of consumer demand for green products. Due to these reasons, mainland scholars envisioned a different future for China's green marketing. While they partially adopted the Western neoliberal model in solving environmental crises with market forces, they did not believe that the market itself had the power to jumpstart a green economy. Many scholars have laid the responsibility on the government, who they believe should take a leadership role and educate the public about the importance of ethical consumption. For instance, Ren (2007) proposes that the government should use extensive propaganda to enhance the "green consciousness" of the consumers, which he believes to be the precondition for behavior change. Similarly, Lv Huicong and Yan Jun (2003) distrust businesses' ability to initiate a structural shift in a market economy and envision a "government-led" green revolution that includes the environmental education of the public, the stipulation of environmental laws, and the innovation of green technologies.

Scholars from Hong Kong, on the other hand, saw a more complex social network that should be involved in leading the green movement. Chan and Lau (2004) lay responsibility on the green marketers, who they believe should "increase their investment in consumer education so as to further raise the environmental consciousness of their target customers" (307). They also believe that marketers should establish wider collaboration by "sponsoring environmental education in schools, and forming alliances with the government and/or environmental groups to promote the ethics of "green" consumption through various propaganda vehicles, such as television and radio broadcasts, exhibitions and seminars" (307). Chan and Lau's vision has largely come true. In the new millennium, business interests enlisted a broad range of support to promote green consumption among the Chinese: environmental NGOs (e.g. Greenpeace China, Friends of Nature's "Green Choice Project" in 2006) hosted press conferences and consumer seminars about the importance of sustainable consumption; trade organizations (e.g. the Sustainability Consortium) and foreign governmental development programs (e.g. EuropeAid's SWITCH-Asia Program) sponsored Green Expos and Green Consumer Fairs to showcase the latest products in the market; international advertising agencies (e.g. Ogilvy & Mather, GlobeScan) or multinational corporations (e.g. Dupont, L'Oreal) conducted green lifestyle surveys and offered marketing strategies for doing green businesses in China. Among these endeavors, the most prominent interest comes from foreign multinationals. According to Fei Xue and Peiqin Zhou (2012), the majority of the environmental advertisements in China are sponsored by foreign brands; it shows that "international advertisers are currently leading the way in China's green movement" (11). In the new millennium, green marketing has become a new avenue for multinationals to potentially "cash in" on China's economic development – in spite of, or because of, its environmental deterioration.

To the marketers' disappointment, nevertheless, these promotional efforts have not reaped satisfying rewards. The majority of Chinese consumers – even the wealthy urban middle class – are still slow in adopting eco-friendly products and services (Ren 2007). To the present day, Chinese car buyers are watching hybrid electric vehicles from the sidelines while choosing to drive home SUVs; many food consumers prefer to spend money on health supplements or snake-oil medicines than on organic foods; environmentally friendly fashion is still secluded in high-end designer studios and is far from entering the mass market. These choices seem to contradict the findings of many sustainable market studies, which claim to register a rising desire for green products among the Chinese. For instance, the 2009 Greendex Survey, sponsored by the National Geographic Society in the US and Globescan Inc. in Canada studied green consumer behavior in 17 countries and claimed that Chinese consumers were among the most concerned about the environment, with 81 percent of respondents willing to pay more for energy-saving products (Kan 2010). In 2012, DuPont China Green Living Survey found "a growing awareness and desire among urban Chinese consumers for green products" and that "a majority are likely to purchase apparel, personal care, hygiene and household products made from bio-based ingredients that offer environmental benefits" (Dupont.com 2012). Similarly, a 2013 study by CCN, China's largest consumer service website, hosted by China Consumer Journal and China Consumer Association, claimed that "90% consumers are willing to pay for sustainable products" and "almost 70% are willing to pay 10% more and 6% are willing to 50% more" (Ren 2013). If so many Chinese have expressed interest in green products, as the studies suggest, why don't they match it up with purchasing behavior?

According to OgilvyEarth (the sustainability branch of the global advertising agency Ogilvy & Mather), this problem is called the "green gap." It refers to the discrepancy between "what consumers say they are doing around sustainably and what they are actually doing" (Ogilvy & Mather 2011). Based on an ethnographic study of 24 families in Shanghai, Tianjin and Wuxi, and a nationwide survey of 1,300 respondents, the O&M report "Get Going with Green" (Sinha & Griffiths 2011) identifies a series of behavioral obstacles that have prevented the Chinese consumers from "buying green." For example, the Chinese often see environmental problems as the responsibility of the government and, to some extent, that of corporations rather than individuals (Ogilvy & Mather 2011). Also, they generally view sustainability practices "as too costly, too inconvenient and therefore unrealistic and impractical for the lives of 'normal' people" (Ogilvy & Mather 2011). In its sister report "Mainstream Green" (Graceann & Williams 2011), researchers point out that this "green gap" is not just a Chinese phenomenon; it also affects many Americans, who seem to have developed pro-environmental attitudes but fail to adopt the purchasing behavior. To close the "green gap," the reports identify a series of strategies for marketers to overcome these barriers, including "mainstream, not model," "products, not policy," "everyday, not just Earth Day," "personal, not planet," "choice, not constraint," etc. (Sinha & Griffiths 78). Overall, the two reports recommend China and the US to take "more similar than different" steps, which "require individual thinking and local action played out on a global scale" (Graceann & Williams 17).

Albeit illuminating, this notion of the "green gap" leaves much to be *desired* (pun intended). First of all, this concept is nothing new: it echoes the "attitude-behavior gap," which social scientists often use to explain the public's inaction toward environmental crises (Kollmuss & Agyeman 2002). Second, this notion of an "attitude-behavior gap" derives from a flawed model of the human mind. It presumes its normative unity and conceptualizes its failure (in coordinating attitude and behavior) as the result of certain contingent and external factors that could be eliminated ("barriers to action"). According to psychoanalyst Renee Lertzman (2011), "the idea of a 'gap' is based on a conception of human psychology that is strongly behavioral and indeed, rationalistic." But the world of consumer psychology is much more complex. Far from being a unified entity, the human mind is full of contradictory impulses and desires and their inner conflicts cannot be reduced to the mere appearance of faulty behavior. As Lertzman (2011) points out, oftentimes, people's seeming "inaction" or "apathy" toward the environmental crisis might be masking deeper struggles in the psyche:

> [A] lack of action or follow-through can be easily the result of deeply conflicting desires woven into our identities, relationships, lifestyles and social networks. Or the result of contradictory pushes and pulls – desires for objects we know are not green, or practices we know are contributing to the larger problems. Throw in some guilt or anxiety – news about a tsunami or severe weather events – and things get even more complicated and less straight forward. Anxieties and fears can seize us up, and lead to a sense of profound powerlessness and overwhelm (para. 6).

Following Lertzman, I argue that Chinese (and American) consumers' hesitancy toward purchasing green products also suggest inner conflicts and ambivalences that are not easily accessible through face-to-face surveys or behavioral observations. Their "inaction" should not be treated as behavioral obstacles to circumvent, but should be read as manifestations of deeper psychosocial problems that have been embedded in consumer culture. The right direction to go, thus, is to turn toward the "internal" question of desire and subjectivity. Moreover, as we move away from the "external" question of behavior, we are able to realize the ideological underpinning of the corporate pursuit of behavior change: that it prescribes consumption as the universal solution to the ecological crisis and sees "buying green" as a panacea to global environmental problems. However, the environmental efficacy of green consumerism is highly uncertain. The next section will review the literature that has called it into question.

Backlash against Green Marketing in the US

Aside from the challenges that green consumerism faces in China, it has been criticized in the US for its dubious role in environmental improvement. The first group of critics, among the three that I identify, disputes the accuracy of green advertising claims. During the early stage of American green marketing, false claims flooded the market. Kangun, Carlson, and Grove (1991) sampled 250 green ads and found that 58 percent of them contained misleading or deceptive claims. In *Toxic Sludge Is Good for You!* (1995), Stauber and Rampton probed underneath corporations' public relations campaigns to uncover their hidden environmentally destructive practices. Such corporate abuse of green claims was called "greenwashing," a term coined by Jay Westerveld in 1986 to describe hotels' practice of putting green placards in their rooms. To control fact falsification in green advertising, the Federal Trade Commission started to enforce regulations on advertising's environmental claims in 1996. But since then, corporate "greenwashing" took on more sophisticated forms, either by making ambiguous environmental product claims or by distorting companies' actual environmental performance. In *The Myth of Green Marketing* (1998), Toby Smith observes that Shell Chemicals' advertising "congratulates itself for its contribution to village life in Africa," while in fact the company made most of its profit from selling products consistently associated with environmental degradation (124). In 2010, the environmental consulting company TerraChoice identified "seven sins of greenwashing," including "the sin of the hidden trade-off," "the sin of no proof," "the sin of vagueness," "the sin of worshiping false labels," "the sin of irrelevance," "the sin of lesser of two evils," and "the sin of fibbing" (Terrachoice 2010). The pervasiveness of "greenwashing" exposes advertiser's tendency to misrepresent product information, which could defeat the very purpose of the green consumerist movement.

The second group of criticisms focuses not on the deception of the marketers but on the hypocrisy of the consumers. Several studies have shown that, quite contrary to the environmentally friendly claims, green consumerism often leads to more consumption and tends to perpetuate societies' existing wasteful lifestyles. Meister and Brown (2006), for example, argue that green consumerism "may increase public awareness about environmental issues" but "also increases public demand for nature 'as a product,' whereby nature becomes a reflection of consumer desires" (98). Williams (2007) points out that "green" labels take the guilt away from consumption and make people consume more than what they normally would have. He calls this the "SnackWell's moment," a similar effect as eating low-fat snacks contributing more calorie-intake and thus more weight-gain. Monbiot (2002) approaches the issue from a different angle. He observes the phenomenon of "conspicuous green consumption," in which consumers treat ecofriendly products as status symbols to boast their hyper-moralized self-image. This phenomenon was also addressed by Sexton and Sexton (2011) in the paper "Conspicuous Conservation: The Prius Effect and the Willingness to Pay for Environmental Bona Fides." The authors argue that the market success of Prius over other hybrids largely owes to its distinctive "hybrid" design, which offers a conspicuous value for consumers to show off. In fact, *South Park* (2006) has famously mocked this "Prius Effect" in its "Smug Alert" episode: after a fictional town embraced the hybrid car "Pious," the drivers produced so much "smug" that it eventually led to "global laming" and the devastation of half of the nation. This sarcastic allegory echoes what Monbiot (2002) calls "eco-narcissism:" that "green lifestyle obsession" produces a lot of feel-good effects for the bourgeois consumer but does little actual good for the environment.

These questionable motives in green consumerism (e.g. guilt-complex, eco-narcissism, lifestyle obsession) have lead to questionable social and environmental impact. As Williams (2007) points out, it has directed the public's attention away from the political and economic roots of the environmental crisis and toward trivial commodity choices and lifestyle changes. "The things causing climate changes are more caused by politics and the economy than individual behavior," states Michel Gelbter, "it has to do with mass transit, housing density… it has to do with the war and subsidies for the coal and fossil fuel industry" (quoted in Williams 2007). Moreover, green consumerism is criticized for deepening the existing class division and intensifying social inequality. The bourgeois "eco-carnival," for Monbiot (2002), drowns out the voices of grassroots activists and alienates the working class from the popular basis of environmentalism. This exclusion also exists on a global level – between affluent consuming nations in Europe and North America and poor producing nations in Asia, Africa, and South America. The wealth gap has certainly contributed to the different levels of interest in green consumerism between China and the US.

Overall, most of the critics cited above expose the limits of the corporate marketers' consciousness raising and behavioral change models. While developing "consciousness" does not always lead to intended behavior, the intended behavior, once achieved, might not always lead to beneficial social and environmental impact. In fact, as Monbiot (2002) and Williams (2007) show, it sometimes induces negative effects such as class division and over-consumption. What, then, is the force that derails the consciousness-raiser and behaviorist's plan? Borrowing insights from psychoanalysis, this book proposes an answer: desire. Desire, as the fundamental force that drives our being, does not operate according to conscious reason and nor does it succumb to behavior control. As the French psychoanalyst Jacques Lacan has stated, desire is a lack; it does not belong to any positive, observable order of things and exists only as a negative force that motivates our actions. In consumer culture, it drives overconsumption and leads to social inequality and ecological destruction, among other problems. For psychoanalysis, desire is also the place where ethics lies. A healthier relationship with the objects of our desire contributes to psychic, social, and ecological wellbeing, and a pathological one might contribute to crises on all other levels of existence. The next section will outline the psychoanalytic approach to desire and its function as a critical methodology. I will also review the literature that has applied psychoanalysis to ecological critique and examine the interconnections between the psychic system and the social and ecological systems.

When Psychoanalysis Meets Ecological Critique

According to Raymond Williams (1985), the word "critical" is a loaded term: it first pertains to *criticism*, which refers to commentaries on literature, denoting a form of judgment (especially unfavorable, fault-finding judgment); second it also relates to *crisis*, which was initially a medical term, referring to the turning point of a disease or the decisive moment in a course of events when immediate action is needed (85). Psychoanalysis is "critical" in both its medical and literary connotations: on the one hand, it responds to the psychosomatic crisis of the patient and tries to change the course of the disease; on the other hand, it reads the patient as a text, finds "faults" with it (pathological phenomena), and seeks the cause of these "faults." In ecological critique, the two meanings of "critical" also convene: the critic not only responds to the ecological crises and tries to intervene, but also reads the "sick" Earth as a text and interprets the cause of its "symptoms." The methodological parallel between ecological critique and psychoanalysis makes the latter highly suitable to tackle the former. In a sense, psychoanalysis belongs to the category that Cox (2007) calls "crisis disciplines," which aims to "offer recommendations for management or intervention to protect imperiled species, biological communities, or ecosystems, under conditions of urgency" (6). Yet its unique contribution locates the cause of ecological disorder in the pathologies of the human mind and the social-political systems. As Joseph Dodds states in *Psychoanalysis and Ecology At the Edge of Chaos* (2011), psychoanalysis "explores the interpellation of inner and outer worlds, of object relations and social relations [...] to the point where terms such as internal and external, inside and outside, psyche and society, lose some of their simple binary character without abandoning the specificity of each domain" (13). Indeed, psychoanalysis insists that psychic, social, and ecological systems are interconnected; yet how exactly has it migrated from the medical-literary context to the social-ecological context is a process that deserves closer examination.

The basic methodology of psychoanalysis, as introduced by Freud, is to find "faults" in textual constructions and interpret their cause(s) (Breuer and Freud, 2000). In examining hysterical patients' narrations about their illness, Freud focuses on the mistakes, gaps, and incongruences in their accounts; these are the *symptoms* – secret passageways to a separate, unknown mental state, i.e. the unconscious, where desires and wishes are repressed and stored. Usually triggered by traumatic events, these repressed contents are too painful to be allowed direct entry into the consciousness; they thus return in the form of symptoms that distort the surface of consciousness. In response to this psychic blockage, Freud invents the "talking cure," which is to verbalize the trauma that triggered the repression and thereby remove the symptoms. His subsequent work (1980; 1990; 1990) continues to search for traces of the unconscious in symbolic constructions, such as dreams, jokes, slips of the tongue, acts of forgetting, etc. He establishes that the unconscious exists in every individual (mentally ill or "healthy") and that findings from pathological cases can be used to explain "normal" psychic functioning.

Based on his theory of etiology (i.e. causation of diseases), Freud's next step (1990; 2000) is to build the structure of the psyche. Human beings are, according to him, a bundle of instincts and drives that seek their satisfaction. The drives, in particular, derive enjoyment from encircling their objects— bodily organs such as the breast, phallus, mouth, or anus—many of which developed through our intimate contact with the mother (or any caretaker figure) during childhood. However, socialization, by way of inhibitions (such as parental injunctions, social conventions, and the law), separates us from these objects. It launches our lifelong pursuit of things and people that remind us of these "lost objects," and constitutes desire. Thus, what we consciously recognize as the objects of our desire are only reminders of the primal "object-cause of desire" that is forever lost to us. Based on the opposition between drives and inhibitions, Freud (1990) conceptualizes the tripartite structure of the human psyche, between the *id* (the reservoir of instincts, drives, and repressed desires), the *superego* (internalized social inhibitions which function as a judge or a censor of the contents of the id), and the *ego* (the mediating agency between the id and the superego, which is usually perceived as the "Self") (Laplanche and Pontalis 1973). These psychic agencies interact with each other to resolve the fundamental conflict between instinctual enjoyment and social pressures. Different psychopathologies (such as neurosis, psychosis, and perversion – terms that Lacan later uses to develop his topology of desire) are manifested, depending on how these relationships are configured.

Freud's structure of the psyche, however, gradually gained a bad reputation. The so-called orthodox Freudianism in literary analysis is known for turning these terms into universalized interpretive themes and impose them onto literatures to interpret the authors' private family dramas: "find the devouring mother, detect the inevitable castration anxiety, listen between the syllables of verse for the squeaking bedsprings of the primal scene" (Crews, 1975; cited in Jameson 1977, 342). According to Jameson (1977), this ahistorical and systematizing method "remain[s] locked within the categories of the individual and of individual experience" and deprives psychoanalysis of the ability to account for the social and historical contexts of the literary work (342). Yet the question is: if the unconscious is strictly private and secluded in the mind of an individual, how could the critic make claims about its content? What is the nature of the unconscious and how mysterious is it really?

According to Jacques Lacan, the answer is: not very mysterious. In proposing that "the unconscious is structured like a language," Lacan suggests that there is nothing private or secluded about the unconscious. Unlike Freud, who sees the unconscious as a repertoire of primal instincts and drives, Lacan sees it as an effect of language or language-like structures created during our insertion into the social-symbolic network. This conceptualization flattens Freud's depth model of the psyche (instincts vs. inhibitions) into a symbolic matrix where streams of signifiers happen to repress one another (discourse vs. discourse) (Fink 1996). Consequently, the conventional divide between the individual and the social disintegrates. Out of the empty place of the "individual" rises the Lacanian subject – a subject that has no hidden core of desire to be uncovered, other than the very socio-linguistic structure that constitutes him (Fink 1996). This realization allows the critic to analyze the symbolic play within the text that gives rise to the desire of the subject. Moreover, Lacan argues that rhetorical devices, such as *metonymy* and *metaphor* (refashioned from Freud's *condensation* and *displacement* in dream analysis), are key ways through which desire is structured. This allows the critic to conduct rhetorical analysis of the text and study the psycho-topologies (or "tropologies" as the rhetoricians call it) that constitute the subject's desire.

Based on Freud's id-ego-superego model, Lacan conceives his structure of the psyche with another tripartite model of the *real*, the *imaginary*, and the *symbolic*. The *real* is the place of psychic trauma (or a fundamental loss) that sets the subject's dynamics of desire in motion; to defend against the anxiety emanated from the real, the subject resorts to the *symbolic* – social-linguistic orders that position her in relations to other subjects – to shield herself from the psychic trauma; these symbolic constructs, while circling around the real, are experienced as the *imaginary*—coherent narratives that we live by every-day (i.e. identities, values, beliefs, worldviews, and even the so-called reality itself). Among the many applications of Lacan's real-imaginary-symbolic model, one of the most popular is the application of the notion of "fantasy" (or *phantasy*) to explain the functioning of ideology. *Fantasy* is a mechanism that simultaneously operates in all three registers: While it presents itself as an idealistic fiction in the realm of the imaginary (the realm of dreams and illu-sions), it is supported by a symbolic structure that keeps the subject in safe distance from the real trauma (the motor of her desire). In *The Sublime Object of Ideology*, Žižek (1989) points out that ideology *is* fantasy; moreover, that "the fundamental level of ideology… is not of an illusion masking the real state of things but that of an (unconscious) fantasy structuring our social reality itself" (33). That is to say, the most essential dimension of ideology is not the conscious illusions that we mistake as reality, but the unconscious structure – i.e. the symbolic scaffolding that holds up what we take as reality.

The notion of the ideological fantasy is highly relevant to my analysis of environmental advertising. Advertising projects the collective "dreams" of a society (Williams 1980) and is a perfect example of such fantasy structure. On the surface, advertising promotes ludicrous imaginations and magical wish-fulfillment that are attached to various products and services; underneath, it is strictly governed by an (unconscious) symbolic structure that regulates the collective pleasures and enjoyment of a society. At the heart of this symbolic structure lies the absent center – the *lost object* of our desire that sets the libidinal economy (and the consumer economy) in motion. But the question is, how could the critic analyze the symbolic and the real dimensions of advertising, which are largely unconscious? The answer is: by looking into the symptoms. Here the old Freudian dream analysis technique becomes relevant again. Since the repressed returns and causes disruptions (gaps, mistakes, inconsistencies) in the fabric of consciousness, the critic can use these *symp-toms* as gateways to access the desire that undergird the ideological text. In environmental advertising, these symptoms are very pervasive. They usually appear as absurdities and inconsistencies that contradict the commonsensical "good" logic of advertising. As I will later show, some examples include a mud-made car that falls apart in a hybrid car commercial (Chapter 2), a cow that invites humans to consume itself in an organic milk ad (Chapter 3), or a broken product "life cycle" flow chart in an eco-fashion ad (Chapter 5). These symptoms seem counterintuitive at first but in fact signal the conflicts and ambivalences in the consumer psyche. Their odd imageries circle around the trauma in the real that the advertising text cannot risk representing in its stark, naked honesty.

Now, what does all of this have to do with the environment? A quick answer is: the trauma that has generated our psychic lack has also led to the ecological crises that afflict our planet. During the last decade, a growing group of scholars have started to use psychoanalysis to inform ecological critique (for a thorough literature review, see Dodds' *Psychoanalysis and Ecology at the Edge of Chaos*, 2011). I divide this literature mainly into two groups: one examines the psychic significance of environmental crises, and the other focuses on the ecological significance of psychopathologies. The first group, including Lertzman (2008 & 2011), Randall (2005), Rust (2008), and Hoggett (2009), analyzes humans' psychological reactions toward environmental trauma. As stated above, Lertzman (2008), in her *Guardian* article "The Myth of Apathy," dissects the psychodynamics underlying the so-called "environmental apathy" and suggests that such "apathy" might be a defense mechanism against the deeper anxiety or loss generated by the environmental trauma. If not properly acknowledged, this loss ("not only of loved ones, but also of a place, species, or favorite tree") can take the forms of "denial, projection, paranoia, grandiosity or an acute sense of inferiority" (16). In "A New Climate for Psychotherapy," Randall (2005) states that the public's anxiety from "stories of war, destruction and pain" (168) might give birth to excessive shopping or eco-narcissism (a concept also mentioned by Monbiot) that could appease the consumers' inner fear or guilt. In "Climate on the Couch," Rust (2008) also points out that "the very thing that is causing our crisis – over consumption – has become our palliative, to soothe away our anxieties about the damage we are doing to the world" (7). According to these scholars, the first step we should take toward effective environmental change is to address the unconscious loss pertaining to widespread ecological trauma before tackling behavioral change with consumption.

The second group applies psychoanalysis more broadly to account for the anthropogenic cause of ecological crisis in the first place. In the landmark essay "The Rhetoric of Environmental Hysteria" (1995), rhetoricians Killingsworth and Palmer apply the Freudian model of repression to explain how human technology exercises domination over the ecological system and generates the trauma that afflicts all life forms on Earth. Calling modern civilization the "ego" of the Earth, the authors seek the return of repressed "great earthly unconscious" (e.g. the land, the forest, the animals, the people) in the "hysterical" rhetoric of the 1960s American environmentalists (48). Rodney Giblett, on the other hand, proposes the study of psychoanalytic ecology in his series of books (e.g. *Postmodern Wetlands* 1997, *Sublime Communication Technologies* 2008, *Landscapes of Culture and Nature* 2009, *People and Places of Nature and Culture* 2011) to examine the psychological underpinnings of ecologically destructive behavior. His projects specifically analyze the "orally and anally sadistic" desires of modern machines and the role technology plays in generating ecological and psycho-cultural crises. In a similar vein, Wolfgang Ley

(2008) articulates psychoanalysis and ecology by establishing a causal relationship between the two "natures" – "our inner, psychosomatic human nature" and ecological nature (1285). When the former loses balance, Ley argues, the latter also becomes chaotic:

> The major mishaps in our dealings with the natural world [manifest] a socially generated form of destructive narcissism, an unwillingness to acknowledge the autonomous integrity and libidinously cathected intrinsic value of natural objects – including the integrity and value of the indivisible somatic and psychological structures and dynamics of human nature (1286).

Overall, Ley (2008), Giblett (1997, 2008, 2009, 2011), and Killingsworth and Palmer (1995), among others, suggest that our problem is much larger than the inability of individual minds to acknowledge and react to environmental crises. Rather, it lies in the broader psychopathologies that are embedded in the technological and economical (infra-)structures of modern civilization. What psychoanalysis can do, thus, is not just to provide therapeutic treatment for individuals to manage their anxiety; more importantly, it needs to theorize ethical principles that could be implemented to adjust humans' general attitude toward technology and modernization in order to have wider ecological impact.

Chapter Synopsis

The chapters of this book are organized around four iconic "eco-friendly" products: hybrid cars, green home products, organic foods, and eco-fashion. They correspond to what the Chinese consider as the four basic human needs: "*yi, shi, zhu, xing*" (衣, 食, 住, 行 clothing, food, shelter, and transportation). The order of the chapters is arbitrary. My analysis of these advertisements combines both groups of psychoanalytical ecocriticism outlined above and focus on the psychic impact of environmental crises as well as the environmental impact of psychopathologies. Viewed from the first perspective, advertising can be seen as a collection of ideological fantasies that helps consumers cope with the psychic trauma generated by environmental crises (e. g. air pollution, toxins in home, food contamination, waste overflow, etc.); viewed from the second perspective, advertising belongs to a market system that generates the very desire for the technology that are causing these environmental crises (e.g. automobiles, home décor and cleaning agents, industrialized farming, and fast fashion). Combined together, advertising forms a perpetual loop of traumatization and defense that puts consumer society in a downward spiral. In this cross-cultural comparative study, I will explore how this downward spiral takes different forms in Chinese and American green consumer cultures.

In Chapter 2, "Morphing the Self," I analyze the advertising for hybrid electric cars. The automobile technology has long been known for its traumatization effects on the environment, as well as the health and safety of drivers and pedestrians. To appease the public anxiety about cars' negative environmental impact, hybrid car advertising in the US and China set out to construct a different set of commercial fantasies. The American ads predominantly appeal to the harmony and welfare of the society and ecosystem, but the Chinese ads mostly dwell on the appeal to the health and prestige of the individual. Applying Lacan's typology of desire, I show that underneath the American pursuit of ecological harmony, there lies a desire to hide the Self from the gaze of the Other, and underneath the Chinese pursuit of individual prestige, there is a desire for the Self to be recognized and acknowledged by the Other. I discuss the implications of these psychic structures and propose a more nuanced understanding of American-Chinese cultural differences beyond a simple binary of individualism versus collectivism.

Chapter 3, "Detoxing the Private," examines the advertising for green home products. Home is the birthplace of subjectivity and how we imagine the "greening" of the home speaks volumes about how we imagine the "greening" of the world. Due to the different levels of maturity for Chinese and American markets, I compare green home décor products in China (e.g. toxin-free wall paint, flooring, furniture) and green cleaning products in the US (e.g. eco-friendly dish and laundry detergent, multipurpose cleaner). Both groups construct the ideological fantasy of a toxic-free "green home" to defend consumers against the trauma caused by toxic chemicals invading the private home. Yet these fantasies are underpinned by different psychosocial relationship within the family and psycho-spatial relationship between the inside and outside of the house (or apartment). My investigation shows how these relationships cultivate varying worldviews about private and public, purity and contamination, domestic and wild, which are passed on from parents to children.

Chapter 4, "The Organi-vore's Dilemma," moves onto organic foods. Just like cars and houses, food is another aspect of consumer culture that marks the junction between individual and collective, private and public. This chapter focuses on milk, which holds a special place in the organics industry due to milk's deep entrenchment in human physiological growth and notions of security. Organic milk ads in both countries promise all-natural, chemical-free agriculture to ease the consumer anxiety about the food security crisis. The Chinese ads often present the product as a luxury for the urban, upper-middle class while the American ads highlight the image of the hardworking, local and independent farmers. Two ideologies stand out between these groups of ads: hierarchy versus equality. They affect how consumers view the relationships between humans, as well as the relationships between humans and animals, humans and nature.

Chapter 5, "The 'Useless' Sustainability," approaches the subject of eco-fashion. As one of the least sustainable industries of the consumer culture fashion companies proclaim the ambition to minimize their negative impact on the environment and the welfare of workers and consumers. I compare the eco-fashion advertisements by major US corporations and the design work of the leading eco-fashion designer in China, Ma Ke. The American ads, as I will show, reveal an ideological fantasy of utilitarianism and see garments as a tabula rasa that can be infinitely reused, repurposed, and recycled. By contrast, Ma Ke consciously diverges from the utilitarian ideology. Entitling her brand as "Useless," she proposes that we conceive our relationship with the material world not in terms of utility, but in terms of memory and history. Her work portrays textiles as a humble medium that records the past and invites consumers to cherish their historical connection with material objects. Ma Ke's conceptualization of eco-fashion, I argue, issues a profound critique against the utilitarian ideology of corporate green culture. It points us toward an alternative ethics of consumption that does not rely on the "wise use" of environmental resources, but on the loyalty we show toward our intimate environment that had historically constituted our desire.

A Note on Advertisement Selection

Advertisements analyzed in this book were collected and photographed through data-gathering in two Chinese cities (Shanghai and Beijing) and three American cities (Boston, MA; Iowa City, IA; Durham, NC). Due to the low resolution of some photographed prints, I replaced them with the digital versions of the same ads located online. All of them can be viewed through the author's private blog "Environmental Advertising in China and the USA" (which can be located by a simple Google search.) Three grants from Babson College's Babson Faculty Research Funds (BFRF, 2011–2014) have assisted me in collecting the majority of the materials in this book. Despite the large size of the collected data for this project, only a small number of advertisements are selected to be included in this book. Three criteria were used to determine their selection – *representative value, comparative value*, and *symptomatic value*.

Representative value means that advertisements selected must contain common features shared by other ads of the similar category. For example, an American ad for Toyota Prius representing the hybrid car with a cartoon icon will be selected since cartoon is a frequently used technique in ads of the same cultural category, but an American ad for Fisker Karma (an electric vehicle) picturing a sexy woman dancing around the electric car will not be included, since sex appeal is rare among eco-friendly car ads. Representative value is the primary principle of selection and ranks higher than the following two criteria.

Comparative value indicates that the advertisements selected should preferably display features diverging from the ads in a comparative group. For example, a Chinese ad inviting consumers to emulate a celebrity in drinking organic milk will be selected as it contrasts with its American counterpart which often pleads consumers to support local and independent organic farmers; on the other hand, a Chinese organic food ad accidentally featuring a picture of a happy farmer will not be selected as it overlaps with its comparative group (but more importantly because it is a rare occurrence, and thus cannot pass the first principle of selection).

The third principle – *symptomatic value* – is strictly derived from the requirement of the psychoanalytic method. As stated above, psychoanalysis sees advertising texts as compromises between rational, conscious thought and irrational, unconscious desires in consumer societies. After all, happy compromises are rare and, more often than not, advertising manifests the underlying psychic conflicts in the form of absurdities and incongruities (i.e. "symptoms"). For example, a Toyota Prius commercial portrays a mud-made car that slowly dissipates into the wind: to a conventional car consumer, such imagery could trigger feelings of insecurity as it implies the car's unreliability in protecting the driver; to a green consumer, nevertheless, it promises to sooth guilt from operating an environmentally damaging machine and reveals an unconscious desire to obliterate the Self from the critical gaze of the social collective. Symptoms of this sort are very persuasive in environmental advertising. They help identify the pathologies embedded in green consumerism and offer us a deeper understanding of the psychodynamics that undergird consumers' desire for green products.

Note

1 Kim Humphery (2012) identifies five strands of anti-consumerism in the West: one is "culture jamming," which uses advertising to subvert the ideology of consumerism; the second is a "civic politics of ethical consumption" that encourages individuals to consume in ways that are mindful of impacts on others and the environment; the third is a "life politics" that promotes the shift in existential satisfaction by working and spending less (such as downshifting, slow living, and voluntary simplicity; the fourth is a "community-oriented politics" focused on affirming local collective initiatives and constructing or maintaining particular communities; the fifth is a "systemic politics" stemming "from advocacy of legislative measure to control advertising, impose environmental taxes on consumer goods and regulate production to more radical calls for the reorganization of work practices, the subordination of market imperatives of social goals and the tackling of economic inequality and social fragmentation" (50). Green marketing belongs to the second strand.

References

Andreasen, A. R. (1995). *Marketing Social Change: Changing Behavior to Promote Health, Social Development, and the Environment*. Jossey-Bass.

Barton, D. (2013, May 30). Half a billion: China's middle-class consumers. *The Diplomat*. Retrieved from http://thediplomat.com/2013/05/half-a-billion-chinas-middle-class-consumers/

Breuer, J. & Freud, S. (2000). *Studies on Hysteria*. 1st edition, Basic books.

Calfee, J. E. (1998). How advertising informs to our benefit. *Consumers Research Magazine*, April.

Carson, R. (1962). *Silent Spring*. Mariner Books.

Chan, R. Y.K. & Lau, L. B. Y. (2004). The effectiveness of environmental claims among Chinese consumers: Influences of claim type, country disposition and ecocentric orientation. *Journal of Marketing Management*, 20, 273–319.

Club of Rome. (1974). *The Limits to Growth: A Report for the Club of Rome's Project on the Predicament of Mankind*. Pan Books.

Crews, F. (1975). Reductionism and its discontents. *Critical Inquiry*, 1(3), March, 543–558.

Cox, R. (2007). Nature's "crisis disciplines:" Does environmental communication have an ethical duty? *Environmental Communication*, 1(1), 5–20.

Cox, R (2012). *Environmental Communication and the Public Sphere*, 3rd edition. Sage.

Dasgupta, S. & Wheeler, D. (1996). Citizen complaints as environmental indicators: Evidence from China. Policy Research Working Paper. *New ideas in pollution regulation*, 3. The World Bank. Washington, D. C.

Doctoroff, T. (2013). *What Chinese Want: Culture, Communism, and China's Modern Consumer*. New York, NY: Palgrave Macmilan.

Dodds, J. (2011). *Psychoanalysis and ecology at the edge of chaos: Complexity theory, Deleuze|Guattari and psychoanalysis for a climate in crisis*. New York, NY: Routledge.

Economy, E. C. (1999). Painting China green: The next Sino-American tussle. *Foreign Affairs*, March/April. Retrieved from: https://www.foreignaffairs.com/articles/asia/1999-03-01/painting-china-green-next-sino-american-tussle

Ehrlich, P. R. (1968). *The Population Bomb*. San Francisco: Sierra Club Books.

Fink, B. (1996). *The Lacanian Subject: Between Language and Jouissance*. Princeton University Press.

Freud, S. (1980). *The Interpretation of Dreams*. 27th edition, Avon.

Freud, S (1990). *Jokes and Their Relation to the Unconscious*. The standard edition. W.W. Norton & Company.

Freud, S (1990). *The Psychopathology of Everyday Life*. The standard edition. W.W. Norton & Company.

Freud, S (1990). *The Ego and the Id*. The standard edition. W.W. Norton & Company.

Freud, S (2000). *Three Essays on the Theory of Sexuality*. Revised edition. Basic Books.

Gerth, K. (2010). *As China Goes, So Goes the World: How Chinese Consumers are Transforming Everything*. Hill and Wang.

Giblett, R. J. (1997). *Postmodern Wetlands: Culture, History, Ecology*. Edinburgh University Press.

Giblett, R (2008). *Sublime Communication Technologies*. Palgrave Macmillan.

Giblett, R (2009). *Landscapes of Culture and Nature*. Palgrave Macmillan.

Giblett, R (2011). *People and Places of Nature and Culture*. Intellect Books.

Graceann, B. & Williams, F. (2011). Mainstream green: Moving sustainability from niche to normal. *Ogilvy.com*. Retrieved from: https://assets.ogilvy.com/truffles_email/ogilvyearth/Mainstream_Green.pdf

Hailes, J. (1998). Understanding the green consumer. Presentation at the International Symposium on Consumption and the Environment on February 26 in Tokyo, Japan. Retrieved from: http://www.gdrc.org/uem/green-consumer.html

Herman, E. S. and Robert W. McChesney (1997). The Global Media: The New Missionaries of Global Capitalism, London: Cassell.

Irvine, S. (1989). *Beyond Green Consumerism*. London: Friends of the Earth.

Jameson, F. (1977). Imaginary and symbolic in Lacan: Marxism, psychoanalytic criticism, and the problem of the subject. *Yale French Studies*, 55/56, 338–395.

Jhally, S. (1997). *Advertising and The End of the World* [Documentary]. Media Education Foundation.

Jhally, S (2000). Advertising at the edge of the Apocalypse. *Critical Studies in Media Commericalism*. Ed. Robin Anderson and Lance Strate. Oxford University Press, USA.

Jing, J. (1997). Environmental protests in rural China. *Chinese Society: Change, Conflict, and Resistance*. Ed. Perry, E. J. & Selden, M. London: Routledge.

Kan, J. (2010, May 2). Environmentally friendly consumers emerge. *China Business Review*. Retrieved from: http://www.chinabusinessreview.com/environmentally-friendly-consumers-emerge/

Kangun, N., Carlson, L. & Grove, S. J. (1991). Environmental advertising claims: A preliminary investigation. *Journal of Public Policy and Marketing*, 10(20), 57–68.

Killingsworth, M. J. & Palmer, J. S. (1995). The discourse of "environmental hysteria." *Quarterly Journal of Speech*, 81(1), 1–19.

Kollmuss, A. & Agyeman, J. (2002). Mind the Gap: Why do people act environmentally and what are the barriers to pro-environmental behavior? *Environmental Education Research*, 8(3), 239–260.

Kunal Sinha & Michael Griffiths (2011). Get going with green: Closing the sustainability gap. *Ogilvy.com*. Retrieved from: https://assets.ogilvy.com/truffles_email/ogilvyearth/Get_Going_with_Green_-_English.pdf

Laplache, J. & Pontalis, J-B. (1974). *The Language of Psychoanalysis*. W. W. Norton & Company.

Lertzman, R. (2008, June 19). The myth of apathy. *The Ecologist*. Retrieved from http://www.theecologist.org/blogs_and_comments/commentators/other_comments/269433/the_myth_of_apathy.html

Lertzman, R (2011, May 25). Mind the "Gap." Sustainablebrands.com. Retrieved from: http://www.sustainablebrands.com/news_and_views/articles/mind-gap.

Ley, W. (2008). The ecological dimension of psychoanalysis and the concept of inner sustainability. *Journal of the American Psychoanalytic Association*, 56(4), 1279–1307.

Li, R. (2006). Green marketing: A review of national research. *Green Economy*, 1.

Lu, X. & Simons, H. W. (2006). Transitional rhetoric of Chinese Communist Party leaders in the post-Mao reform period: Dilemmas and strategies. *Quarterly Journal of Speech*, 92(3), 262–286.

Lv, H. & Yan, J. (2003). Green marketing: Reform, conflict, and strategies. *Accounting Research*, 3.

McIntosh, A (1991). The impact of environmental issues on marketing and politics in the 1990s. *Journal of the Market Research Society*, 33(3), 205–217.

Meister, M., Chamberlain, K. & Brown, A. (2006). Rejuvenating nature in commercial culture and the implications of the green commodity form. *The Environmental Communication Yearbook*. 3, (e.d. Depoe, S.)

Melton, J. G. (1989). *New Age Encyclopaedia*. Routledge.

Monbiot, G. (2002). Eco-junk. *Monbiot.com*. Retrieved from: http://www.monbiot.com/archives/2007/07/24/eco-junk/

Neimark, M. K. (1995). The selling of ethics: The ethics of business meets the business of ethics. *Accounting, Auditing & Accountability Journal*, 8(3), 81–96.

O'Barr, W. M. (2007). Advertising in China. *Advertising & Society Review*, 8(3). Retrieved from: https://muse.jhu.edu/journals/advertising_and_society_review/v008/8.3unit14.html

Ogilvy & Mather. (2011, April 18). Corporations not cashing in on Chinese consumers' desire for sustainability. *Ogilvy.com*. Retrieved from: http://www.ogilvy.com/News/Press-Releases/April-2011-Corporations-Not-Cashing-In-On-Chinese-Consumers-Desire-For-Sustainability.aspx

Parker, T. (2006, March 29). Smug alert! *South Park*: Season 10, Episode 2.

Prothero, A. (2000). Greening capitalism: Opportunities for a green commodity. *Journal of Macromarketing*, 20: 46–56.

Randall, R. (2005). A new climate for psychotherapy? *Psychotherapy and Politics International*, 3(3), September, 165–179.

Ren, Z. (2007). A research on current status, obstacles, and solutions in Chinese green marketing. *Chifeng College Journal*, 28(5).

Ren, Z (2013, January 28). Jiucheng xiaofeizhe yuanwei kechixu xiaofei maidan [90 Percent of consumers willing to pay for sustainable consumption]. *China Consumption Network*. Retrieved from: http://www.ccn.com.cn/news/yaowen/2013/0128/466375.html

Report for selected countries and subjects (2013, April 16). *IMF.* Retrieved from: http://www.imf.org/external/pubs/ft/weo/2013/01/weodata/weorept.aspx?sy=1980&ey=2018&sort=country&ds=.&br=1&pr1.x=40&pr1.y=0&c=924&s=NGDP_RPCH%2CPPPPC&grp=0&a=

Rust, M-J. (2008). Climate on the couch: Unconscious processes in relation to our environmental crisis. *Psychotherapy and Politics International*, 6(3), October, 157–170.

Scott, L. & PeñalozaL. (2006). Matriarchal marketing: a manifesto. *Journal of Strategic Marketing*, 14, March: 57–67.

Sexton, S. & Sexton, A. (2011). Conspicuous conservation: The Prius effect and willingness to pay for environmental bona fides. *The Selected Works of Steven E. Sexton*. Retrieved from: http://works.bepress.com/sexton/11

Si, L. (2002). An analysis of concepts and practices of green marketing in national businesses. *Commercial Economics and Management*, 6.

Smith, R. (1997). Creative destruction: Capitalist development and China's environment. *New Left Review*, I(222), March-April.

Smith, T. M. (1998). *The Myth of Green Marketing: Tending Our Goats at the Edge of the Apocalypse*. Toronto: University of Toronto Press.

"Shiyiwu" zhuanti xilie zhi ke chixu fazhan [Special series on the Eleventh Five Year Plan – sustainable development]. (2006, January). *China.com.cn*. Retrieved from http://www.china.com.cn/chinese/zhuanti/chixufz/1111876.htm

Stauber, J. & Rampton, S. (1995). *Toxic Sludge is Good for You!: Lies, Damn Lies and the Public Relations Industry*. Monroe ME: Common Courage Press.

Survey reveals China's growing desire for green products. (2012, December 5). *Dupont Industrial Biosciences*. Retrieved from: http://biosciences.dupont.com/media/news-archive/news/2012/survey-reveals-chinas-growing-desire-for-green-products/

Terrachoice Environmental Marketing Inc. (2010). The sins of greenwashing: Home and family edition. *Sinsofgreenwashing.com*. Retrieved from: http://sinsofgreenwashing.com/index35c6.pdf

Watts, J. (2010). *When A Billion Chinese Jump: How China Will Save Mankind or Destroy it*. Scribner.

Wei, M. & Si, L. (2001). An analysis of basic categories of green marketing. *Jianxi Social Science*. 6.

Williams, A. (2007, July 1). Buying into the green movement. *The New York Times*. Retrieved from: http://www.nytimes.com/2007/07/01/fashion/01green.html

Williams, R. (1980). Advertising: the magic system. *Problems in Materialism and Culture*. London: Verso.

Williams, R (1985). *Keywords: A Vocabulary of Culture and Society*. Oxford University Press.

Xue, F. & Zhou, P. (2012). Greener on the other side? – A comparative content analysis of environmental claims in magazine advertisements in China and the United States. *Journal of Magazine & New Media Research*, 13(2), 1–18.

Zhao, B. (1997). Consumerism, Confucianism, Communism: Making sense of China today. *New Left Review*, 222, 43–59.

Žižek, S. (1989). *The Sublime Object of Ideology*. Verso.

2 Morphing the Self

Hybrid Car Advertising and the (Dis)Appearing Ego

"What's good for General Motors is good for America." These words commonly (mis)attributed to Charlie Wilson, the former chairman of GM in 1953, speak volumes about the economic, cultural, and ideological importance of the motorcar in the United States (Hyde 2008). Embedded in the fabric of modern capitalism, the automobile industry initiated Fordism, the manufacturing methods of standardization and high worker wages, and contributed to the formation of the society of mass production and consumption. As the waves of modernization sweep across the world, the automobile technology also traverses national borders. John Urry (2004) sees the car culture as "viral," "appearing first in North America and then virulently spreading into, and taking over, most parts of the body social within all corners of the globe" (27). This "car virus" is especially infectious in China, a burgeoning consumerist society with a growing desire to emulate Western lifestyles. Over the past two decades, the Chinese government has built thousands of miles of new highways, allowing the rising middle class to commute to their suburban homes and travel recreationally to the countryside. Car aficionados organize hundreds of driving clubs throughout the country. Drive-through fast food restaurants and car washes, as well as drive-in movie theaters are appearing (Fan, 2008). ABC News reporter Mark Litke (2002) comments: "The China car craze has become a mirror image of America's automobile experience."

While the Chinese are embracing an Americanized, car-centered lifestyle, the Western car markets have undergone structural changes. Consumers became increasingly aware of the rising gasoline prices and the environmental impact of gas-powered cars, and began to purchase alternative energy vehicles. As an iconic technology of green consumerism, hybrid electric cars achieved considerable success in the West and are widely hailed as an efficient environmental solution. The same high hopes were touted when the first hybrid model Toyota Prius was introduced to China in 2006.[1] The Chinese government released subsidy programs to promote hybrids, hoping to mitigate the environmental impact of the millions of new vehicles each year ("China to subsidize" 2010). The result, however, was disappointing: Prius, whose sales reached nearly 300,000 in the U.S. in 2007, only sold around 300 in China ("Qiche ran 'lv' chengfeng" 2008). Honda's Civic Hybrid and GM's Buick

LaCrosse Hybrid also experienced sluggish sales since their launch (Qu 2009). According to a report from the China Association of Automobile Manufacturers, the sales of alternative energy vehicles during 2012 only accounted for 0.2% of the entire auto sales of the country ("New energy cars" 2012). Meanwhile, the Chinese swarmed to purchase gas-guzzlers such as sports utilitiy vehicles and all-terrain vehicles. *Tencent Auto* reports that SUV sales for 2012 took up 13.9% of the national market share, with a 22.7% increase from 2011, and continued to increase (Zhou 2013).

Why have not the Chinese embraced the "eco-friendly" hybrid despite their longstanding habit to emulate Western consumption? What are the cultural, historical, and psychic differences that resist the translation of Western "eco-friendly" appeals to China? This chapter analyzes the advertising for hybrid cars and compares the underlying structures of desires that (fail to) motivate Chinese and American consumers to "go green." In psychoanalytic critique, advertising has long been used as an artifact to study consumer desire. Vince Packard (1957) and Ernest Dichter (1960) pioneered the application of Freudian concepts to analyze advertising and desire for the purpose of commercial persuasion and cultural criticism. Judith Williamson, in *Decoding Advertisements* (1978), coined the concept "advertising-work"—inspired by Freud's "dream-work"—to examine the symbolic process through which unconscious desires are structured by commercial discourse. When placed in an ecological context, advertising enables us to examine the psychopathologies of modern technologies that they sell as well as their broader ecological implications. This chapter extends this eco-psychoanalytic framework via a cross-cultural comparative study. I examine the psychopathologies associated with the automobile technology and study the fantasies these advertisements construct to mask consumers' rising anxieties about the environmental crisis.

Before I proceed, one word of caution must be mentioned: In proposing this study, I do not assume that hybrids are necessarily more "eco-friendly" than conventional cars. According to media reports, hybrid's batteries demand rare-earths, which are often mined illegally with environmentally damanging methods (Bradsher 2009); many hybrid SUVs (such as the Hybrid Ford Escape) have lower gas milage (23mpg) than conventional compact cars (such as Toyota Yaris, at 45mpg); moreover, electric cars are not necessarily "greener" in countries like China, as 90% of its electricity comes from coal-fired power plants. However, the questionable environmental impact of the hybrids does not interfere with the present analysis. Independent from the actual products they sell, hybrid car advertising is an illuminating environmental discourse as it resonates with the desire of mainstream American green consumers and the sales figures confirm this resonance. Its success offers an interesting comparative case to the Chinese consumers, who still lack passion for the hybrid cars. The electric vehicles (EVs), on the other hand, are a rather different story. Perhaps a more ecofriendly technology, some electric cars (e.g. Chevy Volt, Tesla, Fisker Karma) or even the more recent hybrid car models (e.g. Hyundai Sonata Hybrid, Lexus CT Hybrid) are not marketed as explicitly environmental products in either the US or China (see discussion at the end). Their advertisements are less revealing of the desire structures for the "green" consumers and will not be the focus of this study.

The Paradox of the Driving Self

"The automobile is much more than a mere means of transportation," Wolfgang Sachs writes in *For Love of the Automobile* (1992), "it is wholly imbued with feelings and desires that raise it to the level of a cultural symbol" (vii). Indeed, the car embodies many modern consumerist dreams – e.g. comfort, speed, glamor, status, and power – but most importantly, it exemplifies autonomy. Compared to means of mass transportation, the car allows the driver to occupy an enclosed personal space and offers the possibility to control the mobility of the individual body. But how autonomous does the car *actually* make us? The prefix "auto-" in the word "automobile," according to John Urry (2004), captures a double-sense, both of the sovereign self (as in "auto-biography" or "autoerotic") and of objects or machines that possess a capacity for spontaneous movement (as in "automatic" and "automaton"). The dual-meaning of "auto-" reveals a paradox: on the one hand, the car asserts the Self by giving the driver control of her mobility; on the other hand, it negates the Self by running independently from human control. This paradox con-tributes to a driver's ambivalent relationship with the steering wheel: when firmly gripped in-hand, it can bring tremendous pleasure; underneath this pleasure, though, lies a disturbing anxiety about losing control. In 2010, a Prius that allegedly sped up to more than 90 miles per hour on its own on a California highway caused intense panic in the public. Commenting on a Youtube video that only showed the aftermath of the incident, a crisis manager said: "People [...] really haven't seen the car out of control. [But] it doesn't matter if they think they did. It's planted in their heads" (Spagat 2010). This crisis manager spelled out the precise meaning of the Lacanian *real*—trauma that is not necessarily connected to our actual experiences. Structurally embedded in our heads, it haunts us not through what we see but through what we do *not* see. Since the anxiety about the car running amok is present in the drivers' collective psyche, it can easily be awakened and turned into a nightmare for all—whether or not the individual driver has experienced the actual accident.

Both pleasurable and horrifying, the driving experience gives rise to a new type of subjectivity (Freund and Martin 1993; Giblett 2008). First, the driver must identify with the body of the car, whose size and speed empowers her by expanding the physiological limits of the human body. She is freed from previous time and space constraints and her eyes can swiftly "travel over the panoramic landscape laid out before it" (Giblett, 95). Yet these new freedoms also entail new constraints.[2] The driver must now be "in-*car*-cerated" (Giblett, 107), that is, enclosed in a cocooned capsule and tightly strapped onto the car seat. Her sensory perceptions are limited and she can only communicate with other drivers with "the limited language of horn and lights" (Giblett, 94).

Infrastructural constraints further limit the driver: parking deficiency, traffic jams, and car accidents not only inhibit her mobility, but also threaten her physical health and personal safety. But the ultimate victims of the automobile technology are not the ones inside the car, but those outside – the pedestrians, cyclists, urban and rural communities, animals, landscapes, atmospheres, etc. – the sum of which we call, the "environment." In fact, the shell of the car divides its interior from the exterior and materializes the very conflict between the private Self and the public environment. Raymond Williams considers the car as a technology of "mobile privatisation": it allows people to live as private small-family units while also granting "unprecedented mobility of such restricted privacies" (1985, 188). One of the problems of the mobilized privacy is its infringement on public space and its exploitation of shared resourses. As the car carries the cozy home-like compartment across natural and cultural landscapes, it also "privatises the public sphere of the road and the street" (Giblett, 94) and appropirates the global commons of air, land, and water for private enjoyment.

Environmental Rhetoric Disrupts the Driving Self

Now, what is the psychic function of traditional automobile advertisements? It is to divert the consumers from the disturbing anxiety about losing control and to reassert the independent, sovereign Self. To accomplish this, many ads feature close-up shots of the car's body, with a sharp contour singling it out from its background to emphasize self-sufficiency (see Hummer print ad, Figure 2.1 on the author's blog "Environmental Advertising in China and the USA"; same goes with all the following figures). Others use long shots of a car moving swiftly through scenic landscapes to indicate private mobility in public space (Figure 2.2, Volkswagen Polo print ad). These visual strategies create a fantasy world in which the individual driver is in complete control of his environment: he never has to obey traffic laws, share the road with other drivers, or emit toxic gases into the atmosphere. This fantasy function as a symbolic shield to protect the driver from confronting the *real* of driving – that actually he is tightly strapped to his seat, like the infant observed in Lacan's mirror stage theory, barely able to coordinate his motor activity and completely helpless in the cases of traffic jams and accidents.

The commercial rhetoric of car marketers, however, meets powerful challenges from the environmentalists. While increasing concerns are raised about cars' contribution to air pollution, energy shortage, and global warming, environmental rhetoric awakens the very anxieties that advertisers try to veil. "Black Cloud," a public service ad issue by World Wildlife Fund in 2007, exemplifies this subversive function (Figure 2.3). Composed of photo-collages from a public relations event in Beijing, the ad portrays the sequence of the daylong event where the campaigners attached a gigantic balloon to the exhaust pipe of a car and left the engine running for a whole day. As the balloon gradually inflated, a slogan printed on it became visible: "Drive one day less and see how much CO_2 you can keep out of the air we breathe." The expanding black balloon visualizes the "poop" of the car, i.e. its exhaust, and generates a traumatic effect. Slavoj Žižek (2001) describes it as watching an overflowing toilet: when the excrement floats back up, it disrupts the integrity of the body-ego and brings the audience back to the initial state of anxiety. "Drive one day less ..." This slogan appears at the climatic moment and offers the audience a new promise for agency. It re-inserts him into a new fantasy structured around the demand of the "we" and submits him to the power of an idealized collective – the superego that says: "Thou shalt not drive."

The superego, according to psychoanalysis, is the critical agency in the psyche that punishes us with guilt when we fail to meet its impossible demand. In a highly car-dependent society like the U.S., "Thou shall not drive" is *virtually* an impossible demand. According to Urry (2004), the system of automobility coerces a great number of people into driving, and giving up their cars usually equates giving up jobs, relationships, or basic life sustenance. Waller (2005) reports that, in the "exodus" from New Orleans before Hurricane Katrina, whether one had access to a car and enough money for gas directly decided one's chance of survival. After the hurricane, many evacuated to trailer parks did not have a car to get to jobs and were segregated from society. Waller laments: "[I]n a suburbanized country, there is only so much Americans can do to reduce their car usage. To make a living, they have to work. And to get to work, the vast majority of Americans have to drive."

Incapable of meeting the demand of the superego (or we may call it, *super-eco*), the subject is often haunted by guilt, blaming herself for taking the "freedom" to drive – a "freedom" that she has never actually had. Žižek (2007) calls this a "forced choice," or an *empty gesture*, of "pretend[ing] that there is a free choice although effectively there isn't one" (13). An example he gives is the bandit's demand "Your money or your life:" money is not really an option because when you choose the money, you lose your life, which makes you lose the money too. By the same logic, "environment or car" is also a forced choice. If giving up your car practically means giving up your life, environmental benefits become largely meaningless. For Žižek, the forced choice is a typical ideological strategy. Here we can see this car-centered ideology being inscribed in the very infrastructure that tears the nation (or, city, neighborhood) apart.

Viewed in a larger cultural context, "Thou shalt not drive" is not the only moral injunction issued in American popular environmental discourse. From environmental news and documentaries to NGO ads and green consumer guides, one frequently hears admonitions such as "Thou shalt not – fly, eat meat, drink GMO soy milk, buy chemically doused vegetables, wear sweatshop clothes, etc." Each injunction implies certain harm being done to some abstract and distant Other – be it the developing-country workers, near-extinction species, future generations, ecosystems, etc. – and their suffering being added to the psychic debt of the shoppers. For Lacan, this uppercase "Other" is distinguished from the lowercase "other": while the former refers to an abstract and empty symbolic position that wields power without interacting with the subject, the latter refers to actual, living persons that the subject knows, interacts with, and forms relationships with. The big Other, according to psychoanalysis, is the place where the superego speaks from. Representing the benefits of abstract social-ecological collectives, the *supereco'* injunction ensures that consumers constantly experience guilt and try all means to redeem themselves.

Erasing the Self in American (Western) Hybrid Car Advertisements

As environmentalists spoil the commercial fantasy of the autonomous "me," marketers aim to construct a new fantasy around the harmonious "we" – a utopian community or ecosystem that exist in perfect harmony. "Why not?", a 30-second Toyota Prius commercial produced for the American market in 2007, is a good example of this strategy (Figure 2.4). The commercial sets the scene on a vast prairie at the foot of the Rocky Mountains. Accompanied by slow-paced acoustic guitar music, three people dressed like pioneer settlers enter and use organic materials such as branches, grasses, and mud to build a car-shaped object. After building, the settlers leave the scene. The camera then slowly circles around the "car," showing it being transformed into a Prius. As the camera continues to turn, the natural background around the Prius changes quickly, indicating the passage of time. A few more rotations later, the Prius turns back into a mud-made object and starts to disintegrate. Eventually it vanishes into the wind and returns the prairie to the original state of pristine beauty. The voiceover says, "Can a car company grow in harmony with the environment? Why not? At Toyota, we're not only working toward cars with zero emissions. We're also striving for zero waste in every-thing else we do. ... The best way to have an impact on the environment is to have as little impact as possible."

First of all, the Rockies, the acoustic guitar, and the pioneer settlers evoke a nostalgic feeling of the American Old West and the building and maintaining of local communities. The Prius, as implied here, embodies a type of com-munal and ecological harmony. Yet something potentially disturbing can be detected; that is – the rather peculiar displacement of a solid, steel-built car with a flimsy, mud-made car that falls apart. To traditional car consumers, the fragility of the Prius might bring back the traumatic feeling of vulner-ability and its immobility might trigger the memories of traffic jams or engine breakdowns. Both violate the unsaid taboos of traditional car commercials. However, viewed from a psychoanalytic perspective, these peculiarities are symptoms and suggest deeper conflicts in the unconscious. Their meaning can be interpreted by considering the desire of the eco-subject: Since he is con-stantly punished by the *supereco* for occupying the collective space with his personal presence, he desires certain relief from such punishment; thus, by erasing the car's body from an image of ecological utopia (a *"supereco-ic"* look into what the world should be), he is able to erase the Self from the critical gaze of the *supereco* and be temporarily freed from guilt.

But the technique of erasure alone does not sufficiently explain the psycho-dynamics of this commercial. More insights can be revealed by analyzing its cinematic technique: first, the camera makes a 360 degrees circle around the Prius – like a magician turning his cart around showing that he is not hiding anything – then, it employs a time-lapse technique to portray the slow disin-tegration of the Prius. The camera movement creates a panorama in space and time and establishes a fantasy of total invisibility. Yet the most pleasurable part of the erasure is not so much the end goal of invisibility, but the process of disappearing – the intermediate stage when the car has already started distintegrating but is still maintaining its contour. As Lacan (1977) points out, desire is constituted by a symbolic split. Similarly, the contour of the car splits the driving subject into two: On the one hand, there is a *conscious* ego that strives to maintain her identity in the eyes of the Other (by preserving the car's outer edge) and, on the other, there is an *unconscious* desire that wishes that she never existed in this world or rather was already dead to the Other (by hollowing out the insides of the car). The Other is also split – between an imagined community/ecosystem of perfect harmony and a sadistic gaze of the *supereco,* who derives perverse enjoyment from punishing the subject for not doing its duty. This split generates a fundamental ambivalence in the subject: that she would diligently pursue the imagined harmony but would never want it fully realized – as it would put an end to the enjoyment of her *supereco.* In the commercial's punch line, the same ambivalence can be observed. Rather than saying "no impact at all," it emphasizes that one should have "as little impact as possible." The infinitesimal margin is exactly where desire survives and flourishes: through the lingering contour of the vanishing car, the eco-con-sumer "child" plays the "fort-da" game (a childish game of disappearance and return, as observed by Freud) with "mother" nature by prolonging the process of self-erasure.

In Lacan's typology of desire, this type of subjectivity is best described as obsession. Always consumed by guilt, the obsessive is convinced of his individual autonomy and performs compulsive rituals to *singlehandedly* prevent some terrible disasters from happening. The obsessive's solution to crisis is always solitary: he copes with his guilt internally and refuses to enlist help from others. He allows his powerful ego to cut himself off from the dependence on others and places an impersonal Other in the "backseat" as a passive observer of his actions. Fink (2004) wrote, "while [the obses-sive's] ego participates in the games – that is, in the spectacle staged for the Other – his desire, his unconscious desire, remains on the sidelines as if it did not exist" (p. 28). Instead of confronting the unpredictable *desire* of the Other, the obsessive prefers to deal with the its explicit, fixed *demands.* He would rather follow long lists of behavioral instructions than engaging in interpersonal contact with other members of the community. Moreover, he always picks impossible ideals to strive for; that way his object can always stay "lost," his desire remains unsatisfied, and his guilty pleasure persists. For Lacan, the obsessive is fundamentally troubled by an existential question: "Am I dead or alive?" The half-erased body of the Prius is a perfect metaphor for this dilemma – a permanent tug-of-war between the wishes to annihilate and assert the Self.

The technique of *incomplete* erasure can be widely observed in Western hybrid car advertisements, which commonly remove the image of the hybrid and replace it with a piece of leaf, a post-consumer cardboard, a cartoon image, or a surrealist icon (see Figure 2.5-2.10: Toyota Prius print ads "Being Followed," "Paper Clip," and "Good Ideas Grow, Literally," Volkswagen Polo Blue-Motion print ads "Can A Car Ever Be Eco-friendly?" and "Absurdly low consumption," Volkswagen pint ad "The Car Recycling Drop Box"). Yet the most extreme example is the 2012 Mercedes-Benz commercial for the F-CELL hydrogen fuel cell powered car (Figure 2.11). Although German, it demonstrates a similar obsessive subjectivity shared by American green consumers. Titled the "invisible Mercedes," this commercial shows a car that not only disappears in front of the camera but also "vanishes" before a casual observer physically standing next to it. To achieve this effect, technicians covered the car with $263,000 worth of flexible LED mats and programmed the lights to reproduce the image from the other side of car (Hyde 2012). The commercial follows the "invisible" car on a tour across Germany to capture the shocking expression of pedestrians. As it moved along the streets, many people ignored it first but soon noticed its car-shaped contour and could not take their eyes off of this uncanny object. After capturing the viewers' attention, the car flickered a few times and assumed its original form; then a slogan flashed across the screen: "0.0 emission, invisible to the environment." This commercial demonstrates that what the eco-subject desires is not full invisibility, but the process of disappearing and re-appearing, which produces endless enjoyment.

Despite all the enjoyment it generates, the obsessional structure is fundamentally problematic: it entraps the green consumer in a solipsistic fantasy and directs her libidinal energy towards maintaining the integrity of the ego. It instructs her to see environmental destruction as a failure in individual responsibility and demands her to "do her part" by consuming even more. In Foucauldian critique, the rhetoric of individual responsibility has been identified as a key technology of neoliberal governmentality (Lemke 2002). From a psychoanalytic perspective, nevertheless, the neoliberal construction of the Self is supported by its obverse side – an unconscious death wish that desires to erase the self from the authoritarian gaze of the Other. The death wish is pervasive in the rhetoric of American green consumerism: from zero-calorie water, biodegradable chip bags, to zero-waste homes and zero-carbon cities, all of these "container technologies" (Mumford, 1961) imply the symbolic "death" of the subject since they are metonymically connected with the body-ego of the consumer.

The desire to self-annihilate must be repressed from consciousness. Once brought out to the open, it may generate subversive effects. A great example is the "No Impact Man," which attracted broad media attention in 2009. In an experiment to lead a life with zero eco-footprint, New York City writer Colin Beavan and his family tried to live a year without electricity, cars, or even toilet paper. Clearly an obsessive attempt, Beavan's project aimed to leave "zero waste in the ground, zero pollution in the air, zero resources sucked from the earth, zero toxins in the water" (14)—an impossible goal that he decidedly failed at and felt guilty about. His book and website provided detailed to-do-lists for readers to minimize their eco-footprint in all aspects of consumer lives. "No Impact Man's" initial plan was to establish a behavioral exemplar for the wasteful mass consumers (note the smugness in his superhero / *supereco*-ic stunt name). But as the project continued it received so much criticism about the absurdity of its rationale that Beavan (2009) worried that he had "single-handedly managed to make a mockery of the entire environmental movement" (164, cited in Kolbert, 2009). In a sense, his quandary results from him inadvertently eliminating the distance between fantasy and reality. As mentioned before, ideology wields power by making an empty gesture (to the *real*) that is meant to be rejected. Beavan, however, took up this empty offer and brought the supposedly symbolic self-erasure to the level of the *real*. By trying to "live the impossible," his experiment exposed the unconscious supplement of green consumerism, i.e. a death wish; it suggests that one must literally die to leave no "footprint" on the environment and exposes the potential cruelty that the supereco imposes on its green consumer subjects.

***

China's Historical Encounter with the Automobile Technology

After analyzing American hybrid car ads, I now look into their Chinese counterparts. Chinese people's desire for cars can be traced to the country's different historical encounter with the automobile technology. Emerging at the end days of feudalism and the high times of Western imperialism, cars were presented as exotic foreign goods (*bolaipin*) and perceived as a status symbol for the top tier of society. The alleged "first car" introduced into China was a tribute offered to the Empress Dowager of the Qing Dynasty in 1901 by the politician Yuan Shikai ("*Fengyu bainian,*" 1996). During the same year, the Hungarian merchant Li Enshi (Leine) also transported two American cars to Shanghai and created a huge buzz on the streets ("*Zhongguo qiche lishi de cangsang bianqian,*" 2005). After the establishment of PRC, China's First Automobile Works manufactured the first domestically produced sedan, the "Red Flag Sedan" (*hongqi jiaoche*), in 1958 solely for the usage of central party leaders. The sedan became a national emblem and a symbol of highest communist leadership. In the 1980s, as foreign cultures flooded in, American television shows (e.g. *Knight Rider,* 1982–1986, *Hunter,* 1984–1991, and *Growing Pains,* 1985–1992) exposed the Chinese to modernized, car-centered Western lifestyles. David Hasselhoff's *Knight Rider,* in particular, portrayed a high-tech, impenetrable "super car" that became engrained in the collective memory of the Generation X. Zhao (2007), a blog writer, recalls how as a kid he wished to have Hasselhoff's car:

> During 1995 when I was still in primary school, every Tuesday at 7:30pm I had to tune in to CCTV2 and wait for the Knight Rider to come on… Simply looking at these posters makes me feel nostalgic. Those years all my dreams were to own that omnipotent, talking, super NB[3] car.

Many Chinese who had watched that show shared Zhao's aspiration. If cars previously seemed unattainable in the hands of feudal lords and party officials, now they appeared within close reach through the vivid portrayal of these TV shows. However, most people at the time were still unable to afford cars; this only exacerbated their discontent about the existing public transportation. Daniel Lerner (1973) describes this phenomenon as the "revolution of rising frustrations," where the exposure to Western media raised the expectations in the people of developing countries and led to frustrations about their current living conditions. By "dangling" the glamorous car-centered lifestyles in front of the Chinese eyes, these TV shows only worsened the repression of their long-standing desire for the automobile.

In the late 1990s, when the private car finally became affordable to the economic elite, the century-long repression became undone and the Chinese middle class bought into the automobile culture with vengeance. Many purchased private cars to gain "face" (*mianzi*) – i.e. to show off their wealth and status within their social circles. "Face" (*mianzi*), a central value in traditional Chinese culture, refers to "a reputation achieved through getting on in life, through success and ostentation" (Hu, 1944, 45). The pursuit of "face" was interrupted by Mao's egalitarian communism but returned after China's economic reform. In post-reform China, it became one of the most important motivations behind extravagant spending on imported foreign goods – from cigarettes and liquor to home electronics and cars (Zhao 1997). In the car market, the link between "face value" and exoticness is highly prominent. According to Doctoroff (2005), despite the fact that the Chinese auto-industry is protected by governmental economic policies, the majority of the consumers still prefer foreign cars to domestic ones. Wang and Yang (2008) confirm that Chinese car consumers' brand perception and purchase intention are significantly influenced by the automobiles' country of origin – that is, products from developed nations are viewed as more superior than those from developing ones.

As the cost of owning a car decreased in the twenty-first century, cars gradually became one of the essential commodities in urban China. Lim (2009) states, "Back in the 1980s, young married couples in China aspired to own a bicycle, a sewing machine, a watch and a radio. These days, many Chinese men believe they must first own a car, house and a laptop before they can think about getting into a serious relationship." Young urbanites bought them for fun, as well as the experience of "freedom" and "independence." A car club founder said: "the car brings to my life … convenience, freedom, flexibility, a quick rhythm; I can't imagine life without it" (Fan 2008). Campanella (2008) explains why the Chinese are particularly attracted to the appeal of "freedom:"

> In a society where travel was once highly restricted and much of life circum-scribed by the state, driving your own car – wherever and whenever you wish – offers a compelling sense of agency and self-determination. [...] It may well be that the car is a kind of placebo for freedoms yet ungained in China (218).

Substituting social and political changes with changes in consumer brands is a common hegemonic strategy of global consumerism. The advertising industry, writes Janus (1983), frequently preaches Western ideologies such as "happiness, youth, success, status, luxury, fashion" to developing countries to mask their social and class conflicts. In the same vein, car manufacturers successfully sold the ideas of "freedom" and "independence" to Chinese (and American) consumers whose lives are tangibly constricted.

As argued before, "freedom" should never be taken at its face value. The fantasy of the autonomous driver only diverts attention away from driving-related anxieties. Moreover, driving in China is a particularly anxiety-indu-cing experience. According to Peter Hessler (2009), since most Chinese are yesterday's pedestrians, they often "drive the way they walk:"

> They like to move in packs, and they tailgate whenever possible. They rarely use turn signals [...] They convert sidewalks into passing lanes, and they'll approach a round-about in reverse direction if it seems faster. If they miss an exist on a highway, they simply pull onto the shoulder, shift into reverse and get it right the second time (28).

Bad driving habits, coupled with the sheer volume of cars on the road, make the traffic conditions highly chaotic: accidents, traffic jams,[4] and parking problems abound; road rage, phobias, and post-traumatic stress pervade. Most importantly, air quality severely worsens in the past decade and respiratory diseases now constitute China's biggest public health threat (Watts 2012). These anxieties deeply upset the car consumers, who cling to their autonomous ego even more.

Multiplying the Self in Chinese Hybrid Car Advertisements

"The car of tomorrow" is a 2007 print ad that introduced Prius, the first hybrid car, to the Chinese market (Figure 2.12). It pictures a Prius parked against a glass wall (of possibly a modern building); the wall mirrors the car and captures some of its background in the view – blue sky over a line of high-rises in the distant horizon. Almost immediately, one can observe a striking difference from the American ads: the hybrid's "in-your-face" kind of presence. The Prius takes up 1/6 of the ad's space and the mirror doubles its size. The car dons a chrome surface, which appears futuristic and impenetrable. Its bullet-shaped design suggests velocity, mobility, and tenacity. Digitally superimposed fluorescent lines, suggesting technological advantage, wrap around its mirrored image. In addition, in the view of the mirror, there are an extra patch of grass, a small bush, and a slightly bluer sky. "The car belongs to today, the heart belongs tomorrow:" the tag line on top suggests that the two cars represent the contrast between the technology of "today" and that of "tomorrow."

Compared to the American hybrid car ads, this one contains surprisingly few environmental cues. Visually, the only references are the marginally bluer sky in the mirrored view along with the tiny patch of grass and small bush. These features look like garnish on a hamburger platter and can easily go unnoticed. Verbally, the hybrid's environmental benefits are mentioned in the small font copy at the bottom, but they are also downplayed:

> This is the car of tomorrow. Its advanced technology is sufficient to benefit the next generation. Since Prius' birth in 1997, it has never stopped amazing the automobile world. And today the first domestically assembled Toyota hybrid electric vehicle Prius brings a series of more noteworthy extraordinary performance such as smooth and powerful acceleration and quiet driving atmosphere. Meanwhile, its energy consumption and gas emission are also lowered in order to reduce its environmental impact. Now, the car of tomorrow has truly arrived.

The first emphasis of this paragraph is the technological advancement of the Prius and its prestige in the international market. The phrase "the worldly renowned _____ has finally arrived" is frequently used in modern Chinese advertising slogans: it presents the product as a signifier of Western lifestyles and taste, which makes it a status symbol among the Chinese. As the copy continues, it outlines the performance of the hybrid – "smooth and powerful acceleration" and "quiet driving atmosphere" – both enhance the individual's driving pleasure and have nothing to do with the environment. Finally, the environmental advantage of the hybrid is mentioned in a minimalistic fashion: "its energy consumption and gas emission are lowered in order to reduce its environmental impact." And the copy affirms, again, the greatness of technological innovation: "Now, the car of tomorrow has truly arrived."

Having studied the cultural and psychic significance of cars in China, it is not hard to understand why this ad made its sales pitch. Since the automobile has always been portrayed as exotic foreign goods, the hybrid must also be first presented as the signifier of the Westerners' desire – in order for it to have exchange ("face") value among the Chinese. Moreover, in modern mainstream media, Westerners' desire has been uniformly represented as that of technological progress, economic development, and high consumerism. As governmental propaganda repeatedly stated, modernization and indus- trialization are historical necessities and, without them, nations would weaken and fall prey to the modernized ones – like China's humiliation by the West since the eighteenth-century Opium Wars. Following the trajectory of economic development and technological progress, therefore, is not only desirable but also patriotic – as one would be contributing to the great revival of the Chinese nation. This ideology of modernization is clearly present in the slogan of the "Car of Tomorrow." It implies that the direction of linear tech- nological progress, as determined by the affluent Western countries, is now pointing toward the hybrid technology. Purchasing it would allow one to climb up the ladder of modernity and approach the pinnacle of human welfare.

Underlying this blatant ideology, nevertheless, there exist some symptoms that reveal deeper psychic conflicts. One may notice them in two small visual details in the ad – the glass wall that mirrors the Prius and the fluorescent lines that wrap around its mirrored image. Without these features, this ad would be almost identical to the aforementioned American Hummer ad – in the larger-than-life portrait of the car and the lack of environmental refer- ences. But these small details (the mirror and the lines) change the whole story: they confine the Prius in a narrow space and contradict the promise of the car as a symbol of autonomy and freedom. Instead of setting it as a sin- gular, autonomous object against an infinite horizon (as the Hummer ad does), they corner the hybrid against a wall, double its image with a mirror, and wrap its mirrored body with spider-web-like fluorescent lines. If being alone and whole in an open space suggests a Western theme of rugged mas- culinity, then being confined, mirrored, and tightly wrapped represents a classic treatment of the female body. A body that is bound and shadowed by a double is not autonomous. The fluorescent lines register the Western, mas- culine gaze of modern science that cuts into the feminized body of the Prius. They scrutinize, dissect, and measure the Chinese driver's body-ego and mark his desire to be recognized, examined, and acknowledged by the Other (the West).

This type of subjectivity, again within Lacan's psycho-topology, can be characterized as hysteria. Hysteria is another kind of neurosis that, in many ways, opposes obsession. Both succumb to repression, i.e. the "Thou shalt not" injunction of the Other, but they adopt different symbolic measures to cope with it. While the obsessive asserts the autonomous Self and rejects the desire of the Other, the hysteric identifies with the desire of the Other and renounces her own desire. The hysteric is troubled by a gender question: "Am I a man or a woman?" Unsure of her sexual identity (one Freudian example is Dora, who is unsure whether to identify with her father, whom she secretly desires, or her father's mistress, who is the desire of her father), she is entrapped in the web of the Other's desire and divided about which subjective position she should identify with. This radical uncertainty is manifested in the multiplied and fragmented body of the Prius. By constantly switching angles to view herself, the subject is able to morph into multiple body-egos in order to capture the unknown desire of the Other (the Western technological gaze). Moreover, as the hysteric strives to be the object of the Other's desire, she also withholds herself to avoid letting the Other reach full satisfaction, as too much satisfaction would kill desire (Fink, 1997). While having sex with her partner, the hysteric would "imagine that some woman other than herself is in the bed" (Fink 1997, 127).[5] The thought that "I am not there" is evident in the slogan: "The car belongs to today, the heart belongs to tomorrow." It indicates that "although you can have my body, you cannot have my heart" – a typical hysterical gesture to never fully give herself up to the Other. In a sense, when the obsessive derives enjoyment from prolonging the process of self-erasure, the hysteric gets her enjoyment from prolonging the process of consummating with the Other.

The second ad for the hybrid luxury SUV – Lexus RX 400h – also adopts a similar self-multiplication strategy (Figure 2.13). Featuring the tagline "It moves and purifies; it accompanies you to perfection," the 2008 ad consists of a large-bodied SUV printed across an extravagant two-page spread. Although SUV sales have declined in the U.S. during recent years, they – along with other large, high-emission gas-guzzlers – saw a steady increase in China. A Hummer H2 owner told the *Washington Post*: "In China, size matters. People want to have a car that shows off their status in society. No one wants to buy small" (Cha 2008). The consumer desire for size also manifests the hysteric desire to seek recognition. It is revealed in this ad, again, through the "mirror treatment": the SUV sits on top of a reflective surface; through the surface we can see its internal engine and battery system from the bottom up. Fluorescent lines illuminate these mechanic parts, resembling an X-ray image whose technical gaze penetrates the surface of the car. In a sense, the "see-through" shot of the engine has no practical value for the consumer, nor does it have display value in enhancing an individual's social status. The uselessness of the image marks exactly the desire of the hysteric – the temptation to see what the Other sees but remains hidden from his own eyes. The sophisticated appearance of the engine welcomes the gaze of the engineer but remains opaque to the consumers – it throws the subject out of its dominating position and marks his utter loss of mastery.

The strange appearance of the engine is also found in the 2010 Honda Hybrid ad (Figure 2.14). Entitled "1+1=3?" the ad indicates that this hybrid car not only "enhances driving pleasure" and "improves energy efficiency" but also helps consumers reap the third, bonus benefit – "environmentally friendliness." Thus the environmental benefit is only portrayed as a byproduct generated by having fun driving and saving money on gas. Also, unlike the previous ad that cuts through the car's surface to show the engine, this ad simply takes the engine out of the car for display. Similar to a scientific exhibit, two indication lines were drawn between two particular parts of the engine and the smaller captions read: "i-VTEC hybrid engine" and the "DC brushless motor". The out-of-body engine is a perfect metaphor for the hysteric's decentered structure of desire: since the engine is removed, the car can only sit passively in shop windows for show. The fetishized engine also echoes the recurring theme of feminization: just like the female body which is too often fragmented and parted, the hybrid car's body is similarly cut apart and reduced to the worth of its partial objects.

The fourth example of Buick Lacross Hybrid's ad contains more environmental references than the previous three (Figure 2.15). Entitled "Take off right now," the ad portrays a car driving on a road that flies over a lush green forest. The road's polished surface, once again, mirrors the bottom of the car and resembles a runway that invites scrutiny of the car's body from multiple angles. The far end of the road connects to a gigantic "O^2" sign; behind the sign, one sees the silhouette of an industrial city with tall chimneys and skyscrapers in the distant horizon. The city image alludes to urban air pollution; but instead of proposing to save the environment, the ad suggests that the urbanites run away to the countryside to enjoy fresh forest air. At the bottom of the ad, a few tourism spots are shown in pictures such as the Ancient Tea Road and the Xinjiang Kanas Lake, most of which are located in the underdeveloped region of China where the rich urbanites go for vacation. Here the hybrid is marketed not as a "silver bullet" to save the public environment, but as an individual "escape pod" for the economic elite to flee to their private utopia. The slogan confirms the escapist impulse: "H(ybrid)-plan: Take off right now, and return to the pure world in your heart." Rather than supporting the conservation of the ecosystem, the hybrid is promoted as a vehicle to bring aggressive ecotourism to nature to further disturb its fragile harmony.

To summarize, the Chinese ads analyzed above contain varying levels of environmental references, but they all promote an anthropocentric view of the environment and see the environment as merely a signifier for technological progress or an object of consumption or recreation. These ads unanimously feature full-size displays of the hybrid and maximize its visibility by means of mirrors, fluorescent lines, "see-through" X-ray images, scientific exhibits of the engine, etc. Combined with digitally constructed artificial backgrounds and opaque technical jargons, these techniques represent a Westernized, scientific, male gaze over the feminized body of the hybrid and capitalize on its popularity in international markets. In the last ad, the most "eco-friendly" one I found, an ecological utopia is staged to promote the environmental benefit of the hybrid car. At a glance, this utopia parallels the one in American hybrid car ads: both construct fantasies of eco-harmony to mask the rising anxiety about environmental pollution. But different structures of desire underlie the two utopias: the former, associated with obsession, internalizes the critical gaze of the *supereco* and blames the Self for not doing its duty; the latter, linked to hysteria, positions the Self as an object of the Other's desire and withdraws her presence to maintain her desirability. Both are cases of neuroses and succumb to repression; but when the repressed returns, "obsessives react with guilt and aversion, whereas hysterics react with disgust or revulsion" (Fink 1997, 117). When encountering pollution, waste, and the toxin-loaded neighborhoods, the American ads respond with guilt and self-blame while the Chinese ones react with disgust and escapism.

Why Don't Some Chinese Buy Hybrids (and Electric Cars)?

Due to the Chinese pursuit for "face," size, and status, it is unsurprising that hybrid electric cars have yet to achieve commercial success in this country. As stated above, Toyota Prius only sold over 300 in China during 2007 when its global sales came close to 200,000. Six years later, in 2013, the national sales for all hybrids went up to just above 3,000, but it was still a miniscule portion compared to the country's total auto sales – over 20 million ("2013 China new energy vehicle sales figures released" 2014). Yet the low sales figure did not indicate the consumers' initial lack of interest in the car. In fact, when Prius first appeared in Chinese Toyota dealerships in 2006, many showed up and stood in long lines to test-drive it. Most were amazed by the hybrid technology, but very few ended up buying it. The same fate is facing the newly emerged fully electric vehicles, such as the EVs (Electric Vehicles) and PHEVs (Plug-in Hybrid Electric Vehicles). Most Chinese consumers still stand on the sidelines and watch; even generous governmental subsidies could not make them easily open their wallets (Zhang 2012).

Why haven't the Chinese embraced the hybrid (or electric) car as a Western novelty like they did with the SUVs, Hennessey X, and iPhones? In "Why don't I buy electric cars," the *Guangzhou Daily* journalist Qing (2014) wrote: "the reason why the market doesn't accept [alternative energy vehicles], is not because they are not environmental friendly, but because they cannot meet people's needs." He complained that electric vehicles take too long to charge and he "needed" his car to be ready to go at all times. Qing's grievance evokes the long-held view that Chinese consumers are pragmatic and tend to judge a product's worth by its utilitarian value rather than its idealistic value. Chan (2004), for instance, argues that the Chinese lacks passion towards environmental marketing because of their "pragmatism":

> The traditionally "pragmatic" Chinese [...] philosophical teachings are based on the practicalities of everyday ethics, politics, and social relations, the Chinese people have long been characterized by pragmatism and realism (Sue & Kirk, 1972). Classical psychological research has demonstrated that, compared with Americans, Chinese people have a tendency to evaluate ideas according to practical and utilitarian values (Hellersberg, 1953), and are therefore more likely to emphasize the informational contents of advertisements, rather than the entertaining features (Zhao & Shen, 1995).

"Pragmatism" has been more frequently associated with China since Deng Xiaoping's economic reform in the early 1990s. Even Deng himself was famous for evoking the folk adage, "Black cat, white cat, it's a good cat if it catches the mouse" (meaning, "capitalism, socialism, it's a good system if it develops the economy") ("Truth behind the folk saying," 2008). Killion (2006) writes, "Chinese pragmatism is not so much an issue of an evolution to pragmatism in the politics of modern China, rather than the old, becoming the new again." (48).

But what is this "utility" that the Chinese "pragmatists" are after? Critical theory has often deemed "utility" as a problematic concept. Karl Marx famously distinguishes between "use value" and "exchange value": while the former refers to the ability of a commodity to satisfy (supposedly biological or objective) human wants or needs, the latter refers to its constructed value generated through social exchange. Based on Marx, Jean Baudrillard (1981) takes a step further and dissolves this opposition into a single category – "sign value;" he suggests that there is no such thing as "use value," since commodity values are intersubjective constructions that have no grounds in objective reality or biological needs. For Copjec (2004), utilitarianism "believ[es] naively that complete satisfaction is attainable by anyone who [...] sets about realizing a rational plan" (168). But this completely rational subject who amasses satisfaction for pure self-benefiting, biological needs does not exist. From the psychoanalytic viewpoint, utilitarianism is an ideological fantasy conditioned upon a misrecognition of the structure of human enjoyment, which is fundamentally irrational and sometimes self-destructive (this topic will be explored in depth in Chapter 5 on eco-fashion). The so-called "utility" is only an ideological construction. So the question is: if Chinese consumers' "pragmatism" does not rise from an objective, unbiased value system, then what is it based on? The answer is, an alternative, intersubjective system shaped through social interactions.

In an interview with *New Finance Economics* (*Xin Caijin*) (Ding 2008), Ms. Song, a Prius owner, expressed her dissatisfaction that all her family and friends thought she could have bought a much higher-capacity car at this price. One day, when drag-racing a friend on the highway, she lagged far behind her friend's VW Passat. "Comparing with my friend's car," said Ms. Song, "I feel that I have lost face (*mei mianzi*)." Another consumer complained about the size of the Prius: "the car has such a small body. It is no different from other two door cars. If you buy a Reiz [a high-power sedan with a V6 engine and all-wheel drive] with this much money, how much magnificent air (*daqi*) will you gain!" These testimonials demonstrate the immense power of interpersonal influence on Chinese consumers' decision-making processes. In Song's case, her family's disapproval dampened her spirits and her friend's scorn made her feel shame. It seems that her pursuits of identity and social status ("face" and "magnificent air") are to seek approval from this intimate social circle and any commodity choice that fails to obtain their approval is impugned as "not worth the price." Nevertheless, this interpersonal dynamic does not nullify advertising's effect on the consumers; in fact, as suggested by Lazarsfeld et al.'s (1944) two-step flow theory, media effects are often indirectly established through the personal influence of opinion leaders. Moreover, media messages are the most powerful when they confirm – rather than contradict—the existing beliefs of the opinion leaders. In the case of the hybrid car, advertising does introduce the abstract gaze of the Western *Other*, but its effects are compromised by the opinions of specific *others* (e.g. family and friends) who limit the influence of mass media. Although this interpersonal dynamic might seem to be a conservative (anti-environmental) force in the case at hand, it can potentially serve as the locale for consumer resistance in the global spread of Western green consumerist ideologies.

Conclusion

After analyzing American and Chinese hybrid car ads, I find that the former seeks to *erase* the Self from a fantasy of eco-harmony, while the latter strives to *expand* and *multiply* the Self in the technical gaze of the Other (West). By eliminating the car, a guilt-laden symbol in environmental rhetoric, American ads provides emotional redemption for the liberal-minded, middle-class consumers; the Chinese ads, however, significantly downplay the hybrid's environmental values and portray the technology as another status symbol to augment the ego of the urban rich. "Guilt" versus "pride:" Steve Asma (2010) traces this set of affects to the contrast between Christianity and Paganism:

> For the pagans, honor and pride were valued, but for the Christians it is meekness and humility; for the pagans it was public shame, for Christians, private guilt; for pagans there was a celebration of hierarchy, with superior and inferior people, but for Christians there is egalitarianism (para. 5).

Although it will be reductionist to explain American and Chinese cultural differences solely with the opposition of Christianity and Paganism, Asma's comparison is illuminating: it makes a powerful point that political and religious ideologies could shape cultural psyches and in turn influence consumer psychology. If the psychic structure of the American environmental rhetoric suggests the heritage of Judeo-Christianity, then the Chinese consumer-subjectivity bears certain imprint of Confucianism. Occupying the status of China's "civil religion" (Bellah 1975), Confucianism not only values the pursuit of pride and prestige but also advocates social hierarchy and the centrality of the family. The hybrid car is predictably subjected to this as well as many other philosophies that blossomed on China's historical territory (e.g. Chapter 5 will explore the influence of Daoism on Chinese ecological thought).

The last point of the chapter is to revisit the traditional distinction between individualism and collectivism through the perspective of psychoanalysis. In numerous American-Chinese cultural comparisons (e.g. Triandis 1993; Zhang & Neelankavil 1997; Lin 2001), the two are frequently identified by this set of binary, but my juxtaposition of the hybrid car ads seems to suggest the opposite. American culture, famous for its individualism, sees green consumerism as a collectivist calling, while Chinese culture, known for its collectivism, tends to consume green products for individual benefits. Now, who is the collectivist and who is the individualist? Are both cultures turning into their polar opposites in an apocalyptic frenzy? (In *The Simpsons Movie* 2007, there is an End-of-the-World scene in which all churchgoers run into bars and all bar-goers escape into the church.) The answer is, not quite. To understand desire, the psychoanalytic lesson is to move beyond the manifest content of cultural imaginaries and abandon the superficial categorization of "collectivism" versus "individualism." As my analysis shows, the American version of "collectivism" is in fact pursued in an individualistic fashion – avoiding the engagement with one's communities – while the Chinese version of "individualism" depends on the desires of the communal members, as consumers relentlessly search for approval from their families and friends. Rather than labeling cultures according to their overt "values" or "beliefs," we should characterize them according to the underlying structures of desire – for example, obsession and hysteria. While the obsessive performs solitary rituals by the self to avert terrible disasters, the hysteric is entrapped in the web of desire with others and cannot determine which subject positions to identify with.

With that said, I do not mean to assert that all consumers coming from one country are driven by one type of desire. Human desires are ultimately heterogeneous and cannot be determined by one single discursive structure. And advertising discourse within each of these gigantic nations is fragmented and their symbolic structures change with time. Thus, the reader should keep the complexity of culture and history in mind when viewing the above findings. In fact, due to the evolving nature of cultures and the forces of globalization, cross-cultural comparisons like this are always dealing with outliers or mutations that cannot fit in. For example, in the US, ads for the newly emerged EVs such as Chevy Volt, Tesla, and Fisker Karma diverge largely in strategy from the early group of hybrid cars ads (Prius, Honda Hybrid). They often capitalize on the car's energy-efficiency, high speed, slick design, or even sex appeal and give very little emphasis on the car's environmental values. These advertisements focus on selling to the tech-savvy, image-aware mainstream American drivers, rather than targeting at the usual tree-huggers. In a sense, they very much resemble the Chinese ads that we have reviewed in this chapter. They cannot be strictly considered as environmental advertisements and thus are not the focus of this chapter. This has proven my earlier point (in the beginning) that technologies and the popular representations are two different matters entirely. Judging by the technology, electric cars (plug-ins) might be more eco-friendly than the gas-electric hybrid cars. Judging by the advertisements, nonetheless, electric cars (and the new hybrids) are not mainly marketed as an eco-friendly product and are often purchased as a technological novelty for the conventional consumers who seek traditional values in their cars.

To end this chapter, I would like to call attention to the apocalyptic irony of this cross-cultural comparison that has inspired this book in the first place: it seems that no matter which structure of desire the consumer is embedded in, the environment of both the US and China (and thus the world) still loses out. Is it possible to truly engage the environment at all? Or will our desires always lead us astray? Can there be true environmental communication between cultures and countries? Or will we always be trapped in our ideological bubbles and can never truly communicate with each other? These questions will be explored further in the following chapters in the contexts of green homes, organic food, and eco-fashion.

Notes

1 The Prius became the first hybrid vehicle manufactured in China under the national hybrid vehicle certification system, which came into effect on October 1, 2005. See: http://www.funponsel.com/blog/news/first-hybrid-cars-in-china-the-toyota-prius.html
2 "Media are the extensions of Man," says Marshall McLuhan; yet he also points out that media induce the amputation of Man. Functioning as a medium between the body and the environment, the automobile technology brings us both the pleasures of "extension" and the threats of "amputation."
3 NB is the short form for *niubi*, a Chinese colloquial expression meaning "incredible" or "super cool."
4 In 2010, China had the world's longest and biggest traffic jam which lasted for 9 days and extended over 60 miles. See: "Nightmarish nine-day traffic Jam: In China, cars crawl along 60- mile stretch" by David Gura at NPR. Retrieved from http://www.npr.org/blogs/thetwo-way/2010/08/23/129376194/traffic-jam-beijing-tibet
5 Although the Lacanian metaphors of the hysteric and the obsessional are highly sexualized, I am using them to describe gender neutral desire that can be shared by men and women.

References

Asma, S. T. (2010, January 10). Green guilt. *The Chronicle Review: The Chronicle of Higher Education*. Retrieved from: http://chronicle.com/article/Green-Guilt/63447/

Beavan, C. (2009). *No Impact man: The Adventures of a Guilty Liberal Who Attempts to Save the Planet, and the Discoveries He Makes about Himself and Our Way of Life in the Process*. New York, NY: Farrar, Straus and Giroux.

Bellah, R. (1975). *The Broken Covenant: American Civil Religion in A Time of Trial*. New York, NY: Seabury Press.

Cha, A. E. (2008, July 2). China's cars, accelerating a global demand for fuel. *The Washington Post*. Retrieved from: http://www.washingtonpost.com/wp-dyn/content/article/2008/07/27/AR2008072701911_pf.html

China to subsidize electric, hybrid car purchases in five cities. (2010, June 1). *People's Daily*. Retrieved from: http://english.peopledaily.com.cn/90001/90778/90860/7008240.html

Ding. (2008, June). Huanbao qiche zai zhongguo [Environmental-friendly cars in China]. *Xin Caijing [New Finance Economics]*. Retrieved from: http://www.chinavalue.net/Media/Article.aspx?ArticleId=26652

Dichter, E. (1960). *The Strategies of Desire*. New York, NY: Doubleday.

Doctoroff, T. (2005). *Billions: Selling to the new Chinese consumer*. New York, NY: Palgrave Macmilan.

Fan, M. (2008, January 21). Creating a car culture in China: New owners among growing middle class find sense of freedom, "Taste the fun." *Washington Post Foreign Service*. Retrieved from: http://www.washingtonpost.com/wp-dyn/content/article/2008/01/20/AR2008012002388.html.

Fengyu bainian: Laofoye che shenshi [One hundred years of turmoil: The life of Empress Dowager's car]. (1996, January 1). *Chinese Auto Pictorial*, 1, 1–20.

Fink, B. (1997). *A Clinical Introduction to Lacanian Psychoanalysis: Theory and Technique.* Cambridge, MA: Harvard University Press.

Fink, B (2004). *Lacan to the letter: Reading Écrits closely.* Minneapolis, MN: University of Minnesota Press.

Freund, P., & Martin, G. (1993). *The Ecology of the Automobile.* Montreal: Black Rose Books.

Giblett, R. J. (2008). *Sublime communication technologies.* Basingstoke, England: Palgrave Macmillan.

Heimao maobao lun – minyan hou de zhenli. [The Black-Cat-White-Cat Theory: Truth Behind the Folk Saying] (2008, May 4). *People's Daily.* Retrieved from: http://finance.people.com.cn/GB/8215/103889/121891/7194003.html

Hessler, P. (2009). *Country Driving: A Journey Through China From Farm to Factory.* New York, NY: Harper Collins.

Hyde, J. (2008, September 14). "GM's 'Engine Charlie' Wilson learned to live with a misquote". *Detroit Free Press.* Retrived from: http://www.freep.com/article/20080914/BUSINESS01/809140308/GM-s-Engine-Charlie-Wilson-learned-live-misquote

Hyde, J. (2012, March 7). Invisible Mercedes brings James Bond technology to life. *Motoramic* at *Yahoo! Blogs.* Retrieved from: http://autos.yahoo.com/blogs/motoramic/invisible-mercedes-brings-james-bond-technology-life-171557818.html

Janus, N. (1983 Summer) Advertising and global culture. *Cultural Survival Quarterly,* 7.2, The Electronic Era.

Kolbert, E. (2009, August 31). Green like me. *The New Yorker.* Retrieved from: http://www.newyorker.com/arts/critics/atlarge/2009/08/31/090831crat_atlarge_kolbert?currentPage=all#ixzz0i7JE7nfs

Lacan, J. (1977). *The Four Fundamental Concepts of Psychoanalysis.* Ed. Miller, J., Trans. Sheridan, A. New York, NY: Norton.

Larzarsfeld, P. F., Berelson, B., & GaudetH. (1944). *The People's Choice: How the Voter Makes Up His Mind in a Presidential Campaign.* New York: Columbia University Press.

Lemke, T. (2002). Foucault, governmentality, and critique. *Rethinking Marxism, 14(3),* 49–64.

Lerner, D. (1973). Notes on communication and the nation state. *The Public Opinion Quarterly,* 37(4), 541–550.

Lim, L. (2009, February 10). Car ownership changes Chinese society. *National Public Radio.* Retrieved from: http://www.npr.org/templates/story/story.php?storyId=100497742

Lin, C. (2001). Cultural values reflected in Chinese and American television advertising. *Journal of Advertising, 30(4), Winter,* 83–94.

Litke, M. (2002, December 21). American car culture invades China. *ABC News.* Retrieved from: http://abcnews.go.com/WNT/story?id=129934

Morton, T. (2007). *Ecology Without Nature: Rethinking Environmental Aesthetics.* Cambridge, MA: Harvard University Press.

Mumford, L. (1961). *The City in History: Its Origins, Its Transformations, and Its Prospects.* New York, NY: Harcourt, Brace and Jovanovitch.

New energy cars are praised but not purchased; sales only count for 0.2%. (2012, April 17). *NetEase,* the automobile section. Retrieved from: http://auto.163.com/12/0417/07/7V9DTS0800084TV1.html

Packard, V. (1957). *The Hidden Persuaders.* London: Random House.

Qiche ran "lv" chengfeng: Xin nengyuan che weihe jiaohao bu Jiaozuo [Why are alternative energy cars praised but not purchased]. (2009, August 13). *Information Times.* Retrieved from: http://news.ucar.cn/details.aspx?nid=96515

Qing, Z. (2014, December 8). Wo weishenme bu mai diandongche [Why don't I buy electric cars]. Guangzhou Daily. Retrieved from: http://gzdaily.dayoo.com/html/2014-12/08/content_2816652.htm

Qu, X. (2009, May 20). Hybrid-power vehicle sales experience embarrassing situation in China. *People's Daily*. Retrieved from: http://english.peopledaily.com.cn/90001/90776/90884/6661849.html

Sachs, W. (1992). *For Love of the Automobile: Looking Back into the History of our Desires* (Reneau, D. Trans.). Berkeley, CA: The University of California Press.

Spagat, E. (2010, March 10). Feds to probe cause of runaway Prius in California. *Associated Press*. Retrieved from: http://news.yahoo.com/s/ap/20100310/ap_on_bi_ge/us_runaway_prius

Triandis, H. C. (1993). Collectivism and individualism as cultural syndromes. *Cross-cultural research, 22(3–4)*, 150–180.

Urry, J. (2004). The "system" of automobility. *Theory, Culture & Society, 21(4/5)*, 25–39.

Waller, M. (2005). Auto-Mobility. *Washington Monthly*, Oct/Nov, 37, 10–11.

Wang, X. & Yang, Z. (2008). Does country-of-origin matter in the relationship between brand personality and purchase intention in emerging economies? Evidence from China's auto industry. *International Marketing Review, 25(4)*, 458–474.

Watts, J. (2012, March 16). Air pollution could become China's biggest health threat, expert warns. *The Guardian*. Retrived from: http://www.guardian.co.uk/environment/2012/mar/16/air-pollution-biggest-threat-china

Williams, R. (1985). *The country and the city*. London: The Hogarth Press.

Williamson, J. (1978). *Decoding advertisements: Ideology and meaning in advertising*. London: Boyars.

Žižek, S. (2001). *Enjoy your symptom!: Jacques Lacan in Hollywood and out*. New York, NY: Routledge.

Žižek, S (2007). *How to read Lacan*. New York, NY: W.W. Norton & Company.

Zhang, Y., & Neelankavil, J. P. (1997). The influence of culture on advertising effectiveness in China and the USA: A cross-cultural study. *European Journal of Marketing, 31(2)*, 134–149.

Zhang, S. (2012, October 29). Diandongche xiaoliang di, dianchiye bian tangshou shanyu? [Electric vehicles sales low, battery business becoming hot potato?] *Sohu Auto*. Retrieved from: http://auto.sohu.com/20121029/n355993227.shtml

Zhao, B. (1997). Consumerism, Confucianism, communism: Making sense of China today. *New Left Review, 222*, 43–59.

Zhao, B. (2007, August 14). Youren jide zhebu meiju ma? [Can anybody remember this American TV show?] [Web log message]. Retrieved from http://www.mtime.com/my/781648/blog/506197/

Zhongguo qiche lishi de cangsang bianqian [The vicissitudes of China's automobile history] [Online forum comment]. (2005, January 18). *Che Tianxia*. Retrieved from http://bbs.chetx.com/149/57_921039_921039.htm

Zhou, L. (2013, January 17). 2012 nian SUV shichang xiaoliang 183.7 wanliang, tongbi zeng 22.7% [2012 SUV sales reach 1.837 million, an increase of 22.4% from the previous year]. *Tengxun Qiche* [Tencent Auto]. Retrieved from: http://auto.qq.com/a/20130117/000127.htm

Zhongguo xinnengyuan qiche xiaoliang chulu [2013 China new energy vehicle sales figures released] (2014, January 10). *Diandong Qiche Shidai* [Electric Vehicles Times]. Retrieved from: http://www.evdays.com/html/2014/0109/zb44725.html

3 Detoxing the Private
Parenting Philosophy in Green Home Product Advertising

"A home is the foundation of all consciousness because it allows us to perceive the world," says the media philosopher Vilém Flusser (2004, 102). Indeed, as the primary locus of socialization, home is where we develop our beliefs, values, and worldviews. How we imagine the "greening" of our homes speaks volumes about how we envision the "greening" of the world, or what is "green" in general. The relationship between the home and the world is always fraught with contradictions and instability. In the English term "homeland" or the Chinese "*jiaguo*" (home-state), home is used as a metaphor for the state, implying an alignment of interests between the two. Yet home can also exist as a counter-point to the state. It represents private welfare and sometimes comes into conflict with the public welfare of the community, the nation, or the world. In this sense, the relationship between the home and its environment is at stake in green consumerism. This chapter compares Chinese and American green home product advertising. It analyzes the different structures of desire that underlie the ideological fantasy of a "green home" and the implication of these structures (as either facilitators or obstacles) for the "greening" of homemaking worldwide.

During the past decade, both China and the US have witnessed the rise of a green home product industry. Advertising, lifestyle magazines, and business literature in both countries tout the eco-friendliness of home decoration and household products and provide tips or DIY instructions for consumers to "green" their homes. Product categories in this market are miscellaneous, including energy-saving electronics, water-saving toiletry and kitchen appliances, recycled and sustainably-produced wood flooring and furniture, toxin-free wall paint and covering, green cleaning products, and more. Due to the rich variety of products available, it is important to first define the "green home" agenda. The US Environmental Protection Agency (EPA) describes this agenda through six imperatives:

> [1] reduc[e] home energy use and using renewable energy; [2] reduc[e] home water use and protecting water resources; [3] select the most environmental friendly location for a new home; [4] choos[e] greener home building materials and household products; [5] reduc[e] waste from home construction and household activates and increasing recycling; [6] protect

your health from environmental hazards that occur in homes ("Green homes overview," 2012).

This comprehensive list covers a broad range of ecological impact of the private home, from building construction, energy and resource consumption, to waste generation and household maintenance. In China, the Ministry of Environmental Protection (MEP) has not issued an official mandate for "green home," yet Baidu Baike (China's equivalent of Wikipedia) lists two definitions. The first one, added as early as 2006, refers to "the idea of bringing in a microscopic view of nature in order to enliven the home space," particularly through the growing of green plants indoors ("Lvse jiaju," 2006). Interpreting the term "green home" literally, this definition "is extremely important for urban dwellers, who have long been separated from nature to fulfill their psychological need to 'return to Nature'" (ibid). This definition clearly diverges from the American version and concerns more with the benefit of the home dwellers inside than the wellbeing of the ecosystems outside. The second definition, published more recently in 2014, presents a more Westernized notion: "the use of environmentally friendly materials in home decoration, furniture, electronics, and home remodeling." Although the meaning of "environmentally friendly" is not specified, it shows the evolution of the Chinese term toward a potentially more comprehensive and ecological direction.

The varying definitions of what makes a home product "green" in the US and China, respectively, correspond with different market structures. In the US, "all-natural" and "eco-friendly" household cleaning products (e.g. dish and laundry detergent, multipurpose cleaner, toilet cleaner) prevail in terms of sales, advertising rates, and media attention they receive; in China, "toxin-free" green home décor products (e.g. toxin-free wall paint, flooring, and furniture) take the lead in similar dimensions. Accordingly, I will compare advertisements for cleaning products in the US and home décor products in China. Interestingly, both of the bestselling green home products in the two countries respond to the same environmental crisis – toxic chemicals polluting the domestic space – and construct the fantasy of a home free of contamination. These ideological fantasies are underpinned by differing psychosocial relationship within the family and psycho-spatial relationship inside and outside of the house. I explore how these relationships cultivate different worldviews about private and public, domestic and wild, purity and contamination, and how they are passed on from parents to children to have ecological implications.

Home, House, Family, and their Environmental Implications

The study of domestic life or "home" is by nature multidisciplinary. It has been examined in sociology, anthropology, economics, architecture, housing studies, women's studies, consumer culture studies, philosophy, and psychoanalysis, among others. According to British sociologists Saunders and Williams (1988), home is a "spatial-social system:" It contains the spatial unit of the *house* (or apartment) on the one hand and the social unit of the *household* or *family* on the other (83). The home is irreducible to either dimension. This interlocking relationship allows sociologists to study the social and cultural practices of the family by analyzing the physical and spatial aspects of the house, it also allows architects to design the spatial structure of the house based on the social and cultural values of those inside. For example, in Saunders and Williams' study of English housing culture, they point out that English families usually live in detached and privately owned houses and often show less interest in "collectivized living strategies (e.g. in the parks and cafes)" than their European neighbors such as France or the Netherlands (87). This type of housing structure, they claim, can be traced to the English political tradition, which sees home as the "symbolic antithesis of the state" and seeks to "limit the intrusion of the state into the private affairs of its subjects" (88). This pursuit of household autonomy can also be seen from the architectural design of American and Australian houses. Sharing the same Anglo-Saxon roots, both cultures are characterized by massive suburban sprawl, "composed of individual houses set proudly in their own plots and with relatively low levels of collective infrastructural and service provision" (ibid).

In the same vein, anthropologist Francis L. K. Hsu (1981) compares the architectural design of American and Chinese houses in his classic *Americans & Chinese*. His analysis examines how the home relates to its outside environment as well as the environment within. On the exterior, Hsu observed, American houses seem more open to their surroundings. They usually have a yard and maybe a hedge, and have nothing but window curtains or blinds to protect the interior from exterior view (78). Most Chinese houses, by contrast, are strictly separated from the outside. High walls and solid gates usually surround them. Sometimes a "shadow wall" behind the gate would shield the interior courtyard from the glances of the passerby (ibid). On the interior, however, the open-closed dynamic in Chinese and American houses is inverted. The American houses uphold privacy, not only through the division of the function of the rooms (e.g. bathrooms, bedrooms, living room, kitchen) but also through the demarcation of space and possessions between parents and children. "Parents have little liberty in the rooms of the children, and children cannot do what they want in those parts of the house regarded as preeminently their parents' domain" (79). Inside the Chinese homes, on the other hand, privacy hardly exists between family members. Chinese children often share the same room with their parents until they reach adolescence. "Not only do parents have freedom of action with reference to the children's belongings, but the youngsters can also use the possessions of the parents if they can lay their hands on them" (ibid). For Hsu, the spatial arrangements of the house correlate with the social structures of the family. In China, the parents who share the same space with children also prefers children who think and act more like them. The ideal Chinese child is valued for her maturity in understanding the adult culture and sophistication in maneuvering interpersonal relationships. In the

US, the parents who occupy separate spaces from their children prefer to "let children be children" – i.e. expect them to follow their own interests and passions without adult interference. The ideal American child is cherished for her innocence to social relationships and her connection to her own enjoyment. In summary, the American home establishes strong discipline for the child indoors, but does little to separate him from the outside world; the Chinese home, however, strictly separates the child from the outside world, but maintains little restriction for him indoors.

In comparison to Sanders & Williams' and Hsu's social-spatial approach, psychoanalysis adopts a third position and studies the psychic dimension of domestic life. For Freud, like Flusser, family is the primary locus of socialization. Childhood experiences, most of which take place through interactions with parents, shape the adult psyche. In his theory of psychic formation (e.g. infantile sexuality, castration anxiety, Oedipus Complex, etc.), a child's relationship with parental authorities shapes his experience of the home as well as his future experience with the world. For Lacan, family is primarily constituted by the linguistic play between parents and child. Parental injunctions lay out the ground rules for the child's relationship with the Law and with his own enjoyment. What would it look like when we apply this psycho-social approach to examine the spatial structure of the house? A simple analysis can be seen, for example, in the family ritual of grounding – a common parenting technique already hinted in Hsu's description above. When the parents issue the injunction "Thou shall not leave home," the physical boundary of the house (i.e. the wall or the gate) thus gains psychic significance and becomes a barrier against the child's own enjoyment of the outside world; it could also channel his libido to the building of family relationships and potentially cultivate his concerns for private rather than public welfares. Indeed, parental instructions powerfully shape children's evolving relationship with the world. Since these educational philosophies are ideological and are shared within a culture, they inevitably manifest in advertising discourse. Hence, I ask: How do these green home ads depict an ideal parent-child relationship within the Chinese and American families? How is this relationship projected onto the relationship between the inside and outside of the home? What does this mean for the toxins that cross the boundary between the home and its environment, and the "detox" solutions projected in the ads? What can these ads tell us about the evolving conjunction between home and environment in the world's two most powerful countries?

Building the Private "Oasis" in Chinese Housing Culture

I will begin my analysis of China with a brief overview of the traditional notion of "home" and the modern infrastructure that both challenged and reinforced it. The Chinese character for home is *jia* (家), an ideogrammic compound made up of two parts – 宀 and 豕. When put together, they mean "a pig under the roof" (Huang & Huang 2011).[1] Since pigs were the symbol of wealth for rural families and formerly lived under houses on stilts, the character indicates that family is a basic social unit with its own economic foundation and spatial territory. In modern Chinese, *jia* indicates, first, house, home, and residence, and second, family. It not only includes the container or the shell, but also the social relationships it contains (Fleischer 2007, 296). Home occupies an important position in Confucianism. It was the primary locale where hier-archies of the feudal society were established. In *San Gang* (Three Guiding Principles), the Confucian moral and political requirements are crystallized into three sets of subordinations: first, *zhong* (忠 loyalty) – the minister must serve his emperor; second, *xiao* (孝 filialness) – a son must serve his father; and third, *zhen* (贞 fidelity) – a wife must serve her husband (Yao 2000, 34). As a metaphor of the state, home bears the responsibility to cultivate obedient children who will become obedient subjects to the emperor.

China's encounter with the modern home can be traced to the Maoist period, when socialist planning radically altered the infrastructure in which people lived and worked. Two housing policies were used to control domestic life. The *hukou* (household registration) system restricted residents in their native birthplaces and prohibits them from moving elsewhere (Davis 1995, 2). The *danwei* (work units) system – state-run production-centered compounds for urban workers and their families – provided the necessities of daily life, such as working, shopping, eating, social services, child rearing, elderly care, and eliminated their need to leave the collective space. (Fleischer, 290). During the Maoist period, these policies created the "residential immobility" that dominated China's housing situation. Housing was not a trade-able commodity but a welfare benefit distributed to the most deserving "supplicants" in a public housing queue (Davis, 698).

In the post-1978 economic reform, nevertheless, housing policies dramatically shifted. On the one hand, the state encouraged people to leave their work units and find jobs and housing on the free market (Fleischer, 290). On the other hand, land reforms in the late 1980s re-introduced land prices and relegated housing construction to private contractors. This reform led to massive upgrading in the quality of urban homes and the privatization of nearly all residential properties by 2002. The housing boom quickly filled up the cities and led to the emergence of suburbs. Similar to the urban developments in US cities after World War II, China's suburbanization appeared under the conditions of improved transportation, rapid urban growth, inner city renovation, and rising incomes (Wang & Zhou, 1999, cited in Fleischer, ibid).

In the mass consumerist boom of the 1990s and 2000s, the private home emerged as a major commodity and a key marker of socio-economic status. "More important than ownership of a car, travel, and leisure activities in general, children's schools, and clothing styles, where and how one lives is an indicator of one's financial well-being" (Fleischer, 297). The home also becomes the central consumer item around which other items cluster. According to Fraser, purchas-ing a luxurious apartment leads to "the Diderot effect" – the urge to upgrade all other commodities such as furniture, home appliances, electronics (Grant McCracken's term, quoted in Fraser, 32). In the new residential environment, privacy and anonymity become the most valued characteristics. Unlike the old courtyard houses (e.g. Beijing's *hutong* or Shanghai's *shikumen*) where people share communal showers, bathrooms, or kitchens, these new residences are Westernized – i.e. composed of self-contained flats, with internal walls and doors subdividing the interior space into several functionally-specific enclosed spaces (Davis, 701). The latest housing structure reduces the chance of interaction between neighbors, and leads to the segregation of residential communities according to age, income, education, etc (ibid).

Housing advertisements in this new era capitalize on privacy and alienation from public and communal life. David Fraser (2000) examines Shanghai's luxury apartment ads from the 1990s and observes the frequent portrayal of the private home as an urban "oasis" – "a green, pleasant, personal space as a buffer zone between the individual apartment and its larger social and spatial contexts" (27). Politically, the private "oasis" functions as a space beyond the all-seeing gaze of the state. Unlike work units that used to closely monitor and direct personal activity and behavior, private homes become the locale "where one enjoys increased personal autonomy from state control and can consume and act in a relatively free way" (43). Yet the "oasis" also performs a more important function: to shelter the residents from environmental pollution. As industrialization and urbanization quickly deteriorated China's environment, air and noise pollution in Chinese cities reached unbearable levels. Fraser (2000) recounts the noise pollution in Shanghai in the 1990s: "car, truck, bus, and motorcycle horns honk constantly [and] construction noise drowns the chime of bicycle bells" (45). Air pollution poses an even worse problem: thick smog envelops the streets and the buildings and sends thousands to the hospital each day with respiratory diseases. Seeking protection from the polluted urban environment, many city dwellers see the private home as the last frontier – a safer and cleaner "inside" to shelter them and their families from the repressive and dirty "outside." Advertisements often carry the promise of "respite, greenery, and peace," and tout the adjacency of real estate to urban gardens, parks, and lawns and its access to cool wind and fresh air. The "oasified" homes temporarily relieve the residents' separation anxiety from nature and provide an imagined "cushion [against] the clamorous world of commerce and transport" (46).

However, the imagined "oasis" is no fortress. Pollution is still seeping from the "outside" in, invading the homeowner's safety cocoon. Compared to the notoriously polluted outdoor air, China's indoor air pollution is often 5 to 10 times worse ("2.2 million young Chinese die," 2010). One of the main culprits is *zhuangxiu* – interior design and decoration products and practices. The *zhuangxiu* culture is a unique byproduct of China's housing boom. Since most new Chinese apartments are sold as concrete shells (*mao pei*) with no interior wiring, floors, finished walls, or doorframes (Davis, 706), new residents need to purchase and install every item to make the shelter a livable space. As new homeowners decorate their dream homes, they often unknowingly purchase low-quality products such as wall paint, furniture, and flooring that introduce high levels of toxic chemicals into their homes. Soon after moving into their newly decorated homes, many residents develop the "Sick Building

Syndrome," with symptoms ranging from respiratory diseases to mental impairment and cancer. Most affected are children and the elderly – the most vulnerable members of the family. According to China's Centre for Disease Control and Prevention, indoor air pollution kills 2.2 million Chinese youth each year (ibid). Many children developed leukemia after their parents decorated their homes. Most of these casualties owe to their exposure to benzene, ammonia, radon, and formaldehyde – pollutants found in home décor products (Li 2005).

Toxic contamination of the private homes is traumatizing to Chinese homeowners on many levels. On the spatial level, it shatters the ideological fantasy of a private "oasis" which protects them from environmental pollution in public spaces. As pollution enters from the "outside" to the "inside," the repressed threat returns in the form of toxins and exposes the fictitiousness of the boundary between the private home and the public environment. On the social level, toxic contamination of the homes harms children – the core of China's modern nuclear family. Since China's one-child policy went into effect in 1979, the single child became the exclusive embodiment of the hopes and dreams of a family. Were the child to fall ill, it would threaten another ideological fantasy of Chinese culture – that of procreation and family lineage – and would be detrimental to a Chinese family.

"Thou Shall Not Go Out:" Chinese Green Home Decor Product Advertising

In response to the widespread fear about toxic contamination, manufacturers of home décor products aimed to steady the shaken fantasy. Since the mid-2000s, wall paint, furniture, and flooring industries successively launched ecofriendly products, touting their "toxin-free," "zero-formaldehyde," and "pollution absorbing" features. My analysis will focus on the advertisements for "toxin-free" wall paint, because paint manufacturers advertise more aggressively than furniture and flooring makers. Similar to the soap industry in the US (which I explore below), the wall paint industry has been one of the earliest and biggest advertisers in post-reform China.[2] The current market is dominated by two foreign brands – Nippon, a Japanese brand entering China in 1992, and Dulux, a British brand entering in 1994. Named as the "Coke and Pepsi" of the paint market, these two brands have the combined market shares of 95.88 percent – far above all domestic brands which totaled less than 5 percent (Chen 2013). Dulux and Nippon started their advertising campaigns on national television in the late 1990s. Many consumers today can still recall the slogan "Nippon Paint works beautifully everywhere" or the enormous English sheep dog in the Dulux commercials. Their aggressive advertising had contributed to their leading sales figures ("Guanggao xuan-chuan boyi," 2014). When asked about why most people prefer foreign over domestic brands, a consumer once explained: "It's not that I don't want to support domestic products. Dulux and Nippon's are just always on TV" ("Duoleshi PK Libang Qi," 2010).

In the mid-2000s, Dulux and Nippon both launched their ecofriendly versions of wall paint and released their national advertising campaigns. The first ad we turn to is a 30-second commercial "Runaway Baby" for the Dulux Life Master/Clean Air Choice released in 2007 (see Figure 3.1 on the author's blog "Environmental Advertising in China and the USA"; same goes with all the following figures). "Life Master" is one of the three "Eco Well-being" Paint products that Dulux released in 2007 (the other two being "Forest Breath" and "All Around Guard"). The commercial begins with a young father painting a living room wall and his toddler daughter coughing. "It's chocking me. Doggy, let's go!" She dresses herself up and walks toward the door. The signature Dulux dog follows her. Mother enters and brings the toddler back. She blames her husband: "The paint smells so bad, no wonder our baby wants to run away!" The father turns around, surprised: "What?!" The camera zooms in on the wall only to find computer animated toxic chemical "devils" bearing their teeth. The narrator's voice enters: "Use Dulux Lifemaster Clean Air Choice. It contains a new eco-friendly odor-less formula, with no added benzene, mercury, and lead. Keep new homes away from the smell of paint." Meanwhile, a fleet of green leaves comes out of a can of Dulux and flies across the room. It encircles the parents, baby, and dog, as they sit down happily together in a picture-perfect modern living room. "Eco-friendly and odorless, safe and comfortable, Dulux Lifemaster Clean Air Choice." After the brand name flashes across the screen, the baby is shown kissing the wall. Then, she turns around with a big smile: "Really no smell!"

This commercial constructs a harmonious, toxin-free "green home" by centering on the image of the happy, healthy child. This strategic choice corresponds largely to the desire of the parent-consumers. Using Lacanian vocabulary, children are the big Other for their parents. Identifying with the desire of the Other, however, leads to a lifetime of anxiety. Starting from the baby's first cry, parents have to interpret: does she need to eat, drink, or poop? As the child grows up, parents have to spend tremendous energy planning around her schooling, career, marriage, etc. But there is no guarantee that the child's desire will match parental plans. This commercial revolves around this exact conflict between the child's desire and that of the parents. In an ideal private home as portrayed in the home décor magazines, parents are engaging in *zhuangxiu* and are anticipating the completion of their safety cocoon. Conflict, however, arises when the child wants to go "outside." This immediately spells trouble for the parents. As mentioned above, most Chinese urban dwellers deem the "outside" as an antagonistic place full of pollution, surveillance, crime, and other unpredictable danger. The thought of a toddler going "outside" all by herself presents unthinkable horror. To resolve this conflict, the mother closes the door behind her and issues the injunction: "Thou shalt not go out." Moreover, she assumes that she "knows" the reason – indoor air pollution. This assumption rejects the possibility that the child may want to go out for other reasons (e.g. taking a stroll, meeting friends, playing in nature) and denies her of her alternative enjoyment for activities outdoors. Here Hsu's point becomes useful to explain the mother's reasoning: since in traditional Chinese culture, an ideal child is an obedient child. The child must desire what her parents desire – to live in the newly decorated apartment. If she ever tries to escape, she "must" be running *away* from the indoors, rather than running *toward* the outdoors. The reason for her attempted departure must be... that there are "toxins" in the wall paint.

The psychoanalytic name for the "toxins" is the symptom – i.e. the antagonistic outsider that sustains (albeit negatively) the fantasy of a harmonious family. Without them, the fantasy would fall apart. Hence the toxins must be brought to existence, through visualization, to prevent the mother from confronting her worst fears (of having a disobedient child). In a sense, the dueling of the parent-child desire is doubled in the battle between the cartoon devils and the green leaves. If the devils embody the child's desire to escape home, then the green leaves that encircle the family's living room represent the mother's desire to protect/entrap the child in her private "oasis." (A similar visualization can be found in Alfred Hitchcock's *Birds*, where the mother's jealousy takes the form of the hovering birds – see Žižek in *The Pervert's Guide to Cinema*, 2006) The green leaves destroy the devils, of course, and the mother's desire triumphs over the child's disturbing potential for autonomy. In the end, the child's reaction confirms the mother's suspicion: after the paint is switched, she euphorically kisses the wall and confirms the wisdom of her choice.

The second commercial we consider is the highly popular 45-second "Why can't I play with you" for Dulux Safe Home Emulsion released in 2009 (Figure 3.2). In an outdoor garden, a toddler boy and a girl of the same age are talking intimately. The boy grabs the girl's hand and asks: "Why don't you let me go to your home any more?" "Hmm..." "Is it because I am not tall enough for you?" "No." The girl shakes her head. "My degree isn't high enough for you?" "No..." "My salary isn't high enough for you?" "That's not it, either..." The boy bursts into tears: "Then why? Why? Why on earth can't I play at your home?" The girl finally tells the truth: "Because... my home smells like gasoline!" The camera switches to a can of Dulux paint, where a fleet of green leaves flies out and fills a living room. The little boy's voice is heard in the background: "Don't worry, your home uses Dulux Safe Home Emulsion Wall Paint. It has the innovative Clean Air formula. No gasoline smells. Safe and eco-friendly." These children are now sitting on the floor of the girl's living room, with the English sheep dog between them, admiring the newly-painted wall. Both children bury their noses in the wall and turn around saying: "Really, no smell!"

This commercial begins with an outdoor scene, where the boy and the girl seem to be having a secret meeting without their parents' knowledge. But their entire discussion revolves around how to return to the indoors. If indoors is the territory of the parents and outdoors is the territory of the children, then the children here desire what the adults desire. Moreover, they behave like adults too: the boy and the girl are engaging in a courting ritual that is too mature for their age. He lays out his mating capital one after another (e.g. height, degree, salary, etc.) and she denies them all and plays hard-to-get. When the girl finally airs her apprehension, the mystery is solved and the courting ritual comes to a happy close. In the living room, the boy and the girl – with the addition of the dog – form a new heterosexual family triad and live happily ever after. It is clear that this commercial represents another triumph of the parents' desire over that of the child. Although children have inchoate sexuality and often develop "puppy love," their sexual desires have not been "castrated" by the rules of the marriage market. But their parents' desires have. In Chinese traditional culture, extending the family's genealogical line has paramount importance; children are expected to marry and procreate as soon as they reach the suitable age. This commercial exaggerates this tradition. On the surface, it seems ridiculous and absurd, but it in fact fulfills an unconscious wish of the parents (in feudal China it used to be standard practice for parents to arrange marriages before the birth of their babies; see "Belly-Pointing Marriage," 2014). Here, toxic chemicals are presented as an obstacle to the traditional fantasy of procreation and family line extension and getting rid of them consummates the fantasy.

The third example we consider is the 30-second commercial "Forest," created for Dulux Bamboo Charcoal Forest Breath Emulsion Paint in 2012 (Figure 3.3). It features the Dulux sheep dog running through a boundless, green bamboo forest. As the camera sweeps across, the audience sees furniture pieces (e.g. sofa, coffee table, bed) sitting in the open forest space. Suddenly, the dog stops in front of a door, which oddly stands in the middle of the forest. The door opens and a young couple enters from the other side. Then the forest magically morphs into a living room. The husband speaks to the infant in his wife's arms: "Look, this is the new home daddy painted for you!" The wife: "It's so refreshing!" The camera zooms in on the living room wall and shows black clouds ("formaldehyde, benzene, and bacteria") being extinguished by green leaves ("bamboo charcoal and silver ions"). A male voiceover enters: "Dulux Bamboo Charcoal Forest Breath Emulsion: it contains bamboo charcoal elements that purify formaldehyde and benzene and silver ions that resist strong bacteria. Natural and refreshing home. Adds color to your new life." Finally, the parents, child, and dog happily huddle together in the newly painted living room and the Dulux brand name appears.

Unlike the first two examples, this commercial begins with an idealized image of the outdoors. The pet dog, as a member of the family (a symbolic double of the child), is running wildly in the forest and thoroughly enjoying himself – as a child might. However, parents appear and the "dream" ends: the audience realizes that the outdoors is really the indoors. The bamboo forest is just a concoction of the imagination. The space the father proudly presents to his child is nothing but a modern living room. This drop in expectation expresses an ambivalence harbored by Chinese homeowners. As mentioned above, the private apartment is usually seen as a protective shelter against the polluted outdoor environment. However, this shelter also functions as a cage – the dialectic opposite of a shelter – and traps the residents indoors and deprives them of nature and open space. This dilemma makes urban dwellers simultaneously crave and fear the outdoors. The "dream" of the bamboo forest perfectly manifests this ambivalence: it is both indoors and outdoors and allows the family to enjoy the benefits of the public environment (fresh air, nature views) without all the elements that disturb the fantasy of the private home (e.g. streets, buildings, people, pollution, noise, surveillance).

This half-indoor, half-outdoor space can be widely observed in Chinese green home décor product ads (see Figures 3.4–3.10 for the print ads for Dulux's All Around Guard Emulsion Paint, Nippon's Odorless All-in-One Paint, Three Trees Healthy Paint, and Huarun Eco-Friendly All-in-One Paint, as well as the print ads for Hexiang Zero-Formaldehyde Flooring and HCG Water-Saving Toilet). All of these ads present picturesque nature images in the background and a happy nuclear family (and their modern furniture) in the foreground. On the one hand, this expresses Chinese' people's claustrophobia and their desire for the outdoor space. But on the other hand, the outdoor space alone is not enough: it must also be utterly private, where externalities – e.g. streets, pollution, noise, people – do not exist. This indicates that the so-called "claustrophobia" of the Chinese is not really fear for an enclosed physical space, but fear for an enclosed social space. It is a response to psychic cramming, a type of "intersubjective claustrophobia" that results from modernization and urbanization (Copjec 1989).

The last advertisement I present is the 15-second commercial for Nippon Odorless All-In-One Paint: "I want to live in an ocean world" (Figure 3.11). In the daughter's bedroom at night, the parents are sitting next to the bed and reading her bedtime stories. The girl says: "I want to live in the ocean world!" The parents exchange knowing looks and wait for her to fall asleep.Then they paint her bedroom in an ocean theme. Next morning, the girl wakes up and finds her dream becomes "reality." She cheerfully dances in her "ocean world" and happliy embraces her parents. At a glance, this commercial seems to be an example of Chinese parents giving way to the child's desire. But it is not. Instead of bringing the child to the ocean or the aquarium, the parents paint her a simulation of the ocean on the wall. The trompe-l'oeil (deception of the eye) postpones the child's desire for new horizons and saves the parents a trip to the dangerous outdoors (where no such "ocean world" exists). In a way, this wish to keep the child at home is a defense mechanism against the loss of the environmental safety and beauty outdoors; however, in teaching the child to live with indoor simulations, the parents are reducing her very ability to enjoy the "real" natural environment and make her less likely to take actions to protect it when she grows up.

Generally speaking, the parents portrayed in these ads display symptoms of hysteria. Hysteria is one of the two types of neurosis that Lacan has identified (the other one being obsession). As outlined in Chapter 2, the main feature of the hysteric is her attempt to be the object of the Other's desire (Fink 1997, 120). But to maintain the Other's desire, she must not give herself over easily for the Other's enjoyment (*jouissance*). Since too much enjoyment and exposure kills desire, the hysteric constantly deprives the Other, and herself, of enjoyment in order to maintain desire – her source of power. She adheres to the motto: "The Other will never get off on me!" (Fink 123). By refusing to be the cause of the Other's *jouissance*, the hysteric strives to be the cause of the Other's desire (Fink 123). Chinese parents as portrayed in these green home advertisements display such symptoms. Although children often enjoy the outdoors and crave contact with the natural environment, parents painstakingly confine them within the private home and believe that the confinement is for their own benefit. Rather than allowing children to thoroughly enjoy themselves outdoors, parents prefer to withhold the object of the children's desire and leave them wanting. ("These rules are imposed for your own good!" "Too much fun will hurt you." "You will thank me one day.") Moreover, to further master the Other's desire, hysteric parents offer simulations of children's demand and expect to receive recognition and gratitude in return. In the parents' fantasy, children desire what the parents desire and feel grateful for their efforts to manage their enjoyment. However, the fantasy encounters a crisis when the symptom emerges: indoor toxins bring back the disturbing thought that children might refuse the private "oasis" that parents painstakingly construct and that they might desire something entirely different. This thought triggers intense anxiety. To restore their fantasy, these advertisements aim to remove the symptom, i.e. indoor toxins, and generate a "green home" space where the fantasy of an elegant family consensus can be restored. In this case, environmental pollution becomes the embodiment of a much broader fear or social anxiety – the uncanniness of the real family.

The hysteric structure can be used to explain the parenting philosophy in both traditional and contemporary China. In traditional culture (as described by Hsu, among many others), Chinese parents are known for their "cruelty" in educating their children (e.g. confining them in domestic space, arranging their marriages, forcing them into family careers), all to curb the children's enjoyment – even if it brings suffering to both the parents and the child. The infamous "Tiger Mom" parenting technique is typical of such "cruelty": if your child scores less than 100 percent in her math test, hit her hard, but then cry internally as you watch her suffer. Meanwhile, Chinese children are allowed unusual amounts of freedom as long as they obey the essential boundaries set out by their parents. Sometimes such freedom reaches the level of spoiling: in contemporary China, parents are known to have created a generation of "little emperors and empresses" by conceding to their every demand – as long as the children are kept under tight reign within the confines of the home. What is the environmental implication for such "spoiling" practices? For one, they are turning the "little emperors and empresses" into a generation of "indoor men and indoor women" (*zhai nan, zhai nv*). These "indoor" youths cherish a particular love for communication technologies such as smart phones or video games that provide simulation of "outdoor" activities (or, what Raymond Williams calls technologies of "private mobilization"). These technologies direct the libido inward and alienate the subject from the space outside of the home – including the natural environment.[3] However, as Dodds (2011) points out, being in close contact with nature generates biophilia—a love of life or living systems (originally proposed in Fromm 1964)—that powerfully motivates environmental actions. So, how can this young generation ever learn to love and protect nature if they have never experienced what it is?

* * *

The American Obsession with "Cleanliness"

As Chinese families are struggling with the conflict of desires between parents and children, American families face similar domestic challenges. These household dramas also manifest in the cases of toxic home contamination. First of all, toxic contamination is not new to Americans: in 1962, for instance, Rachel Carson introduced the public to the danger of agricultural chemicals in damaging human health and ecosystems; in the 1970s and 80s, Love Canal and Times Beach made national headlines because of toxic chemicals leaking into residential areas causing severe health problems. Over the subsequent two decades, Americans grew increasingly aware of the "toxic sea around us" and the countless ways chemicals can leak into domestic space (Hays 1989). Sometimes, toxins arrive "uninvited" from industrial manufacturing – through a nearby chemical plant, a waste dump, or a fracking well; in other cases, they are unknowingly "invited" into the household – through the purchase of consumer products. Among the various home products that contain chemical contaminants (such as hair sprays, toys, and laundry detergent, wall paint, flooring, and furniture), cleaning products gained an enormous amount of media exposure and consumer attention in the US. Why was so much attention paid to the cleaning products? The reasons are many, but I argue that they primarily have to do with the American obsession with "cleanliness."

According to Suellen Hoy, the author of *Chasing Dirt: The American Pursuit of Cleanliness* (1995), today's America is probably one of the "cleanest" countries of the world. Its sophisticated indoor plumbing and water heating systems, as well as its citizens' fastidious daily showering and grooming habits impress many foreigners who travel here. Yet Americans are not clean *by nature* (pun intended). How the country begot cleanliness is a historical tale of the process of modernization and the migration from agricultural to industrial forms of existence. First, in the pre-Civil War times, Americans lived "filthy" lives. Farm families cherished a love of dirt and saw it as a generator of "life" – in the form of crops – and a sign of honest character (22). Meanwhile, diseases like typhoid and malaria killed tens of thousands each year. During the Civil War, the idea of sanitation and hygiene emerged and public health reformers promoted the miasma theory, which linked the spread of disease to dirt and filth (31). At the end of the nineteenth century, germ theory displaced miasma theory and attributed the cause of disease to infectious organisms that spread through contact (107). Discoveries in bacteriology thus added "germs" to the list of environmental or ambient impurities and raised the American standards of "cleanliness" (123).

The bar to measure "cleanliness" rose again in the 1920s, when business and advertisers took the lead in promoting a national culture of hygiene and sanitation. At the time, manufacturers of soap and other cleaning products encountered a crisis because Americans were already becoming cleaner. Thanks to urbanization and industrialization, machines took over sweaty jobs at work, paved streets and closed cars eliminated dirt through travelling, and electric lights and gas stoves replaced kerosene lamps and coal stoves at home. Less "dirt" meant accordingly less soap, and thus less business. As a result, the soap industry used advertising and school programs to teach Americans that they can *never* be too clean. Magazine advertisements at the time associated personal cleanliness with social acceptability, upward mobility, and even moral rectitude. After WWII, many families settled into their new suburban homes, and advertisers generated new sales pitches and promised to make shirts "whiter than white" and homes "cleaner than clean." Housewives were taught to strive for a blemish-free, "next to godliness" private home space in order to fulfill their duty as a wife, mother, and homemaker.

The "cleaner than clean," however, did not come without a price. To generate the extra cleaning strength that advertising touted, manufacturers often added synthetic chemicals to their products that are hazardous for home use. Walking down the household goods isle of the supermarket, there are many "anti-bacterial," "disinfecting," or "industrial-strength" cleaners that are better suited to a hospital or factory setting than a domestic one. After use, these chemicals remained in the sinks, tubs, and floors, and went on to wreak havoc. According to the EPA, cleaning products had constituted the biggest sources of pollution in American homes ("Environmentally Preferable Purchasing," 2010). Many of the hazardous chemicals not only threaten human health (particularly that of children) but also harm aquatic wildlife when rinsed down the drain and into surrounding waterways.

Mary Douglas (1966) has famously argued that "dirt is matter out of place;" that is, our perceptions of pollution and purity are manifestations of social and symbolic boundaries. In the fantasy of cleanliness, impurities such as dirt, odor, mold, germs, pests, and weeds are all elements that cross the dividing line between the private home and the public environment; therefore they must be eliminated or held radically at bay. From a psychoanalytic perspective, however, the fantasy of cleanliness is motivated by more than just a necessity to police the social-symbolic border. It is, in fact, supported by a surplus pleasure at its core, an ecocidal tendency that aims to eliminate life forces (call it the *death drive*, if you will). Dirt, odor, fungi, germs, pests – all these impurities are not only "matter out of place" but manifestations of alien life forces that have been expelled from the modern domestic space. The ecocidal tendency functions as the perverse core of enjoyment that sustains the fantasy of cleanliness. But the pursuit of "cleanliness" can never reach its goal, as it constantly generates its own obstacles. The synthetic chemicals added to eliminate the impurities, as it turns out, are the new impurities.

Since the mid-2000s, the danger of cleaning products emerged as a heated topic in American popular media. Housekeeping and lifestyle magazines offered instructions about how to avoid indoor toxins and identify hazardous ingredients in cleaning products. Women's interest blogs and websites sported article titles such as "What is lurking in your cleaning products?" or "How toxic are your household cleaning supplies?" Popular talk shows such as Martha Stewart and Oprah Winfrey launched "green cleaning" special episodes to teach housewives how to make their own "all-natural" cleaners. On Oprah's "Earth Day" special program in 2009, she invited a couple to speak about a "wake up call" they received: the couple's son developed asthma at first, but soon recovered after his parents switched from conventional to "green" cleaners. Attributing her son's illness to toxic home cleaners, the mother said:

> Many of us are buying into a "fake clean" [...] we've been convinced overtime to think that clean means pine, fake lemon. Real clean, doesn't have a smell. Real clean is good for our children, good for our families. I've gone out to make sure my family has the safest, healthiest home that I can provide.

These words show that exposing the toxicity of cleaners did not interfere with Americans' collective desire for cleanliness. Rather than relinquishing the impossible fantasy of absolute cleanliness and make peace with the impurities, the green consumers are embracing a new clean that is "all-natural," "non-toxic," and "eco-friendly." In this new discourse, the bar on "cleanliness" is raised once again. "Green cleaning" means no dirt, no odor, no mold, no germs, and – no synthetic chemicals. What used to represent the "cleaner than clean" now joined the long list of suspects and became the new "dirty."[4]

But is this a progressive move? Looking back into America's long pursuit of cleanliness, we see that it is precisely the desire for "clean" that created the new "dirty." Every new "dirty" makes the idea of "clean" more out of reach, and thus more desirable. The obsessive subject is forever running on the treadmill of desire but never reaches his target: the more he strives to achieve perfection, the more imperfect he gets; the more imperfect he gets, the more he strives. Although advocates of green cleaning seem to have arrived at a temporary solution to toxin contamination, the ultimate cycle of desire does not change: we will soon witness the creation of a "new dirty" to keep the libidinal economy going. As Žižek (1989) says: "we always live in an interspace and in borrowed time; every solution is provisional and temporary, a kind of postponing of a fundamental impossibility" (6).

"Enjoy Your Dirt!" American Green Cleaning Product Advertising

High society concern about toxic cleaners gave rise to a bourgeoning green cleaning industry. According to a study from Packaged Facts, the sales of eco-cleaners in the US reached $640 million in 2011 ("Green Cleaning Products in the US," 2012). Although it only counted for three percent of the total household and laundry cleaner retail market, its market share has dramatically increased during the past decade. The current manufacturers range from smaller, specialty "green" brands (such as Seventh Generation and Method), who entered the market a decade or two earlier, and large conventional manufacturers (such as Clorox and S. C. Johnson), who jumped onto the "green wagon" after seeing great potential in the sustainable cleaning market.[5] The participation of big brands suggests the potential for this niche market to grow into a mass market. It also indicates a significant rise in advertising spending in the category of eco-cleaners.

Yet it has not always been easy to market these "green" cleaning products. As suggested above, the desire for clean is supported by an ecocidal tendency that derives enjoyment from eliminating life (or, the *death drive*). "Ecofriendly cleaning," by definition, threatens to remove the perverse core of enjoyment and, therefore, becomes a hard sell. Carl Pope, the Executive Director of Sierra Club who decided to endorse Clorox Green Works with the Sierra brand in 2008, recognized this dilemma:

> One of the reasons green home cleaning products haven't achieved much market penetration [is that] if they came from an environmental brand, people had the sense they won't work – green won't work. And if it came from someone with a cleaning reputation the reaction was: They can't be green (Barringer 2008).[6]

"Green won't work." These words foreshadowed the fateful alliance between Sierra Club and Clorox Green Works. Their collaboration not only brought the environmental group waves of criticism for "selling out" (to Clorox – "one of America's most chemically dangerous companies" according to US PIRG, 2010) but also failed to promote Green Works in the consumer market. While the sales of the new product started strong at $100 million in 2008, it continued to fall and dropped below $32 million in 2012 (Levere 2013). Clorox Green Works was not the only one that did poorly. Arm & Hammer, Windex, Palmolive, Hefty, and Scrubbing Bubbles all saw a drop in their green product sales (Clifford & Martin 2011). Market analysts attributed their failures to the economic recession of 2009, quoting a consumer's words that "green products [are] something you buy and think about when things are going swimmingly" (ibid). From a psychoanalytic perspective, however, financial difficulty is more of a rationalization for the real problem – that perhaps the fantasy of "green cleaning" never really took hold in the minds of the mass consumers.

Yet not all green cleaning brands have fallen victim to this problem. The smaller and more expensive brands – e.g. Seventh Generation and Method – have developed steadily in the last decade. In fact, their sales went up, rather than down, during the recession. How could these brands pull it off? Market analysts argued that they had developed a loyal consumer following who "tended to be more affluent and more wedded to environmental causes" (Clifford & Martin 2011).

This explanation is partially correct. These brands target niche consumer groups – progressive mothers and hipster youths (which I will later show) – who have a different structure of desire. The following paragraphs will examine the advertisements for Seventh Generation and Method. These advertisements share some similarities with Chinese green home advertisements. Both brands adopt the rhetorical appeal of children (or childlikeness) to market the ecofriendly home product to parents. But they also show major differences in the parental structures of desire. My following analysis will focus on how the parent-child duel of desire interacts with the spatial boundaries between indoors and outdoors and the meaning of the toxic chemicals that crossed these boundaries.

The first example I analyze, "Sleeping Baby," is a print ad for the Seventh Generation Laundry Detergent (Figure 3.12). Seventh Generation is a company founded in Burlington, Vermont in 1988. As the brand name suggests, the company emphasizes sustainability and the welfare of future generations. Their advertising campaigns often use children to appeal to the ecologically minded parents. This ad is no exception. It features a close-up shot of a baby, only a few months old, lying on a white bed and sound asleep. On top of the image sits the product. The title reads: "What you spend: one cent a blankie. What you save: [the baby image]."[7] Returning to what I suggested above, children are the big Other for their parents. Their desire plays an important role in determining that of the latter. However, since the very young (infants and babies) have not acquired language to express their desires, parents often have to decipher what they want. The portrayal of the baby emphasizes his silence and vulnerability, which creates a void for the parents to fill: "What do you want, my child? Whatever it is, I will provide." The Seventh Generation product is posed as the answer. This layout presents a choice: your money or your baby? This is obviously a false choice, because it weighs a negligible amount of money (one cent) against your baby – the parents' love, hope, and future. Although the latter is the apparent answer, the structure of a choice still evokes the guilt-inducing thought of choosing the money over the baby. As the ad implies, should you choose not to buy the product, you *are* choosing the money over the baby.

The "vulnerable baby" strategy reappears in many Seventh Generation ads from the early days. One online ad, "Free Your Baby," shows a month-old infant sleeping on a blanket on outdoor grass (Figure 3.13); it is part of a social media campaign that invites mothers to post their babies' images on Instagram, hastag #FreeYourBaby, to "win a six month supply of Seventh Generation's Free and Clear Diapers." Another one, advertising for the Seventh Generation diapers, pictures a baby crawling on outdoor grass – still in a vulnerable pose – and a large diaper supporting his body from behind (Figure 3.14). Even the diaper package features an infant sound asleep (Figure 3.15). All these ads present babies as silent and vulnerable subjects that call for protection. Also, most of them situate the baby in the outdoors – a major difference from the Chinese ads that I will elaborate on below.

The more recent campaigns of Seventh Generation gradually changed their representations of children – from defenseless and silent subjects to bold and outspoken subjects whose demands adults had better heed. These ads reframe children's innocence from vulnerability into as a type of creative boldness that adults no longer possess. In the 30-second Youtube commercial "Au Naturel" (posted in May 2013, Figure 3.16), a toddler is shown running around in a park, completely naked. He shocks the passerby with his private parts but the adults soon excuse his innocent exhibitionism and walk away laughing. He then runs back to his mother, who changes his diaper (Seventh Generation Diapers Au Naturel) on a park bench and sends him back on his naked run. The accompanying soundtrack is a hip-hop song with the lyric: "Your bootie is in a bag, your bootie is in a bag! Bootie attack, bootie attack!" Onscreen subtitles read: "Free from chlorine processing / Free from fragrance / And free from convention / Diapers Au Naturel: incredibly absorbent, naturally kind / Campaign for a toxin-free generation."

This commercial forms an interesting contrast to the Chinese ads analyzed above. First, the American boy is engaging in the last thing that Chinese parents would like to see their children do: running around in a public space, alone, and naked. It can be seen as an ultimate breach of privacy and security. In fact, this behavior might even furrow the eyebrows of conservative American parents. However, adults in this commercial (the passersby and mother) not only permit the child's action but also encourage it. The audio-visual language of the video also endorses his act: alongside the light-hearted hip-hop soundtrack the camera follows the boy around the park – smelling flowers, running by hills and trees, bumping into strangers – and invites the audience to experience his excitement in the outdoors adventure. As the boy runs past the adults and shocks them with his nudity, the subtitle "free from convention" appears, suggesting that children's actions are exempted from rules of the adult world (e.g. wearing clothes, staying indoors, etc.) and are thus tolerated. Moreover, they gain an ethical dimension because they embrace "nature" – in themselves and in their environment – and defy the boundaries of adult civilization.

In contrast to Chinese ads, the indoor-outdoor relationship here has been flipped. While the Chinese ads portray the indoors as a safety cocoon and the outdoors as a place of danger and surveillance, the American ad implies that the indoors is restraining and the outdoors is the realm of freedom. Since indoors represents the territory of adults and outdoors represent that of children, the parent-child relationship has also been inverted. In China, parents expect the child to conform to their desire because, they say, "we know what's best for you," whereas in the US, parents wish to leave the child to his own decisions because "he knows what's best for himself." This parenting method owes much to the progressive thought of John Dewey, which has profoundly shaped modern America's educational philosophy. According to Dewey, education should be tailored to children's interests and talents and parents and teachers should strive to discover their potential and encourage them to realize it. Laws, rules, and logic from the disciplined and doctrinaire adult world should be suspended in the children's world. This progressive philosophy is very much present in the commercial we are considering: instead of scolding the child's socially inappropriate behavior, adults see it as a sign of boldness and originality and encourage him to enjoy himself without inhibition. Even more, the adults derive vicarious pleasure from the child's transgression and momentarily indulge themselves in the suspension of adult rules.

Another 30-second Youtube commercial by Seventh Generation, "Cake Attack" (posted on March 2013, Figure 3.17), follows the same theme of "letting children be children." At a birthday party, a mother sprays the table with All Purpose Natural Cleaner and places a birthday cake on it. A group of children surrounds the table and grabs the cake by hand. Some mush it all over their faces and others lick it off of the table. The mother laughs at the children's behavior, lightheartedly grossed out. The video is composed of montaged shots from different angles of the room – on top of the glass table and from underneath – to signify the wildness and hyperactivity of the kids. The background soundtrack is a pop rock song singing: "We came, to set you free! Don't stop, come a lot y'all! Don't stop, come a lot y'all!" Onscreen subtitles read: "Clean like crazy / Without V.O.C.'s / Or glycol ethers / (Whatever those are) / Life's a party: Without these toxins." The accompanying caption on the Youtube page reads: "Some things never change – like the messes kids create. But powerful plant-based cleaners are changing the way moms clean up after them – and making childhood a very joyful place to be."

The mess portrayed in this cake party is probably enough to make an obsessive "clean freak" mother – Chinese or American – faint. Here, the mother is clearly disgusted, but she gives the cake-eating free-for-all her blessing. The mess has two meanings for her: on the one hand, it is the symbolic "enemy" of her cleaning impulse and must be eliminated right away; on the other hand, it signifies the enjoyment of her children (big Other) and thus must be tolerated. These two opposing meanings represent the conflicting desires of mother and child. But unlike in the Chinese ads above, here the child wins. The mother holds back her disgust and hosts the party. She patiently watches children violating all kinds of sanitary rules – smashing their faces into cake, licking the table, etc. – and lets the mess spread under her watch.

The enjoyment of the children is key in restoring the parents' desire for the ecofriendly cleaning products. As mentioned above, the fantasy of "ecofriendly cleaning" tends to lose its allure because it has removed the antagonistic core – an ecocidal tendency – from the notion of "clean." This commercial, however, restores this antagonistic core through the figure of children – agents of dirt, mud, germs, and disorder. They make a mess indoors and get dirty from playing outdoors. Most traditional Chinese parents will not tolerate these behaviors, but progressive American parents often do. They especially encourage children to go outdoors and play in nature – rolling in mud, skinny-dipping, snow-sledding, etc. Americans cherish a love for the great outdoors that can be traced back to the transcendental philosophy of Henry David Thoreau and Ralph Waldo Emerson, who rebelled against modern civilizations and sought intimacy with nature. For them, dirt no longer represents the "bad" alien life forces that threaten the health of the family; instead it symbolizes the "good" alien life forces – in nature and in children. The mother's relationship with dirt/mess – i.e. the symptom of her impossible fantasy of cleanliness – has transformed: instead of trying to eliminate it, she now enjoys it vicariously through the child. Watching the child enjoy becomes her duty.

The psychic structure here differs from that of the hysteric parents represented in the Chinese ads above. While the Chinese parent derives her enjoyment from being recognized and appreciated by the child (the big Other), the American parent enjoys serving as an instrument for the child's *jouissance* and seems to obtain nothing for herself. This fits Lacan's description of perversion. According to Fink (1997), the fundamental distinction between neurosis (including hysteria and obsession) and perversion is the difference between repression and disavowal (166). If repression is the submission to "castration" by the Law (the cleanliness principle), then disavowal is a denial of "castration" (pretending that it never happened). The infamous formula for disavowal can be rephrased as: "I know very well that such mess is prohibited in my house, but I am going to allow it just because my children are having fun with it." While the neurotic says, 'The Other must not get off on me!,' certain perverts say, 'Let the Other get off on me!' 'Let me become the "instrument of the Other's jouissance"' (Fink 192).

In 2014, Seventh Generation launched a new advertising campaign. It features children dressed in superhero outfits – "Toxic Freedom Fighters" – engaging in mischievous acts to "fight toxins." Two 30-second viral commercials, "Dunk Tank" (Seventh Generation laundry detergent, Figure 3.18) and "Spaghetti Sling" (Seventh Generation dish liquid, Figure 3.19), are structurally very similar to the aforementioned "Cake Attack." In "Dunk Tank," a group of children, dressed in capes, masks, and hats made from colander and aluminum foil, play pranks on Dr. Science, a nerdy adult wearing thick glasses and a white lab coat. They drop him into a full tank of raspberry juice. Dr. Science then puts the stained coat into the washing machine and magically cleans it in a split-second. The coat rotates 360 degrees in front of the camera as a hip-hop song starts to sing: "Let's ride, everybody gear up, put your seat up coz ..." The subtitle says: "Natural laundry detergent / that removes the toughest stains / 100% clean / 0% toxic / now that's superpower." "Spaghetti Sling" has almost the identical storyline: the same group of children throws spaghetti at Dr. Science. He uses a colander and a baking pan to defend himself but still gets covered in tomato sauce. Afterwards, he puts the baking pan into a sink and cleans it instantly. The pan rotates 360 degrees and the subtitle goes: "The power of an overnight soak / in just 5 minutes / 100% clean / 0% toxic / now that's superpower."

These two commercials mark a new high in terms of how much adults yield to children's enjoyment. Dr. Science, though not a parent, performs the parental figure in this commercial. He submits himself as a victim to the children's pranks. He does not seem very amused when the spaghetti sauce splashes all over his face, but he still plays along. His actions hint at certain masochistic tendency (a subcategory of perversion). For Lacan, the masochist is someone who "orchestrates a scenario whereby it is his partner, acting as Other, who lays down the Law – the Law that requires him to give up a certain jouissance" (Fink 187). A masochist is not just someone who loves pain; the pain is a signifier for the reinstatement of the Law, which he never quite really absorbed. In this case, Dr. Science is willing to sacrifice his own love for clean (suggested by his immaculate outfit) in order to bring into being the law of the parental duty – "let children to be children." I am not saying that Dr. Science's masochism applies to all viewers of this commercial. But his character can surely be read as a caricature for certain self-sacrificing parents whom Americans might find familiar.

Now let us turn to Method – the second-best-selling eco-cleaning brand in the US (though recently purchased by the Belgium company Ecover). Method primarily sells to an urban and young – and mostly hipster – demographic and their advertisements feature chic design, colorful scheme, and catchy music. CEO Eric Ryan mentions that their campaign aims to be "fun, human [and] to play up [Method's] status as a 'high aesthetic' brand without becoming sterile and embrace its status as a quirky brand without being perceived as too strange or lacking in efficacy" (Elliot 2012). Method's advertisements do not use an abundance of children's images, but they share a common strategy with Seventh Generation – constantly flirting with "dirt" in a "childlike" state.

Print advertisements from the earlier stages of Method have thoroughly explored the "childlike" innocence of its adult customers. "Protect Your Wetlands" (Figure 3.20) shows a rubber ducky with three eyes (suggesting genetic mutation) sitting near a bathroom tub and asks consumers to switch from toxic cleaners to Method's tub + tile spray to "keep both your shower and your world spotless." "This Is The House That Method Detoxed" (Figure 3.21) riffs on the British nursery rhyme "This is the house that Jack built" to sell the "liquid, pick, purple or green, that's sprayed on the counter to leave it so clean, without any toxins that damage your spleen." "Spray No Evil" (Figure 3.22) appropriates the Japanese proverb "see no evil, hear no evil, speak no evil" and tell consumers to avoid "typical household cleaners [with] toxic chemicals that don't just pollute your home, but your planet as well" (see all three ads on blog). Rubber duckies, nursery rhymes, and succinct proverbs are all references to childhood experiences.

The fourth ad, "Make Floor Love," flirts with the idea of "childlikeness" in a more sophisticated way (Figure 3.23). The ad shows two pairs of legs emerging from behind a wall, suggesting a couple having sex on the floor. A mop leans against the wall, implying that the floor has just been cleaned. The copy reads:

"Make floor love, not floor war: You know those scenes where a couple clears off a table and starts going at it? Sure, it's hot. But awfully messy. We say, save yourself the trouble and do the mommy-daddy dance right on the floor. Method's a-mop and floor cleaners leave floors spotless, without any toxic residues that can ruin a good time. Now *doin' the nasty is anything but*" [emphasis added].

The sexual topic of this ad is certainly not child-friendly, but it is reminiscent of the Seventh Generation ads above: it sells the ecofriendly cleaner as the guardian of an internal boundary against the "inner dirtiness" in all of us – children (playing with dirt outdoors) or adult ("doin' the nasty" with each other). Rather than simply exercising repression ("no sex at all!" because it is "awfully messy"), the perverse subject refuses to give up *jouissance* and disavows the castration ("I know very well that sex messes up the room, but I can still do it as long as it is cleaned up"). *"Doin' the nasty is anything but,"* in this sense, encourages consumers to fulfill their repressed wishes and act as if no limits exist. "Enjoy your dirt!" The injunction of the green cleaning advertisement speaks the voice of the postmodern superego. According to Žižek, in a postmodern society "we are obligated to enjoy; enjoyment becomes some kind of weird, perverted duty that we must fulfill" (*The Pervert's Guide to Ideology*, 2006). However, the problem of perversion is that overindulgence kills desire. Since desire is essentially a lack, too much *jouissance* creates the *lack of a lack,* which generates the most profound, existential anxiety. Žižek (1999) points out that: "Psychoanalysis does not deal with the authoritarian father who prohibits enjoyment, but with the obscene father who enjoins it and thus renders you impotent or frigid." Being ordered to "Enjoy!" at all times, the Other eventually become overwhelmed by *jouissance* and loses the ability to desire.

The voice of the postmodern superego ("Enjoy your inner childishness!") sounds the loudest in the 2012 Method campaign "Clean Happy." The central piece was a two-minute long music video (Figure 3.24). The song is prototypical hipster music, with "indie" vocals and background reverberation mimicking an indoor concert effect. The video is effectively a postmodern visual collage. It is composed of fragmented scenes staged simultaneously in a large studio set: a marching band plays in their undies and socks; a team of "cleaning experts" wash their uniforms in gigantic washing machines; a clown-like singer plays guitar and dances with children in a staged birthday party; a skateboarder rides in and out of a room-sized "sink" filled with balloons; two people dressed as "nose" and "flower" embrace each other as they jump on a trampoline. In the final scene, dozens of people – of different age, gender, and race – prance cheerfully before the camera, join hands, and form the shape of an earth. The caption appears: "We are the people against dirty / Join us / And clean happy / Method."

The audio and visual features of this commercial scream one word – hipsterism. Contemporary hipster culture is a characteristic phenomenon of postmodern multiculturalism, a kind of cultural eclecticism. On the one hand, it distinguishes itself from mainstream culture by adopting alternative music and fashion styles; on the other hand, it embraces the idea of diversity by haphazardly selecting cultural elements regardless of their origins (e.g. people, ideas, art, fashion, music, etc.). The most prominent feature of hipsterism is its refusal to commit to any ideology – in this case, the domestic fantasy of cleanliness. This commercial is deliberately set in a studio space to avoid representing the domestic space and the traditional gender and class roles associated with it. Located neither indoors nor outdoors, it is set in an artificial "non-place" that has "transcended" (or disavowed) the conventional indoor-outdoor, private-public, home-world division. Moreover, the commercial chooses actors of different age, gender, and race to signal cosmopolitanism. When the actors perform, they do so with a type of self-conscious silliness to keep an ironic distance from any characters they play. Permanent irony is a signature attitude of hipsterism (see Onion's Apple Bee's commercial). It displays what Žižek (1989) calls "cynical reason," which features the classic structure of disavowal: "I know very well that castration has already happened, nevertheless;" in this case, the Method consumer is supposed to say: "I know very well (that I'm just abiding the mainstream ideology by selling a cleaning product), but (I am above it because I am conscious of it)" (with the original formula being: "I know very well that castration has already happened, nevertheless…").

Hipsterism epitomizes the neoliberal, all-permissive, "post-ideological" ideology that pervades postmodern consumer culture. In his article "The Death of the Hipster," Rob Horning (2009) states that the hipster might be the "embodiment of postmodernism as a spent force, revealing what happens when pastiche and irony exhaust themselves as aesthetics." On the surface, the hipster seems to create a culture of tolerance, acceptance, and inclusion (adults can engage in children's activities; children can mix and mingle with different races and ethnicity; people from all over the world join together to rally for a common cause); but underneath the fantasy of inclusion lies an internal limit that it imposes on all objects of "tolerance." To be included, the Other must have its radical core removed. In order for adults to indulge in childlike activities, they must be restored to impeccable cleanliness before and after. In order for diverse people to join together, they must uniformly oppose "dirt" and commit to the "universal" fight for purity (see the slogan "People against dirty"). This internal castration, though disavowed, takes the radicalness out of the Other and neutralizes the possible opposition to dominant ideologies. Žižek's (2009) words are particularly relevant here: "Today, we have […] a subject who presents himself as a tolerant hedonist dedicated to the pursuit of happiness, and whose unconscious is the site of prohibitions: what is repressed are not illicit desires or pleasures, but prohibitions themselves." Indeed, in the postmodern, carnivalistic fantasy of "clean happy," the toxins and the detoxing process are nowhere to be found: because repression itself is repressed, the visualization of toxins will only inhibit enjoyment and "crash the party." For this reason, toxins (and their removal) must be prohibited from the perverse fantasy of cleanliness.

Let us use the formula of perversion to examine, once again, Hsu's (1981) analysis of the residential housing structures. We see that the American houses feature a type of false openness to the outside that disavows the division between indoors and outdoors, private and public, home and the environment. "I know very well that this is my private residence and I can lawfully shoot you for trespassing, but visitors and guests are welcome to enter (e.g. dinner parties, house-/baby-/pet-sitting, household maintenance) and my family members are welcome to exit (e.g. play outdoors, eat outdoors, etc.)." However, such external openness is contingent upon the individual's internal respect for boundaries and willingness to surrender enjoyment (or *jouissance*) in the face of the Law (e.g. dinner party guests must not enter the bedrooms, babysitters must not take anything outside the house, maintenance personnel must leave once the job is finished). The Chinese private residences, on the other hand, are strictly guarded against the outside environment (e.g. no strangers such as delivery and maintenance personnel are easily allowed in; and when they do, the host follows them every step of the way). Such external closedness contrasts with a lack of internal restraint within the individual, who refuses to give up enjoyment at the expense of the Law (e.g. there are plenty of instances when delivery personnel or nannies steal valuables on their job).[8]

The majority of the American ads above have shown perverse symptoms, but some ads show redemptive value and demonstrate the potential to break out of the suffocating universe of pure *jouissance* (lack of a lack). Take the Seventh Generation campaign "Toxin Freedom Fighters" for instance. In its full-page *The New York Times* ad (Figure 3.25), it features the "Freedom Fighters" rallying for healthier cleaning products and tougher governmental regulations on household chemicals. Underneath the tag line ("We're hit with 300 toxins before we're even born. You better believe we're coming out swinging"),[9] four children dressed as "Freedom Fighters" make fighting poses with Seventh Generation products in their hands. In the caption below, the ad announces the company's digital and social media campaign to collect 100,000 signatures by Earth Day to support an overhaul of the Federal government's Toxic Substances Control Act (Neff 2014).

The portrayal of children here has advanced from the previous ads of Seventh Generation. Rather than pleasure-thirsty little monsters who require parental figures' protection and supervision in their pranks, these children are taking the issue of pollution into their own hands.[10] They *vocalize their desire* and spelled it out in bold font and cartoon highlights (Figure 3.26–3.28). This symbolic maneuver has important therapeutic implications for the perverse subject. As mentioned above, in perversion, the subject puts himself in complete service to the enjoyment of the Other, believing that he alone will make the Other whole (having no more lack/desire). For Lacan, the therapeutic treatment for perversion is to put a name to the Other's lack/desire. By vocalizing the Other's lack/desire, the pervert realizes that the Other wants something else beyond enjoyment that he himself cannot provide. Such an operation turns the pervert into a desiring subject – from perversion into neurosis. In this case, the name of the children's lack is their demand for legislative change on the Toxic Substances Control Act. It introduces a rupture into the parents' fantasy of domestic harmony and points to a third party that must interfere in the parent-child dyad to make things "whole" – the government. This invitation to petition is potentially subversive to the consumerist fantasy, because it suggests that buying the product is no longer enough; one needs to enter into the signifying chain of social actions and become a subject who never stops desiring for a better world.

Conclusion

Jonathan Foer, the author of *Eating Animals* (2009), confessed that his serious consideration of the environmental consequence of meat-eating began after he knew that his wife was pregnant. Becoming a parent of a newborn baby made him feel that "everything is possible again" (10). Like Foer, many people decide to "go green" because of their children. Chai Jing, the Chinese Central Television journalist who made the controversial documentary *Under the Dome* (2014), also claimed to start her investigation into China's air pollution upon the birth of her daughter. Indeed, desire to establish a family and nurture the next generation provides a fundamental set of motivations for people to develop environmental concerns. Meanwhile, how parents teach their children about the symbolic significance of private versus public, domestic versus wild, purity versus contamination, also gets passed down. In green home product advertising, the fantasy of a "green home" is thus particularly telling; it speaks volumes about how parents desire for and through their children, which in turn has significant environmental implications.

The Chinese and American ads analyzed in this chapter display different representations of the ideal "green home" space in terms of three variables: the threshold between indoors and outdoors, the relationship between parents and children, and the representation of toxins and the detoxing process. First, the Chinese ads portray the indoor as a safety cocoon and the outdoor as a place of danger and surveillance; on the contrary, the American ads represent the outdoor as the realm of freedom and enjoyment and rarely include any direct portrayal of the indoor domestic space. Second, in both the Chinese and American ads, parents play a caring, protective role for their children. But parental care in the Chinese ads entails confining the children in the private indoor space and taming their desire for the outdoors, nature, and the wild. By contrast, parental care in the American ads suggests the freeing of children into the outdoor space and the unleashing of their inner wildness through the interaction with the natural (and public) environment. If the indoor signifies the territory of parental sovereignty and the outdoor signifies the realm of childhood innocence, then these ads suggest different parent-children power relationship. The Chinese parents expect their children to conform to the rules of the adult world whereas the American parents deliberately suspend these rules and encourage children to explore their own interests, talents, enjoyment, and to some extent, their autonomy. It is no surprise that the ideal American children are shown licking cake off the table, while the ideal Chinese children are passionately kissing the wall. The wall, as mentioned before, is a physical embodiment of social and symbolic boundaries of the adult world; thus, a wall-kissing child is a subject that passionately embraces her position in the social symbolic network. If we distill the comparison down to cake-licking vs. wall-kissing, it is apparent that the American ads allow parents to live in children's fantasy and the Chinese ads make children live in the fantasy of their parents.

The different attitudes toward the spatial boundary (between indoors and outdoors) and the social boundary (between adults' and children's worlds) are also reflected in the third element of this analysis – the representation of toxins. The Chinese ads use eye-catching animation to visualize the toxins' emergence and elimination, but the American ads omit their representation altogether. Since toxins are the unwanted intruders that breach the indoor-outdoor spatial border, their visualization reasserts the border; moreover, since toxins potentially violate the parent-children social boundary (they deprive the children of their innocence and their attachment with their home environment), their representation reinforces this boundary – a welcome effect for the Chinese ads, but not the American ads. In the American ads, toxins are omitted to allow the indoor-outdoor, parent-children boundaries to remain under disavowal – a signature attitude that American mainstream culture takes with the internal divisions within its society (as with race, gender, sexuality, etc.).

As I have tried to demonstrate, these ads manifest different structures of desire: the Chinese ads suggest the hysterical subject, who deprives the Other of enjoyment (*jouissance*) of the outdoor public space to cultivate desire for the private family unit. Since too much *jouissance* kills desire, the hysteric strives to limit *jouisance* in order to keep lack/desire alive. The American ads, on the other hand, suggest that of a perverse subject, who allows for unlimited enjoyment on the Other's part and makes it his duty that the Other never lacks/desires. At a glance, the pervert seems more tolerant to the Other's differences than the hysteric, but this is not necessarily the case. While the hysteric imposes external limits on the Other's desire, the pervert does so internally. In the case of toxic home contamination, the toxins represent the radical difference in the Other's desire—they embody the child's silent protest against parents' painstaking effort to maintain a spotless home. In the hysteric fantasy (seen in the Chinese ads), toxins are visualized and elimi-nated, showing repression of the Other's desire; in the perverse fantasy (seen in the American ads), toxins and the detoxing process are nowhere to be found, demonstrating disavowal of the Other's desire (as even repression is repressed)

Up to this point, we have applied, again, topology of desire quite broadly. As I have repeatedly stated, the reader should take these generalized categories with healthy skepticism—especially due to the complexity of culture and his-tory in these two enormous countries. However, these categories are still valu-able because they can help us appreciate the effectiveness of "green" marketing strategies – particularly as they apply to the *home* – and the kinds of deep-seated subjectivities they manipulate and exploit in us. Moreover, these sub-jectivities have much further implications beyond the environmental health of the home. Throughout this chapter, one truth becomes to clear to us: the home and the world are interconnected. Toxins do not need passports or visas when they cross the boundary of the house; pollutants are not on permanently exile when they flow into the public waterways as they sneak back right in through the air we breathe, the water we drink, and the food we eat. The border between the private home and the public environment is artificially imposed. It does little to protect us from the dangers lurking around us. Often times, it is this very installation of the symbolic border that generates the desire (and thus the technology) to produce the pollutants in the first place. To police the boundary between the home and the world, our obsession with cleanliness drove the invention of toxic agents to kill life. To cultivate our offspring's attachment to the family, our hysterical desire invented the toxic wall paint to simulate an artificial world that does not satisfy. Or even worse, our perverse disavowal of the very existence of this division suppressed our desire to take thoughtful steps to protect either home or the world. As Lacan teaches us, the ethics of psychoanalysis lies in the motto: "Never give up on your desire." That is to say, we should maintain our fundamental division and keep desire alive. What exactly does that mean? I will return to this point in the conclusion.

Notes

1 The cultural notion of home in Anglo-Saxon history, however, differs from its Confucian counterparts. The word "home" derives from the Old English *ham*, which means "dwelling, house, estate, village". According to John Berger ("The Meaning of Home"), the English notion of home "became the keystone for a code of domestic morality, safeguarding the property (which included the women) of the family." Although the notion of home sometimes also serves to promote patriotism (as in *homeland*, which one should die for), Berger argues that home originally meant "the center of the world." This notion diverges from the Confucian notion of *jia*, which sees home as a subsidiary to the state.

2 The parallel between soap and paint is apparent: first, both have a low-cost manufacturing process and a large profit margin and can afford to advertise aggressively; second, their products have largely similar qualities and must rely on advertising to distinguish from one brand from another; third, their products are easily transportable, thus allowing for foreign competition and national consolidation.

3 In a sense, the Chinese government also adopts the same "parenting" method to rule the country: as long as the citizens obey the essential boundaries set out by the government (by not attacking the authority of the party, especially by not attacking the party in the eyes of foreigners), they are allowed unusual amounts of freedom in many aspects of their behavior.

4 The "Green Guide" video on National Geographic's website also made a similar point: "Sometimes a cleaner home equals a dirtier environment. Finding the right product makes all the difference." (http://video.nationalgeographic.com/video/green-guide-howdini/green-cleaning-gg)

5 By May 2012, the top five eco-cleaning brands with the largest market shares are: Seventh Generation (23.8%), Method (20%), Purex Natural Elements (16.8%), Clorox Green Works (12.8%), Mrs. Meyer's Clean Day & Caldrea (6.3%). (http://www.greencleaningmagazine.com/new-study-reveals-state-of-green-cleaner- sales/)

6 Although Mr. Pope rightfully pointed out the fundamental dilemma of the problem, he erred in his solution – by putting Sierra Club's logo next to the Clorox brand

(or, more radically, by trying to solve this problem at all). Thinking in an old Pavlovian logic, this marketing strategy hoped to transfer the symbolic capital of one brand to an adjacent one (similar to putting an attractive woman next to a car), but in fact, the actual transference went the opposite direction and undermined the symbolic capital of the first brand (as if the mechanical nature of the car makes the woman look dull and unattractive).

7 Underneath the baby image is the copy: "We know you're concerned about the health of your family and the future of our planet's environment. We are, too. That's why, when we make our natural laundry detergent – and all our other household products – we take great care to leave the dangerous stuff out. Like all the harmful chemicals that can leave behind irritating residues and pollute our earth's air and water for generations to come. Take out all those risky chemicals and what's life? A natural detergent that leaves your clothes just as clean and fresh as ever. Sure, you may spend a tiny bit more on each bottle of Seventh Generation. But take a moment, and consider how much you save."

8 In fact, the hysteric refusal to give up *jouissance* can be observed in the Chinese less-than-civilized behavior in public. The Chinese never hesitate to exploit public resources when no authorities are around (e.g. stealing toilet paper from public bathrooms, scrambling for accidentally scattered fruits in the streets, snatching rubber ducks from outdoor statues in Shanghai and bringing them home as souvenirs, having children pee on the streets of Hong Kong and confronting passerby who found this unacceptable... The incidents are simply too many to count.) It is not that the Chinese have no notion of the public/private divide; far from that, they are perhaps too well acquainted with it and yet refuse to give up their enjoyment because of it. The hysteric always wishes to cheat the Law whenever she thinks the Other is not around. This creates much difficulty for environmental regulations in China.

9 The copy on the bottom includes four paragraphs: "**Judge us not by our diminutive stature, or the fact that we wear pajamas with built-in feet.** We are Toxin Freedom Fighters, here to wreak havoc on a system that needlessly exposes us to toxic chemicals. And by 'wreak havoc,' we mean enter into a constructive dialogue with elected leaders through which we arrive at a mutually beneficial solution. "**We've been dealing with this malarkey since before we were born.** According to experts at the Centers for Disease Control and Prevention, 300 toxic chemicals are showing up in our umbilical cords. Stuff that can hurt our nervous systems, mess with our developing brains and lower our IQs. Really bad stuff that's also linked to cancer, birth defects and asthma. It's enough to drive even the most rational neonate to the cape and tights. "**It's time for a cleaner clean.** The worst part about having these toxic chemicals in consumer products is that we don't need them. Because there are safe alternatives that work just as well. In fact, Seventh Generation has been using green chemistry and plant-based ingredients for over 25 years, working hard to make products that get the job done, without all the sketchy stuff. Listen, we like a clean onesie as much as the next guy – just one that makes us glow in the dark. "**Help us bring Congress to its knees.** It's time for lawmakers to wake up and smell the botanical extracts. It's time for them to do something about all the bad chemicals out there. Because that stuff ends up in our homes, and then in our bodies. So we're doing whatever it takes to get 100,000 signatures by Earth Day, and force a discussion with the government. If that means we have to do some hard time-out, well, it's worth it."

10 When children are outside of language (e.g. sleeping, crying), parents have to strive to decipher their desire; when children speak up and articulate their desire (identifying their position within language), parents' anxiety reduces as they can now regain certainty and follow these exact demands. There is nothing that pleases the more than the ability to follow the Other's unequivocal demands.

References

Barringer, F. (2008, March 26). Clorox courts Sierra Club, and a product is endorsed. *The New York Times*. Retrieved from: http://www.nytimes.com/2008/03/26/business/businessspecial2/26cleanser.html?_r=0

Belly-pointing marriage (2014). *Cultural China*. Retrieved from: http://traditions.cultural-china.com/en/115T342T1263.html

Chen, H. (2013, November 22). *Guatou zhizheng: Libang yu duoleshi de duijue* [Fighting for oligarchy: The duo between Nippon and Dulux]. *Zhongwai Tuliao Wang*. Retrieved from: http://www.27580.cn/sitecn/zs/98037.html

Clifford, S. & Martin, A. (2011, April 21). As consumers cut spending, "green" products lose allure. *The New York Times*. Retrieved from: http://www.nytimes.com/2011/04/22/business/energy-environment/22green.html

Davis, D. (1995). *Urban Spaces in Contemporary China: The Potential for Autonomy and Community in Post-Mao China*. Cambridge University Press.

Douglas, M. (1966). *Purity and Danger: An Analysis of Concepts of Pollution and Taboo*. Routledge and Keegan Paul.

Duoleshi PK Libang Qi: Liangda pinpai shei gengshou xiaofeizhe zhuipeng? [Dulux PK Nippon: Which brand do consumers pursue more?]. (2010, July 28). Zhongguo Jiancai Diyi Wang. Retrieved from: http://sz.jiaju.sina.com.cn/news/1021421957.html

Elliott, S. (2012, March 12). Ads for Method celebrate the madness. *The New York Times*. Retrieved from: http://www.nytimes.com/2012/03/12/business/media/ads-for-method-celebrate-the-madness-campaign-spotlight.html

Environmentally preferable purchasing. (2010, May 12). *US Environmental Protection Agency Official Website*. Retrieved from: http://www.epa.gov/epp/pubs/cleaning.htm

Fiennes, S. (2006) *The Pervert's Guide to Cinema*. Mischief Films & Amoeba Film

Fink, B. (1997). *A Clinical Introduction to Lacanian Psychoanalysis: Theory and Technique*. Cambridge, MA: Harvard University Press.

Fitchen, J. M. (1989). When toxic chemicals pollute residential environments: The cultural meanings of home and homeownership. *Human Organization*, 48(4), 313–324.

Fleischer, F. (2007). "To chose a house means to choose a lifestyle:" The consumption of housing and class-structuration in urban China. *City & Society*, 19(2), 287–311.

Flusser, V. (2004). Taking up residence in homelessness, *Writings (Electronic Mediations Series)*. Ed. Andreas Ströhl. Trans. Erik Eisel. Minneapolis: University of Minnesota Press.

Foer, J. S. (2009). *Eating Animals*. Back Bay Books.

Fraser, D. (2000). Inventing oasis: Luxury housing advertisements and reconfiguring domestic space in Shanghai. *The Consumer Revolution in Urban China*. Ed. Davis, D. University of California Press, 25–53.

Fromm, E. (1964). *The Heart of Man*. New York, NY: Harper & Row.

Green Cleaning Products in the U.S. (2012, August 31). *Packaged Facts*. Retrieved from: http://www.packagedfacts.com/Green-Cleaning-Products-7114196/

Green Homes Overview (2012, December 19). *U.S. Environmental Protection Agency Official Website*. Retrieved from: http://www.epa.gov/greenhomes/overview.htm

Guanggao xuanchuan boyi: Libang VS Duoleshi [Advertising Promotion Faceoff: Nippon VS Dulux] (2014, May 14). *Yixun Wang/Yatai Jiaju*. Retrieved from: http://news.jia360.com/qiamgmian/20140504/1399190211854.html

Hays, S. P. (1989). *Beauty, Health, and Permanence: Environmental Politics in the United States, 1955–1985.* Cambridge University Press.

Horning, R. (2009, April 13). The death of the hipster. *PopMatters.* Retrieved from: http://www.popmatters.com/post/the-death-of-the-hipster-panel/

Hoy, S. (1995). *Chasing Dirt: The American Pursuit of Cleanliness.* Oxford University Press.

Hsu, F. L. K. (1981). *Americans and Chinese: Passages to Differences.* University of Hawaii Press.

Huang, W. & Huang, D. (2011, October 7). Why the character for "family" has a pig inside a house. *China Daily USA.* Retrieved from: http://usa.chinadaily.com.cn/weekly/2011-10/07/content_13843121.htm *2014 nian lvse jiaju shichang guimo jiangda 694.4 yiyuan* [2014 green home products market will reach 69.44 billion RMB] (2014, May 22). *Huaxia Jingwei Wang.* Retrieved from: http://hb.ifeng.com/house/jiajuredian/detail_2014_05/22/2315014_0.shtml

Levere, J. L. (2013, April 21). In an overhaul, Clorox aims to get Green Works out of its niche. *The New York Times.* Retrieved from: http://www.nytimes.com/2013/04/22/business/media/cloroxs-green-works-aims-to-get-out-of-the-niche.html

Li, F. (2005, May 26). Decorating homes may cause leukemia. *China Daily.* Retrieved from: http://www.chinadaily.com.cn/english/doc/2005-05/26/content_445879.htm

Lvse Jiaju [Green Homes] (Accessed on 2014, May 31). *Baidu Baike.* Retrieved from: http://baike.baidu.com/view/175362.htm?fr=aladdin

Neff, J. (2014, March 21). Seventh Generation Unleashes "Toxin Freedom Fighters." *Advertising Age.* Retrieved from: http://adage.com/article/cmo-strategy/seventh-generation-seeks-tougher-toxin-regulations/292266/

Saunders, P. & Williams, P. (1988). The constitution of the home: Towards a research agenda. *Housing Studies,* 3(2), 81–93.

U.S. PIRG (2010, August 5). Chemical insecurity: America's most dangerous companies and the multimillion dollar campaign against common sense solutions. *USPIRG.com.* Retrieved from: http://www.uspirg.org/reports/usp/chemical-insecurity

Wang, F. & Zhou, Y. (1999). Modeling urban population densities in Beijing 1982–1990: Suburbanization and its causes. *Urban Studies,* 36(2), 271–287.

Yao, X. (2000). *An Introduction to Confucianism.* Cambridge University Press.

Žižek, S. (1989). *The Sublime Object of Ideology.* Verso.

Žižek, S (1999, March 18). "You May!" *London Review of Books,* 21(6), 3–6. Retrieved from: http://www.lrb.co.uk/v21/n06/slavoj-zizek/you-may

Žižek, S (2009, April 4). "God is dead, but he doesn't know it:" Lacan plays with Bobok. *Lacan.com.* Retrieved from: http://www.lacan.com/essays/?p=184

2.2 million young Chinese die from indoor pollution: Report. (2010, May 17). *China Daily.* Retrieved from: http://www.chinadaily.com.cn/opinion/2010-05/17/content_9859728.htm

2014 nian lvse jiaju shichang guimo jiangda 694.4 yiyuan [2014 green home products market will reach 69.44 billion RMB] (2014, May 22). *Huaxia Jingwei Wang.* Retrieved from: http://www.huaxia.com/hxjk/wawj/2014/05/3896834.html

4 The "Organi-vore's" Dilemma

Social (In)Equality in Organic
Food Marketing

"Try organic food... or as your grandparents called it, 'food.'" This Internet meme quote circulated recently and widely on healthy eating and sustainable gardening websites. Its irony is apparent: it reveals the absurdity of the modern notion of "organic food" from the perspective of traditional farming and conveys a longing for a time when food was by default tasty, wholesome, and safe to eat. Such nostalgia pervades the contemporary popular discourse on organic food in different parts of the world. "In China," journalist Tan Yingzi observes in *China Daily* (2007), "going organic is nothing new." China's burgeoning organic food business dates back to the Warring States Period (475–221 BC), when farmers used straw and manure as "organic" fertilizers to grow soil and other crops. "We did it thousands of years ago," says a manager of an organic farm who supplied vegetables to the 2008 Beijing Olympics, "and now we are just going back to the traditions with some modern technologies" (Tan 2007).

But are we going back? Heraclitus, the Greek philosopher, would have told us this was impossible: "No man ever steps in the same river twice." Today's "organic food" is not exactly what our ancestors used to call "food." In a globalized world with an exploding population and dwindling resources, production and consumption of food patterns have changed – technologically, logistically, and ecologically. Furthermore, new discourses of food culture have permanently changed the way we perceive, imagine, and enjoy our food. In the hyper-mediated world, we are constantly bombarded with dietary advice, culinary fads, and food spectacles; eating is now more of a cultural than a biological activity. And organic food culture is a significant part of this. From product packages and television commercials to journalistic investigations and farmers' social media updates, the notion of "organic" circulates widely in popular media and shapes the collective imagination of our food, our environment, and our own bodies.

Historically, the term "organic" emerged in a rebellion against the modern industrialization of agriculture (Drinkwater 2009). Coined in 1940 by the English agriculturalist Lord Northbourne, the expression "organic food" first appeared in his *Look to the Land*. Northbourne conceived the farm as an organism with "a biological completeness, ...a unit which has within itself a balanced organic life" (58). Organic agriculture generates productivity through the self-sustaining ecosystem of the farm and stands in contrast to chemical farming, which depends on "imported fertility" (58). The belief in ecological "holism" also drives the "organic bible" – Sir Albert Howard's *An Agricultural Testament* (1940). Howard argues that the health of soil is linked to the health of all creatures depending on it and proposes to manage soil fertility as a living rather than mechanic process. First initiated in England, Germany, and India, organic farming in the new millennium is a global practice (Kristiansen & Taji 2006), pursued by a wide variety of social constituents, including agricultural co-ops, small and independent farmers, urban and suburban residents, and multinational corporations. Still, not all who grow organic food have the power to claim organic status. In most countries, Certified Organic labels are regulated by governments or third-party authorities and are costly to obtain. Those who can afford them play a significant role in shaping the public's perception of the "organic." The same players – namely "Big Organic" companies – are also able to pay for big budget advertising campaigns to further promote their definition of the term.

The current commercial definition of "organic," according to many critics, has far diverged from the original meaning. Michael Pollan (2006), for example, in his renowned *The Omnivore's Dilemma*, exposes the fact that most of the "organic foods" in the supermarket today are produced on large-scale industrial farms, often shipped from distant countries, leaving huge eco-footprints. He contrasts the actual production process with the bucolic images of family farms one finds in organics marketing and found the latter to be deceptive. Following Pollan, mainstream media hurried to unveil "the organic myth" constructed by advertisers and questioned the foods' health and environmental impacts. These critics uniformly read advertising as a device to deceive and manipulate the public. In this chapter, by contrast, I approach these advertisements not as concealers but as revealers. In spite of the factual deception, they speak the truth about our cultural imagination of ethical or responsible eating and are therefore worthy of serious consideration. This chapter focuses specifically on the advertisements for organic milk, which I argue holds a special place in the organics industry due to milk's deep entrenchment in human growth and notions of security. As humans' first food, milk provides the prototypical model of oral consumption. It allows us to examine the relationship between mother and child, humans and nature, self and other – and how these are represented in advertising.

As I will show, the notion of "organic" is, on the one hand, a consumerist fantasy addressing anxieties about health and safety; on the other hand, it is also implicated in deep-seated social inequality and class antagonism that have always motivated the production, distribution, and consumption of food. Contrary to its connotations of holism and harmony, the organics culture in fact plays on the divide between the poor and the rich, the rural and the urban, and the masses and the elites in many parts of the world. These divides exist both on a psycho-cultural level and a political-economic level. Organic food has become a token of social status, a means to vindicate envy and jealousy, and a way to soothe liberal guilt. The story of organic food is not a story of harmony and holism; it is part of a story of struggle over natural resources and political power in crises such as food scarcity, excess, and contamination. Borrowing from Michael Pollan's book title, this is the dilemma of the "organi-vores."

From Too Little to Too Much: China's Food Safety Crisis

The world's food problem is a pendulum that swings between too little and too much. In the developing countries of North Africa and Middle East, chronic hunger and rising food prices have consistently led to outbursts of protests and riots (Winders 2011). Global warming and environmental deterioration exacerbate the food shortage problem by spreading drought and floods to other parts of the world. On the other hand, developed countries such as the US suffer from an overabundance of food. Thanks to the industrialization of agriculture, food increased in quantity but dropped in quality. "Overfed and undernourished" (Squires 2004), Americans suffer from diseases of affluence, such as obesity, diabetes, heart diseases, etc. They also have to withstand the onslaught of growth stimulants and genetically modified foods and fear for the possible consequences of birth defects, infertility, cancer, neurological diseases, and a host of other afflictions.

China's food problem, nevertheless, straddles both worlds. As a country with only seven percent of the world's arable land, Chinese farmers face the burden of feeding 22 percent of the world's population (McBeath & McBeath 2009). From feudal dynasties to Mao's People's Republic of China (PRC), Chinese society had struggled with malnutrition and starvation; Mao's aggressive agri-cultural campaigns Great Leap Forward and Learning From Dazhai aimed to promote crop yields but instead led to nationwide famine (Shapiro 2001). After the 1978 economic reform, the government issued new agricultural policies to solve the food shortage problem and encouraged the adoption of Western industrial farming methods such as mechanization and fertilization. Over the next three decades, the production of Chinese agriculture rose dramatically. In rural regions, starvation was reduced to a minimum; in urban areas, there were not only an ample supply of grains, fruits, and vegetables, but also a wide array of "luxury" foods such as meat, eggs, and seafood (Gerth 2010, 108).

Moving from too little food to too much, too fast, China is encountering problems of the developed world. In adopting Western diets, including fast and processed foods, many develop heart diseases, diabetes, and obesity (ibid). They have also started to suffer the consequences of chemical farming and genetic engineering – even more egregiously than the West does. According to Greenpeace East Asia (2012),

China is the world's number one user of chemical pesticides and fertilisers. Fruits and vegetables are regularly sold across the country containing a hazardous cocktail of pesticides. Discoveries of banned pesticides in food are not uncommon. [...] In 2009, China used more than 54 million tonnes of chemical fertilisers, only 25 to 35% of which can be absorbed by crops. The rest is lost into the environment, and pollutes rivers, lakes and groundwater.

Industrialized farming and food manufacturing not only pollute the environment, but also threaten public health. In the new millennium, food contaminations have regularly made national and local headlines: "melamine milk," "sewage oil," "glow-in-the-dark pork," "exploding watermelons," and more. Each scandal alerted consumers to new toxic commercial adulterants or growth stimulants with adverse health effects.[1]

The food security crisis has exacerbated social conflicts in China. It not only damaged consumer trust in supermarkets, restaurants, corporations, and governmental regulatory agencies, but also deepened the already wide chasm between urban residents and rural farmers. Since Deng Xiaoping's Open Door Policy in the 1990s, a wide wealth distribution gap opened between the cities and the countryside. As urban living standards became higher than rural standards, farmers became envious of urban lifestyles and many migrated to the cities. However, they remained "second-class" citizens. Due to their rural *hukou* (residency), they were often denied social and educational services in the cities and nearly become illegal immigrants in their own country (Park & Xu 2012). Those who remained on the farmland harbored resentment about their lives and sometimes took revenge through the activity they engaged in all day – farming. According to Dintenfass (2011), "Chinese farmers often grow two sets of crops – the harvest for selling is doused with pesticides, and the patch for personal consumption is kept organic." By using excessive amount of pesticides and growth stimulants on the food sold to the cities, these farmers not only maximized profits but also, in a way, avenged themselves on the urban population that had become rich despite growing rural poverty. Still, the more they spray, the more trust they lose. The vicious cycle continues and the antagonism between farmers and consumers deepens.

The Rise of China's Organic Food Culture

Organic farming emerged in the new millennium as one of the answers to the widespread panic about food security. China's organic food culture is a complex, multi-layered phenomenon. It involves at least four categories of foods: First, organic foods produced exclusively for governmental officials. Just as other premium resources in China, healthy and spray-free foods are made available to the country's political elites. As Barbara Demick (2011) reports, the government-run organic gardens in Beijing are locked behind a six-foot fence, with security guards on watch. They produce the best-quality vegetables, which are "sent to Communist Party officials, dining halls reserved for top athletes, foreign diplomats, and others in the elite classes." This special treatment is called *tegong* (special supply), a tradition descended from the 1950s when state-owned enterprises raised their own food and allocated it based on rank. In the new millennium, this practice persisted and became the earliest form of Chinese organic farming. "Organic gardening [in China] is a hush-hush affair," writes Demick, "the cleanest, safest products are largely channeled to the rich and politically connected. Many of the nation's best food companies don't promote or advertise." Protected behind iron gates, these *tegong* foods have hardly influenced the public's view of organic foods because they are hidden from view.

Second are the DIY organic foods. As mentioned above, Chinese farmers often reserve patches of unsprayed land to grow crops for their own consumption. This DIY practice has also gradually been taken up by city dwellers. Terrified by food scandals, many urbanites decided to take matters into their own hands. Some started gardening on their balconies or rooftops; others rent suburban allotments from farm co-ops and pay weekend trips to tend to their vegetables. Some visionary entrepreneurs even gave up high paying salaries in the cities to invest in rural farm properties. An owner of 200 organic farm allotments across China says his customers usually include three types: "families who want to teach their children where food comes from, older people in their retirement, [and] a growing number worried about food safety" (Foster 2011). Most urban farmers have ample wealth – owning a car and thus able to drive to the suburban allotments – or plenty of leisure time. Due to the economic and time constraints, the general public is still exempt from this luxury.

For urbanites that have money but no time, local organic farmers markets are answering their needs. Since 2011, large cities such as Beijing, Shanghai, Xi'an, and Tianjin saw the rise of such markets ("Yu putong caishichang buyiyang," 2012). Organized by citizen food safety advocates, these markets aim to provide a platform for farmers to directly sell to consumers. Consumers are encouraged to talk to their farmers or even visit the farms in person. "Face-to-face is the most important element in building trust," an organizer commented; "some farmers said, because I couldn't see the consumers, I didn't feel much guilt about putting stuff into the milk [...] but in the farmers market where kids call them 'uncle' and 'aunt,' farmers will develop emotional connections with them as if they were kids of their own relatives" (Gao 2012). Still in their nascent stage, these markets are mostly not-for-profit and rely on digital and social media to advertise their products within local communities. They still have a long way to go before reaching a bigger market and facing the potential of being coopted by larger companies. At present, many growers in these markets prefer not to label their foods "organic" – due to the high cost to pursue governmental certification – and call them "healthful" or "natural" foods (Eckhardt & Hagerman 2010).

The fourth type of organic food plays the most significant role in shaping the Chinese public's perception of "organics." They are the corporate-manufactured, mass-produced organic foods. What first motivated the corporations to farm organic was the demand from overseas. Since the turn of the new millennium, China had converted massive amounts of conventional farmland to organic to sell their products to Europe, US, and Japan (Bezlova 2006). From 2000 to 2006, the country moved from forty-fifth to second place worldwide for organic farmland acreage (Dinterfass 2011; Willer, Yussefi & Sorenson 2008). The companies also acquired certification from foreign organizations such as USDA Organic Certification and the Eco-Cert by the EU, in order to sell their food abroad. After the domestic food scares broke out, more companies turned to the internal market. Within a decade, a plethora of organic products had appeared on supermarket shelves. Specialized organic food stores mushroomed both in the streets and online. To the marketers, the first challenge was to reestablish credibility in the ocean of counterfeits and forgery. Two governmental certification systems were established: one is the CDFCC's "Organic Food" (*youji shipin*) label for food products; the other is the "Chinese Organic Product" (*zhongguo youji chanpin*) label for all organic products ("Youji shipin, lvse shipin, wugonghai shipin de qubie," 2010). When introduced to the mass consumer, however, these new labels were often confounded with previous quality control labels such as "Green Food" and "Non Public-harm Eatables" (ibid). From the authorities' perspective, each label corresponds to a very specific set of agricultural standards. "Non Public-harm Eatables" refers to the foods that fulfill the very basic environmental safety and health requirements. "Green Food" refers to the products grown with improved farming methods but still allows for limited use of certain chemicals. "Organic Food" has the highest set of standards and is produced without any pesticides, artificial fertilizers, or GMO technologies. From the consumers' perspective, however, the distinctions between these labels are largely unclear because they all relate to the notion of healthy eating. This makes it difficult to market the notion of "organic" to the public.

China's "Milk Frenzy" and Its Social and Psychic Significance

Among the various types of organic foods on the market, I will focus on one particular type of product because of the special place it occupies in human development. Milk is our original nourishment. As mammals, we rely on mother's milk for survival at the earliest stages of life. Thus, milk is the liquid medium that connects the mother and the child. It is also metonymically related to the breast, which according to psychoanalysis, is the first object of desire. For Freud, the child's "sucking at his mother's breast" is his first experience of pleasure. The act of sucking goes beyond a nutritional purpose; it generates a surplus symbolic enjoyment for being connected to the body of the mother (Other). Most mammals stop drinking milk after infanthood. However, in many human cultures, the habit of milk drinking – substituted by the consumption of animal milk – continues throughout adulthood. According to *Science Daily*, the gene that allows humans to digest lactose beyond infanthood can be traced to the dairy farming communities of Central Europe, some 7,500 years ago. It gradually became more prevalent among people living in Europe and the Middle East. In these cultures, milk took on a more important place and often came to symbolize fertility, prosperity, and spiritual nourishment. In the biblical phrase "the land of milk and honey," for instance, milk stands for the rich yields of a bountiful Earth (Mother) as well as the hope of religious deliverance.

Chinese culture, however, did not have a milk-drinking tradition. Aside from the pastoral regions in northern and western China (such as Inner Mongolia or Xinjiang), animal milk used to be scarce and was not commonly consumed by children or adults. After the Opium Wars of the late nineteenth century, several coastal Chinese cities were forced into foreign trade and dairy products were introduced along with other consumer goods (Fuller, Huang, Ma & Rozelle 2006). In the twentieth century, the idea of milk as a healthy and nutritious food became widespread among the Chinese. Many believed that "Westerners had a better life based on meat and milk, [which made them] physically stronger" (Rohrer 2007). Since China's economic boom in the 1990s, milk supply has become more abundant. Many consumers, having long aspired to Western lifestyles, took to milk drinking as a nutritional supplement to their diet. Parents deemed milk as a magical formula for their children's growth. The government also strongly pushed for milk consumption, seeing it as a symbol of improved living standards.[2] Chinese premier Wen Jiabao once said, "I have a dream to provide every Chinese, especially children, sufficient milk everyday" (ibid). Facing the quickly growing demand, China's domestic dairy industry is making every effort to increase production. By 2007, it rose to the third biggest producer in the world behind the US and India (ibid). In fact, China's rising demand for milk may even threaten to exhaust the world's milk supply and drive up global food prices (Lim 2008).

Ironically, as milk-weaned adults in China are driven back toward their newborn instincts, babies are separated from the intimacy of breastfeeding. If milk is the liquid medium that connects the child with the mother, then modern Chinese mothers are slowly losing this unique connection with their children. According to domestic health authorities, China has the world's lowest rate of breastfeeding for infants under six months – only 28 percent, while the global average is 40 percent and US and India's is about 46 percent (Pasick & Timmons 2013). This development has various societal causes, such as "long working hours, short maternity leaves, the prevalence of mothers who migrate from their villages for work and leave infants with their families and scarce nursing facilities" (ibid). Yet intensive marketing of infant formulas has been identified as a key reason. Sales representatives contact new mothers in hospitals shortly after their birth and offer free samples. Advertisements for infant formulas saturate television, newspapers, magazines, and outdoor billboards. Successful marketing, coupled with changing social conditions, is creating a silent revolution in the most fundamental layer of the Chinese diet. More and more, mothers decide to substitute their utmost intimacy with their children with cans of white powder.

To market to a culture that has been "weaned" off of human milk, cow milk advertisers often stress the product's nutritional value and its ability to strengthen health and enhance growth. Many milk ads feature celebrities (such as an athlete or a movie star) sucking from a milk package and looking satisfied (see Yili Pure Milk print ad, "Olympic Athlete Liu Xiang" (see Figure 4.1 on the author's blog "Environmental Advertising in China and the USA"; same goes with all the following figures). The apparent interpretation is that "you or your child can be as strong or successful as this athlete or movie star." However, there is more to be said about the consumer's desire than the need to identify with the ideal ego (i.e. celebrities). A closer look reveals a deeper anxiety in the milk culture of modern China: in choosing "nutrition" over nurture, "convenience" over connection, the milk drinker must first be alienated from the mother's breast (the nurturing body of the Other) and embrace the *prosthetic breast* of the mechanically farmed cow. In these advertisements, prosthetic breasts are represented as mass-produced, identical-looking milk packages (see Yili Pure Milk print ad, "Discount Package Launched" Figure 4.2). Exchanging for the mother's breast as well as the cow's breasts (which also are perhaps too sensual and too messy to show), these packages are twice removed from the *real* thing and function as prostheses that shore up consumers' separation anxiety. By emphasizing the oral pleasure from sucking, these ads promise to restore the lost unity between mother and child, gesturing toward the rewarding feelings of love and safety.

In the 2008 "melamine milk" scandal, however, the promise of love and safety turned out to be smoke and mirrors. Twenty-two domestic milk manufacturers, including major brands such as Yili and Mengniu, adulterated their baby formula with melamine to give the products higher protein content ("China Seizes 22 Companies," 2008). As a result, over 300,000 children fell ill and six of them died from kidney stones. This tragedy hit low-income families the hardest, as they usually purchased inexpensive local milk powder that were among the most contaminated brands (Branigan 2008). Poisoned milk, unlike poisoned pork or poisoned wine, was particularly unnerving because it awoke the anxiety about the already weakened mother-child bond in China's nuclear families. When the commercial fantasy of cow milk as safety nest went bust, parents were desperate. Having lost confidence in the domestic dairy industry, many frantically bought imported baby formulas. In Hong Kong, Taiwan, Japan, Europe, the US, and elsewhere, Chinese tourists stormed grocery stores and cleared their shelves of milk powder. However, curiously, even after this traumatizing incident, not many mothers shifted back to breastfeeding (Pasick & Timmons 2013). Perhaps the neatly packaged cans of white powder were still, after all, more attractive than the wet, swollen, and achy breasts of the mothers.

"Golden Breast" or "Nature's Breast?" Two Organic Milk Brands in China

As part of the effort to recuperate their reputation, domestic milk manufacturers launched organic product lines. Two leading products in the organic milk market are: Jindian Organic, produced by the Inner Mongolian dairy giant Yili, and Telunsu Organic, produced by Mengniu, another dairy corporation from Inner Mongolia. Yili and Mengniu were the nation's top milk manufactures and both were found responsible in the 2008 melamine scandal. Afterwards, they each added an extra line to their existing high-end brands – Jindian and Telunsu – respectively launched in 2005 and 2006.[3] Although these organic products were sold as subsidiary lines of larger brands, they received heavy promotion through the aggressive advertising machine of Yili and Mengniu. Therefore, it was unsurprising that their market shares were larger than the smaller but exclusively organic brands such as Shengmu and Weilaixing.

Marketed under the high-end brands of Jindian and Telunsu, the new concept of "organic" was wedded with images of luxury from the start. To begin with, both Jindian and Telunsu have "gold" in their brand names. *Jindian* means "golden classic," in Mandarin, and *telunsu* means "gold medal," in Mongolian. The following two advertisements give a glimpse into the marketing techniques of both brands prior to the introduction of the organic lines. The first print ad for Jindian Pure Milk was launched in 2005. Titled "New taste, 'Golden Classic' milk," it displays the milk in a triangular shaped bottle and three wine glasses (Figure 4.3). The bottle is topped with golden leaves and wears an ornamental golden belt around its waist. Commonly used for fine wine or high-end spirits, the bottle and glasses symbolize the superior quality and Western origin of their contents. They also suggest that their contents are not for sucking, but for sipping. In a physiological sense, sipping is more discretionary than sucking, because it allows one to stay detached from the source of nutrition and control her intake. If the sucker yearns for love and intimacy, then the sipper pursues independence and status. This status appeal is also confirmed by the bottle's golden-laced design: If the milk container is a prosthetic breast, then a breast made of gold (a metal breast, essentially) feeds the eye but not the mouth. It does not yield milk itself, yet it looks gorgeous. Here commodity fetishism is manifested at its purest: the milk is abandoned for the breast. The breast is no longer a source of love and intimacy from the mother to the child; in its place stands a golden (phallic) object valued for its symbolic potency for exchanging for more social power and status.

Similar to Jindian, Telunsu's early advertisements also adopted the appeal to class, wealth, and privilege. "Never Stops Pursuing An Outstanding Life," appearing in 2006, uses blue (another royal color, like gold) as the background color and laces it with golden threads (Figure 4.4). It features Lang Lang, a world-renowned pianist from Shanghai, standing next to a milky white grand piano. Under the spotlight, he stands upright and holds a pack of Telunsu milk. Instead of drinking it, he clutches it to his chest as though it is a badge of honor. This milk package is another example of the new "golden breast"; it feeds the eye, but not the mouth. Next to Lang Lang is a line supposedly coming from him: "Never stop pursuing an outstanding life. Follow me and choose Telunsu. Originated from the 40 degrees latitude; molded into 3.3

grams of high-quality protein." On the bottom right, there is the slogan: "Not all milk is called Telunsu." Then there is the invitation to join the "Telunsu VIP club" sitting next to a picture of a large diamond. Lang Lang, piano, diamond, gold thread, and the slogan: all these symbolic elements accentuate the exclusivity and exceptionality of the milk product and its presumed elite consumers.

Following its precedent, Telunsu Organic was also marketed as a brand of wealth and prestige – but with a twist of ecology. "Heavenly Formed, Heavenly Made," created in 2008, shares the same blue and white color scheme as the previous Lang Lang ad (Figure 4.5). Its most conspicuous feature is a large drop of milk dangling from the top. The drop contains a miniature portrait of a pristine river valley. It is positioned right on top of a pack of Telunsu Organic milk, which by implication captures the "essence" of the natural landscape. This layout symbolizes the exclusivity of the product: it is not churned out in large quantities, but is slowly accumulated into a tiny amount. It is the most refined essence – as valuable as gold. It *is* white gold.

Between the drop and the package, a slogan cuts across: "Primordial organic milk, heavenly formed (*tian ran*), heavenly made (*tian cheng*)." The Chinese character *tian* (天) is the key to decipher the slogan: while the word literally means "sky," in the Confucian tradition, it also refers to the sovereign *heaven* and materialist *nature* (Yao 2003). During the feudal dynasties, emperors were called *tian zi* (sons of heaven), since Heaven was deemed the highest sovereignty and source of legitimacy. Rebels, in a similar vein, rose against emperors by claiming that their insurgence followed from *tian ming* (the order of heaven). *Tian,* however, has another connotation in Confucianism – a materialist view of the order of the world without any "theo-volitional qualities" (Berthrong 2003, 377). The double-entendre of the term is exploited in this advertising slogan. "*Tian cheng*" (heavenly made) implies that the organic milk is not only the material concentration of "natural" products, but also a symbol of the highest sovereign power. The revival of the ancient term allows the advertiser to articulate "nature" with class and market organic milk as a luxury product. Following the previous logic of milk being a prosthetic breast, this large milk drop can be interpreted as the "teat of heaven," as it were, through which the elite consumer can suckle for the milk of Mother Nature.

The early advertisements for Jindian Organic – rival of Telunsu Organic – display similar traits. "Zero Pollution, Zero Additive" features the slogan "Zero pollution, zero additive; only that is organic milk; organic all the way" (Figure 4.6). Next to it is a large stamp print; its outer ring reads "Limited production from Yili's No. 7 Organic Pasture;" its inner ring is a sketched picture of cows grazing with a fence in the foreground and a farmhouse in the back. The stamp signifies the approval from authority – not by heaven, but by governmental agencies. The "nature" image in the stamp print is reminiscent of the thumbnail "nature" image in the milk drop: both are entrapped in a small space, meticulously selected and strictly controlled. They evoke the visualization of the hybrid car in the Chinese Prius ads in Chapter 2. Such an image of refinement mirrors the ego of the elite consumers, who are also supposed to have undergone the ruthless Darwinian selection of the Chinese society (from the educational system to the business world and the political world). Even if some of them obtained success through illegal, immoral, or accidental means, this fantasy of elitism retroactively legitimizes the means through which they gained their current wealth and status. This recalls the aforementioned concept of *tegong* or "special supply" in Beijing's government-run organic gardens, where organic is also a privilege of the elites. However, while *tegong* suppliers do not advertise, the commercial manufacturers do so vigorously.

Since 2011, Jindian shifted its direction and started to market itself primarily as an "organic" brand. This led to conspicuous changes in its advertising strategies. In the print ad "Heavenly Endowed Treasure," (Figure 4.7) what first greets the eyes of the viewer is a boundless pasture. In the foreground, a young mother and her daughter are playing in the grass. Judging by their hairstyles, clothes, and complexion, they are urban dwellers probably on a weekend excursion to the countryside. In the background, three cows are grazing, carefree. To their left the tagline reads: "Soil, free of chemical fertilizers; grass, free of pesticide pollution; cows, free ranged." Underneath is the slogan: "ZERO pollution, ZERO additive; only that is ORGANIC MILK." (Capital letters represent the bold font). On the bottom, two governmental organic certification labels preside over the tagline "Heaven-endowed (*tian ci*) treasure. Give it to the ones you love most."

The green pasture first sets this ad apart from its predecessors: "nature" is no longer compacted into an enclosed circle but is released into a wide and open space. The appeal to status and privilege is thereby diminished. Meanwhile, the appeal to love and intimacy increases. This ad portrays an idealistic image of mother and child sharing an intimate moment together in the backdrop of nature. As mentioned above, many Chinese families have forgone breastfeeding and relied on cow milk to rebuild the lost mother-child bond. Yet poisoned milk revealed the inadequacy of the prosthesis and awoken the separation anxiety. This ad, thus, introduces a new prosthesis – "nature" – to restore the mother-child intimacy. "Nature" has itself become a nurturing breast: it feeds all the creatures depending on it – soil, grass, cows, mother, and child – and supports an intimately connected ecosystem without the interference of outsiders ("zero pollution, zero additive"). "Heaven-endowed (*tian ci*) treasure. Give it to the ones you love most." Compared to *tiancheng* (heavenly formed) in the Telunsu ads, *tianci* (heavenly endowed) implies more gratitude than privilege. "Give it to the ones you love most" implies that this product is sold as a gift. Rather than being the buyer's ego, it constructs a fantasy of an ideal relationship between the buyer and the receiver. Thanks to "nature's" breast, the milkless mother can regain the intimacy relationship with her child.

In 2012, Jindian Organic incorporated celebrity endorsement into its advertising campaign. Faye Wong, a well-known Chinese singer-songwriter and actress, became its spokesperson. Often referred to as "*tian hou*" (heavenly queen, or diva), she was ranked the No. 1 female star on the 2011 Forbes China Celebrity List. Marketing analyst from ChinaMedia360.com applauds Jindian's choice: "Jindian Organic targets a high-end consumer market; to match the quality of the product, advertising must correspondingly use high-end celebrities as its spokespersons. Wong's fans are mostly white collar and bourgeois, spanning different age groups. Having her endorsing Jindian Organic manifests the additional value of the product, the lifestyle it promotes, and its 'high-endness'" (Shen 2012).

In Wong's first TV commercial, *"Tianci de Baobei,"* (heavenly endowed treasure) released in 2012 (Figure 4.8), the soundtrack begins with her humming a capella to a simple melody with no lyrics or accompaniment. She leads two young girls – her "daughters" by implication – into a pristine pasture where cows graze.[4] They dance in the wind, blow on dandelions, and pet the dairy cows. Her narration enters: "Caring for family, I have the heavenly endowed treasure. Jindian Organic milk, every drop comes from the pollution-free organic factory. Zero pollution, zero additives. Jindian Organic milk, heavenly endowed treasure, give it to the ones you love most." The commercial ends with the two girls huddle by her side, each suckling a box of Jindian Organic milk.

Wong's endorsement fee for Jingdian Organic was rumored to be as high as 70 million RMB (equals 11.4 million USD). Yet this astronomical fee was apparently justified because "Heavenly Endowed Treasure" became an instant classic. A key reason, in my view, is the interesting resonance between Wong's private life and the role of the "milkless" mother. Despite her diva status, Wong was known for her failed marriages. Her first husband Dou Wei, a famous rockstar, left her for a fashion photographer. After their divorce in 1999, she won widespread sympathy for her husband's disloyalty, but many attributed her husband's departure to her busy career and traveling lifestyle. Wong brought up their daughter by herself and was widely admired as a career mother. In 2005, she remarried, became pregnant again, and went into a career hiatus. Four years later, the second marriage failed and she returned to the entertainment world. Wong's private life, as portrayed in Chinese tabloids, is marked by her struggle to balance career and family. Her experience embodies the dilemma of many Chinese career women, who had to sacrifice family relationships for professional success and social recognition. Selecting her to be the spokesperson wins over the sympathy of these mothers (and fathers), who probably imagine the organic milk to be the solution to their predicament as well.

In 2014, Jindian Organic released a second commercial with Wong (Figure 4.9). It features her and Ella, one of the two young actresses from the first Jindian commercial, sitting in a kitchen. Ella asks in a girlish voice: "What's organic milk?" Wong responds: "It's just like Jindian!" She puts a package of Jindian Organic milk on the table, and a calf magically appears in the middle of their kitchen. Ella is still confused. Wong takes her and the calf out to a green pasture (subtitle appears: "specially owned organic farm"). Her voiceover continues: "These dairy cows grow up healthily in the organic farm." Ella feeds grass to the cow: "So they eat organic feasts?" Both bend down to milk the cow and produce buckets full of milk. "Every drop of milk is organic. Jindian Organic milk, zero pollution, zero additives." The two return to the kitchen. Wong: "Listen, the calf is speaking." Ella: "He says 'I love you.'" Wong: "Jindian: the leader of the organic lifestyle."[5] This commercial shows an intimate moment between mother and daughter who labor together, learn together, and have fun together. Unfortunately, this is an experience that many career parents can only wish for. While many crave to spend more time with their children, such precious time has indeed become luxury that even the rich and successful parents cannot afford.

To sum up the analysis above, I have observed that organic milk in China, at its current stage of mass marketing, is sold as a luxury product targeting the upper and upper-middle class consumer. The term "luxury" could be interpreted both ways—as a high-end status symbol and a promise of a scarce moment of parent-child bonding for the elites. In the former case, "organic" symbolizes exclusivity and privilege and advertisers go as far as naming the products "gold." In the ads, "nature" is visually compressed into an exclusive and enclosed space (e.g. a milk drop, a stamp), which indicates its function as a VIP club, reserved only for elite humans (and elite cows). "Nature" is referenced to by the Confucian term *tian*, as in *tianran* (heavenly formed) or *tiancheng* (heavenly made). Simultaneously meaning materialist "nature" and sovereign "heaven," *tian* signifies the product as the embodiment of both natural nutrition and higher-power endorsement. Overall, "organic" is represented as the outcome of meticulous selection, purification, and refinement. It mirrors the ideal ego of the elite consumer.

In the latter case, the organic milk ads appeal to love and intimacy and present the product as a gift for family and friends. They usually represent "nature" in a wide and open space (e.g. a green pasture, a diary farm) with elite consumers and their children playing in its embrace. Considering how Chinese career mothers often substitute breastfeeding for cow's milk, these ads evoke "nature" as a prosthetic breast to retrieve the lost mother-child bond. In the fantasy of eco-harmony, the all-encompassing "nature" restores mutual intimacy to all elements of the ecosystem, including the human mother and her child. This fantasy allows successful professionals to achieve vicarious intimacy with their estranged family members and gain solace in the dilemma between career and family. It sweetens the somewhat bitter (i.e. alienated) experience of the growing bourgeois demographic. The "organic" here is represented as a gift from heaven: *tianci* (heavenly endowed), which implies less privilege and more gratitude than "*tianran*" (heavenly formed).

Despite their differences, these Chinese advertisements all portray organic milk as a precious resource to be consumed by the privileged. They also share a common exclusion: the dairy farmers, who raise the cows and milk their breasts, cannot be found anywhere in these ads. Their erasure is necessary to sustain the eco-fantasy of the elites due to the historical antagonism between the urban consumers and the rural farmers. As mentioned above, farmers fell to the bottom tier of the Chinese society since the economic reform in 1990s. Urban dwellers often find them an eyesore and describe them as "*tu*" (earth) or "*tuqi*" (earthy) – a pejorative term that refers to one's lack of culture and class. Ironically, the farmers are associated with *earth* and the organic products are linked with *heaven*. The polar opposites signify a tacit disavowal of the "lowly" farmers by the urban elites. If the organics are "divine treasures," then the farmers must not have laid their dusty hands on them. Moreover, after the food security scandals, farmers and small food distributers (e.g. street stands, small restaurants and food factories) became an easy target for urbanites to blame. Although corporations and supermarkets have all taken part in food adulteration and contamination, they often use media and advertising to conduct image repair. Corporations' visibility makes them seem more trust-worthy, while independent farmers' anonymity often becomes a reason for suspicion.[6] All these factors contribute to the exclusion of farmers from organic milk advertisements, which aim to maintain the fantasy of righteous purity for the urban elites.[7]

* * *

The Organic Movement in the US

Due to their divergent histories, organic food advertising in China and the US display very different ideological tendencies. An analogy of marriage status may be helpful to understand their current states within the organic movement: If the Chinese are just entering into their "honeymoon" with organics, then the Americans are perhaps experiencing their "seven year itch" and are pondering "divorce." But the US did have a passionate "affair" with organics. In the 1950s, after authors such as J. I. Rodale and Wendell Berry introduced organic farming from the UK to the US, the practice resonated widely: postwar agriculture triggered increasing concern with its mechanization, fertilization, and pesticides application. During the 1960s and 70s, the organic movement gained momentum by converging with the countercultures. Hippies, feminists, antiwar protesters, and civil rights activists used food as a means to embrace community and pursue social solidarity. Many established food co-ops and farmers markets (see Frances Moore Lappe's *Diet for a Small Planet,* 1971) and others answered the call "back to the land" and migrated to the countryside for a rural life. These new farmers strived to revive Thoreau's philosophy of simple living and Leopold's land ethic to harmonize "man and land."

During the Reagan era, however, the organic's "affair" with the countercultures was disrupted by its "marriage" with the mainstream consumer culture. In 1989, a scandal about Alar – a carcinogenic pesticide used on apple crops – led to a "panic for organic" ("Warning," 1989). Soon afterwards, the US government passed the Organic Foods Production Act (OFPA) to regulate the production, certification, and marketing of organic foods. In the next two decades, organic foods became a multi-billion dollar industry. The term "Certified Organic" became a synonym for governmental and corporate control. Represented by Michael Pollan's *The Omnivore's Dilemma* (2006), critics began to censure the Big Organic and exposed their highly mechanized production methods and global distribution channels. Some other examples include the *Newsweek* cover story "The Organic Myth" (Brady 2006), the documentaries *Food Inc.* (2008), *What's Organic about Organic?* (2010), and *In Organic We Trust* (2012). Accusing corporations for stealing the original spirit of the organics, many proposed that local foods might be truer to the ethics of the 1960s' movement. In 2007, *Time Magazine* published the cover article "Forget Organic: Eat Local" (Cloud 2007). It signaled the rise of the local food movement, where consumers started to calculate food miles instead of finding organic labels on food packages. In no time, local eating experiments and backyard gardening tutorials blossomed in popular media. The new locavores wanted to repoliticize food culture by reviving the ideals of the earlier stages of the organic movement.

Despite the disillusionment from the Left, the mainstream demand for organic continues to grow. According to the "Organic Marketing Report" released in 2014, the American organic industry achieved a 3,400 percent sales increase from 1989 to 2013 and sold $290 billion in 2013 in the domestic market alone (Flynn 2014). This success is backed up by a sophisticated organic marketing industry, which often enlists the support from advocacy groups and the US Department of Agriculture. The following paragraphs will examine ads from leading organic brands. They particularly represent this mainstream consumer explosion and, at the same time, show signs in appropriating the Leftist, anti-hegemonic rhetoric of condemning the Big Organic and promoting local food. To correspond with the Chinese portion of my analysis, I will focus on organic milk first before moving on to briefly consider other types of organic foods and the rhetorical strategies of the companies marketing them.

"Know Your Farmer, Know Your 'Cow'": Two Organic Milk Brands in the US

In the US, the two leading organic milk producers and distributors are Organic Valley and Horizon Organic (Schultz & Huntrods 2013). Organic Valley is a farmers' cooperative established in 1988. Based in Wisconsin, it is now the largest farmers' co-op in the world and sells its products in all 50 states as well as China, Japan, and other foreign countries. Horizon Organic, having started its organic milk production in 1992, is North America's largest organic milk supplier. Acquired in 2004 by Dean Foods, a big agribusiness, Horizon sources its milk from farms around the country and frequently comes under criticisms for failing the organic standards. Organic Valley and Horizon Organic represent the opposition between independent farmers co-ops and "Big Organic." Accordingly, fundamental differences in their advertising strategies can be observed.

Organic Valley's ads highlight its status as a farmers' cooperative and often feature portraits of farmers and their family members. A print ad titled "Organic and farmer-owned; as good as it gets," puts a larger photograph of a rural family – mother, father, and two boys – front and center (Figure 4.10). The father holds the hand of the older boy and the mother carries the younger one in her arms. All four family members wear dirt-stained blue jeans, have tanned faces, and smile at the camera with a simple candor. Behind them, a few dairy cows stand in an open prairie that stretches out to horizon. The color palette of the photograph is "naturalistic" or "earthy," ranging from olive, grey, to yellow-green. The small font on the bottom explains the identity of the family: "The Mikita family, one of the Organic Valley farm families in the Rocky Mountains who co-own our cooperative." The larger font underneath reads: "We are proud to be Colorado farmer owners of the Organic Valley Cooperative. By choosing our organic milk, you are getting the safest, healthiest, most delicious food you can buy, while supporting organic and independent Colorado family farmers well into the future."

Compared to the Chinese ads analyzed above, the first observable difference is the presence of the farmers. Nowhere to be found in the Chinese ads, farmers take center stage and are presented as the ideal product spokespersons. The associated text suggests that buying organic is not just a nutritional statement – "safest, healthiest, and most delicious" – but also a political statement – to "support organic and independent Colorado family farmers." The term "organic" is articulated with three other modifiers—"independent," "Colorado," and "family"—indicating that the farmers are honest, traditional, and responsible. But above all, they are "local" that is, *of the land*. Their "down-to-earthness" evokes the American agrarian fantasy of harmony between man and land. Expressed in Alfred Leopold's land ethic, this aspiration holds that hands-on farming allows humans to achieve unity with nature, which had become the principal ideal of the early organic movement. Also, the farmers' projected identity evokes the ideology of social equality – or, harmony between man and man: "We are proud to…" "by choosing our… you are getting…." The symmetrical structure of "we" and "you" implies a relationship of equal exchange between farmers and consumers. The discourse of equality glorifies the underdog and degrades the ones in power. Being subjected to the oppression of big corporations and big government, these small farmers assume a moral (and marketable) high ground.

The apparent ideological fantasy here – social equality – forms a sharp contrast with the Chinese ideology of hierarchy. While the Chinese ads put celebrities or elites front and center for consumers to emulate, the American ad put farmers or the "common man" in the spotlight for consumers to support. Two types of subjective relationships lie between the images and the consumer-subject. Lacan describes the differences as the *ideal ego* and the *ego ideal*. The *ideal ego* is an image of the perfect Self that the subject strives to become. In Žižek's (2009) words, it is the "the way I would like to be, I would like others to see me." The *ego ideal* is an idealized Other before which the subject wishes to appear perfect. It is the "agency whose gaze I try to impress with my ego image, the big Other who watches over me and propels me to give my best." In the Chinese ads, the celebrities are the ideal ego. Their idealized and healthy figures function as an ideological screen that shields consumers from the chaotic reality of food scares. They carry the promise that elites can always buy their way out of the poisonous web of food, water, and air – and the only way to become an elite is to eat what the celebrities eat, drink what they drink. In the American ads, meanwhile, the farmers are the ego ideal. They are idealized figures (i.e. the big Other) that cast a moral gaze onto the consumer-subject and issue the injunction: "Eat local. Do the right thing." This gaze – proud, warm, and trusting – helps consumers cope with their anxiety from the incessant corporate food scandals. It frames the ecological imbalance as a problem of political imbalance – a familiar discourse to the American public – and calls on them to rectify social inequality by buying from the local farmers.[8]

But the adverse side of the *ego ideal* is the *superego*, warns Lacan – the "revengeful, sadistic, and punishing" side of the moral injunction (ibid). The superego, as stated in Chapter 2, issues impossible demands and punishes the subject with guilt when he fails to live up to its standards. Although the farmers' gaze seems warm in this ad, there is a certain menace lurking behind it. In "Green Like Me" (2009), Elizabeth Kolbert enumerates a number of recent locavore experiments that did the near-impossible to follow the absolute principle of "eating local." One couple, for example, tried to live a year eating only food within 100 miles of their apartment, and eventually had to boil down seawater to make salt and buy stale wheat berries littered with mouse droppings. Another family had to move a family of four from a city to farmland and yet another had to dig into urban dumpsters for hours to find pig feed. These bold souls endured incredible hardship to follow the principle of local eating. They prove that the farmer's gaze, when inscribed into consumers' guilty conscience, could indeed be relentless. In a sense, the fantasy of equality only obscures the real dominance within the psychic realm – of the Farmer (i.e. the big Other) over the consumer. As the Farmer puts the consumer under constant surveillance, the consumer struggles to manage his self-image in the eyes of the Other.

The gaze of the farmer – seeminly warm but potentially cruel – can be found in many American organic food ads. Two more print ads for Organic Valley portray farm families dressed in blue jeans and knee-high boots, standing in their fields, making direct eye contact with the viewer (Figure 4.11–4.12). Another two promotional photos from Earthbound Farm's website show farmers in fields proudly presenting their harvest to the viewers (Figure 4.13–4.14). A fifth website promotional photo for Texas' Greenling Organic Delivery presents "Pedro Schambon," a farmer called "Pedro

Schambon" from "My Father's Farm, Segain, TX" (Figure 4.15). He seems to be talking to the camera and his words are spelled out in bold font: "It's a GREAT FEELING that somebody appreciates what we do."[9] In a sense, who is "Pedro Schambon" or where is "Segain, TX" are of complete irrelevance to the viewer. But the simple fact that he has a real-sounding name nullifies this irrelevance and creates an illusion as if the viewer knows him in person. "Pedro Schambon" is both somebody and nobody: he is a small, specific other that hollows out its content and takes on the role of the big, abstract Other. Simultaneously named and anonymous, this empty farmer figure is situated at the heart of the locavore movement. He occupies the place of the superego and demands the consumer to buy from him so that he can have the "GREAT FEELING that somebody appreciates what we do."

Outside of print media, companies also use social media and larger public relations campaigns as carriers of the farmer's gaze. A webpage from Organic Valley's official website, sporting the large title "Who's Your Farmer?", lets consumers type in their zip codes and search for nearby farms' information, including names and locations, Facebook pages, profile pictures, and exact distance calculated in decimals of miles (Figure 4.16).[10] The digital mapping technology – combined with social media profiles and mileage calculation – empties out the meaning of "local:" it turns what once meant face-to-face interactions into an all-rounded aggregation of private data about some imagined "neighbor" that you have never met, and likely never will.

In conjunction with the mapping webpage, Organic Valley also launched "Who's Your Farmer" Tour in 2010. This annual event puts young organic farmers from farming states – inspiringly called the "Generation Organic" – on biofuel buses going around the country to spread their vision to college students. These nationwide PR tours are ideal for spreading local-*ism*: their fleeting and commercial nature allows consumers to "meet" their farmers without really meeting them, "knowing about" them without really knowing them. Since the fantasy is more based on the imagination of an abstract Other than on embodied contact with real human beings, it is important that the meeting never take place. The moment the consumer knows the farmer as a real person, he ceases to function as the Farmer and his gaze disappears. Moreover, in the new catchphrases for the locavore movement, this farmer's gaze has been disguised in a new form as the "hand." "Shake the hand that feeds you," a quote from Pollan's *In Defense of Food* (2009) became an instant mottle that appeared in many advertisements ("Shake the hands that feed you: Richmond Farm Tour," Figure 4.17, and "Shake the hands that planted your coffee: Barismo Coffee Roaster presents Origin Week;" Figure 4.18). The hand, implying intimate physical contact, intensifies the gaze and escalates the moral stake.

Once the "local" has been wrenched from the concrete context of a local community, the locavore movement is well on its way to being appropriated by large corporations. In recent years, big agribusiness and chain restaurants have increasingly joined in the competition of "who can know their farmers better." National commercials for Lays Chips feature proud "local" farmers from Michigan, Texas, Florida, who have been growing potatoes for Lays on their "(third, fourth, or fifth) generation family farms" (Figure 4.19). In these ads, "local" is stretched to mean "locale, emphasizing the geographic origin of their food" (Sevenson 2009). Chipotle, the multibillion-dollar fast food chain, launched its nationwide "Farmers Market Tour" in 2012, where they set up stands in farmers markets and handed away samples for "their salsa supposedly made with tomatoes from local farmers" (Roth 2012). Here, "local" has become a Trojan horse to transport national and global food ingredients to a setting that is supposed to be reserved for local commerce. In fact, the notion of "Farmers Market Tour" is already an oxymoron: how can one be a local and a tourist at the same time?

Chipotle's "farmer-friendly" advertising strategies never cease to amaze with their absurdity. Since 2011, they built the website "Farm Team" and allowed customers to play online farming games to virtually collaborate with farmers in order to win prizes (Hicks 2011). Supporting a virtual "local" farmer blatantly defeats the purpose of the locavore movement, and might be *the* biggest insult to the consumer intelligence. However, one must not deny its ability to provide a certain perverse enjoyment: since the fantasy is structured around a disembodied Other, the consumer (on an unconscious level) makes no distinction between a real farmer or a virtual farmer. Whether real or virtual, it "gets him off." (Pardon the vulgarity, but this enjoyment can be considered as sexual in a psychoanalytic sense). In Lacanian terms, this general "local-ness" is the symptom pure and simple: it is the knot of enjoyment that reveals the abstract, ghostly core of local-*ism* that contradicts the very idea of "local." "From Farm To Face" is another example of the symptom (Figure 4.20). In this Chipotle's Facebook cover photo, the viewer sees a close-up of a mouthwatering burrito, spilling out its contents. Next to the image was the aforementioned slogan. It appropriates the expression "farm to table" but pushes its logic to an extreme: it shows that at the very end of the consumers' pursuit to minimize the distance from farmers is the desire to devour the farm in whole. This carnivorous imagery presents an ultimate disembodied relationship – the process of biting, ingesting, and digesting the Other – that erases all the differences between the bodies, so that the miserable journey to fulfill the Other's impossible demand can finally end.

Of course not all organic advertising has "gone local." We must also look at another group of advertisements that adopt a different appeal – animal welfare. This strategy frequently appears in the advertisements for the Big Organic brands, such as Horizon Organic, Stonyfield Farm, and Brown Cow, who for some reason cannot (or perhaps choose not to) jump on the localism bandwagon.[11] These advertisements often feature portraits of animated, happy cows talking to the camera. "Prize Winning Cow" presents to the viewers a headshot of a brown cow wearing a tiara standing in an open pasture (Figure 4.21). The copy reads: "What makes me, Lily, so perfect? Is it my looks, or how eloquently I express myself on paper? No. What makes me special is how I make the greatest yogurt in the world." In "Other Cows Don't Like Me," the same cow, Lily, is admiring her own image in a mirror: "Regular cows don't like me because they're jealous. But I keep telling myself, Lily, you were born for a reason and that's to make the greatest yogurt in the world" (Figure 4.22). In "Hello My Name Is," three ads each features a dairy cow wearing a nametag "Moly," "Betsy," or "Amy," with the copy above reads: "Downright, utterly, pure, unadulterated, all-out, sheer, out right, organic yogurt_ Moly/Betsy/Amy approved" (Figure 4.23).

By means of anthropomorphism (e.g. nametags, self-confessions), these ads portray the cows as unique individuals with names and personalities of their own. They roam free in the open pasture and seem proud and happy. These happy cows form a clear contrast with the factory cows depicted in animal rights documentaries (e.g. *Food Inc.* 2008), which are anonymous, crowded in small spaces, and covered in their own feces. They associate the organic milk brand with the notion of animal welfare, which derives from the American animal rights movement. In his classic work *Animal Liberation* (1975), Peter Singer advocates the extension of rights from humans to animals and equates the oppression of animals with the oppression of human minorities. The notion of animal rights (and its compromised version, animal welfare) is also based on the Western ideology of equality. Just like the localism ads, these animal welfare ads are structured around the same fantasy: they place the subjugated Other center stage, who casts a moral gaze onto the subject. These happy cows, "Molly," "Betsy," and "Amy," mirror the proud farmer "Pedro Schambon" – they are the disembodied core of the discourse of equality and stimulate consumer desire by being an essential lack and none other.

Almost inevitably, symptoms emerge. In these ads, they can be found in the absurd form of animals exuberantly presenting their own bodies for human consumption. The I-am-so-delighted-to-be-eaten-by-you tactic is not new; it has long existed in traditional food advertisements. The logo of Starkist Tuna, for example, is a tuna fish happily introducing its meat to the consumers; beef jerky packages portray cows always cheerfully inviting humans to eat them. Likewise, happy cows touting their milk to the consumers cannot escape the irony. Although one might argue that dairy cows are not killed like the other unlucky animals, they are still objects of human consumption and often die from exhaustion by excessive milking. The image of animals welcoming their own exploitation, in my opinion, bespeaks the hypocrisy in American consumer culture. It disguises the necessary violence in the act of consumption – the brutal evolutionary law of predator and prey – as a happy consensus. It disguises a repressive relationship with an illusion of reciprocity, which is a typical example of perversion. As stated in Chapter 3, the pervert disavows the symbolic division and submits himself to be a tool of the Other's enjoyment. Similarly, the tuna says: "I know very well that I will be eaten, nevertheless, I am happy to do it because it will please you, the consumer." By comparison, the Chinese ads – in their appeals to exclusivity and privilege – are more "honest." They candidly represent the brutal truth (or, the *real*) of consumption – a relationship of dominance and subjugation – and even capitalize the inequality embedded in organic farming.

This inequality, I believe, is something that we should first acknowledge. Indeed, compared to conventional foods, organic foods take up more land, more clean water, and more human labor to grow. In a world that faces food shortage and population explosion, they cannot be enjoyed by the masses and have to remain as a privilege for a select few. In China, political and economic elites, as well as urban consumers that have space and time, are mainly the ones that consume organic foods. In the US, the same exclusion exists: natural-organic food stores are often located in wealthy, educated, and white neighborhoods, and farmers markets are usually found in urban communities that have a strong middle-class economy. Although American low-income residents might also have access to affordable organic foods due to governmental programs and community initiatives, from a global perspective they can still be considered as elites when compared to poor residents in developing countries such as China or India. Viewed globally, organic farming is just a symptom of the deep-seated social and ecological inequality that always underlies the production and consumption of food. This fundamental antagonism is the *real* of food that consumers have to confront, and the advertising reviewed in this chapter can be seen as a means of helping them cope. The Chinese cope by confirming and accepting this antagonism, and the American cope by disavowing and avoiding this antagonism.

Conclusion

To summarize, my above analysis has demonstrated significant differences between Chinese and American organic food advertising. In China, "organic" is sold as privilege. Its advertisements often employ celebrities as spokespersons and portray the products the "essence" of nature (or rather, man's privileged relationship to nature). In the US, "organic" is often sold as a form of consumer social advocacy. Its advertisements use farmers or cows as spokespersons and portray the product as an equalizer that can erase the social and environmental injustice embedded in the industrial farming system. In both China and the US, "organic" is constructed as a fantasy of ecological or social harmony (harmony between man and nature, harmony between man and man) to help consumers escape the anxiety-inducing food scares surrounding their lives. For the Chinese consumers, "organic" delivers the promise that the rich can always buy their way out of the poisonous web of food and water; for the American consumers, "organic" suggests that one can trust small farmers and "responsible" food companies and opt out of the corporate-dominated agricultural food systems and all of their ethical compromises.

Despite these grandiose promises, the *real* of organic farming – the fundamental social inequality and ecological imbalance – keeps returning to haunt us. Attributing the root problem to corporate capitalism, Michael Pollan and others try to revitalize the community-centered agriculture that had thrived during the American countercultural movement. However, is industrial capitalism the root of all evil when it comes to food production? According to the studies in archeology and evolutionary biology, we might need to rewind the clock much further back – to the *invention* of agriculture around 10,000 years ago. Jared Diamond (1987), the well-known geologist, calls agriculture "the worst mistake in the history of the human race." For Diamond, agriculture has initiated a host of problems that continue to plague the world today, including famine, malnutrition, social inequality, and population explosion. Comparing to the nomadic, hunter-gatherer lifestyle, agriculture allowed humans to settle down on a piece of land and manipulate the soil into yielding an abundance of crops. Though an efficient way to get more food, it also tempted societies to overly rely on it. The result was the reduction in the diversity and quality of the human diet (shown in shorter statures, weaker health, and more starvation victims) and the rise of institutionalized inequality (as the population freed from food procurement became the bureaucratic class). Food surplus also allowed for population increase, which created more mouths to feed and, thus, the need for more agriculture – a society-wide addiction (Diamond 2013). According to Kolbert (2014), it took humans thousands of years to "recover" from the blow of agriculture; only recently – thanks to industrial agriculture – did Western societies regain the average height of the hunter-gatherer societies. However, they also grew wider and became sicker in a different way – not from food shortage but from food excess and food pollution.

Viewed from this agro-revisionist perspective, the local-organic food movement might not have touched the root of the problem. The harmonious bond between man and land – as boasted in the agrarian ideals of Leopold and Thoreau – had never existed as such. Perhaps, the real problem lies not in the *mechanical* manipulation of soil, but in the desire to *manipulate* soil, and on a larger scale, the wish to manipulate one's environment and one's own body (and the bodies of others). Driven by the desire to control, farming technology has precipitated the inequality between man and land, man and man (and man and woman for that matters). Its trauma lingered throughout history and its symptoms escalated over time. When we fear the impact of GMO technology on today's food, we must not forget that the genetic modification of foods had started thousands of years ago with the invention of agriculture. When we feel indignation about the worldwide food disparity of today, we must not forget that the unequal distribution of food and power originated in early agricultural societies, long before modern industrialization. In a sense, humans had traded quality for quantity a long time ago.

But can we go back? The new Paleolithic movement seems to think so. Just as the organivores who want to rewind history to the pre-industrial stage of agriculture, the Paleo-eaters wish to return to a pre-agricultural past where humans foraged wild plants and hunted wild animals. According to Kolbert (2014), the now trending Paleo-diet seeks to mimic the diet of the hunter-gatherers' by eating mainly meats and vegetables. However, this diet also supports the energy-intensive meat industry that contributes to global warming 40 percent faster than the entire transportation sector (Foer 2009). Ironically, in the attempt to unwind the harmful ecological and social effects of agriculture, the Paleo-eaters only exacerbate it. From the psychoanalytic point of view, I believe that both the organivores and the Paleo-eaters have missed the mark. Technologies of agriculture, sustenance or industrialized, are only symptoms of the human desire to control. Such desire is manifested in the technologies that promise to propel us into the future, or to bring us back to the past. At the outset of the chapter, I mentioned that the organic food culture is dominated by a nostalgia for the pre-industrial past. To tackle the world's present day food problems, however, we must first rid ourselves of this nostalgia, as it manifests the problem that got us into this mess in the first place – the desire to control our food, or environment, and the bodies of others and that of our own.

Notes

1 A spoof diary, "A Typical Day in the Life of A Happy Chinese," went viral on the Chinese web in 2008. It enumerates the recent food scandals of nearly every consumer food item: "I wake up in the morning [...] have a cup of Melamine polluted milk, eat some fried bread sticks (youtiao) cooked in diesel, dipped in some chile source died with Sudan Red, added to a bowl of duck egg gruel with poison rice and egg with large amounts of Lead Oxide." Underneath the sarcasm, one can detect the silent desperation of the Chinese consumers who feel caught in the toxic nexus of contemporary foods, drinks, and medicine. The entrapment is so suffocating that the only way out seems to be death: "I was born a Chinese, and will die a Chinese spirit." Seemingly patriotic, this remark implies just the opposite – the attribution of blame to everything Chinese (e.g. food, farmers, companies, the government, etc.).

2 For 20 years, my father had in fact been receiving a bottle of milk per day from the government, for working in a toxic workshop of a state-owned bed sheet factory. This form of compensation testified to the Chinese belief that milk has detoxification functions and is able to strengthen stamina. I will elaborate on this story in the concluding chapter.

3 In other words, Jindian and Telunsu are not exclusively "organic brands;" they are the larger umbrella brands under which these new organic products are sold. For example, Jindian includes three types of milk products: organic, pure, and low-fat (http://jindian.yili.com/product_list.aspx?proID=0). Telunsu has four: pure, low-fat, organic, and fiber-added (http://baike.baidu.com/view/123039.htm#2). Telunsu Official Website. http://www.telunsu.net/brand.jsp

4 One of the two young actresses, Ella, gained instant fame after the commercial, not only because she appeared in the same commercial with Wong but also because she was known as a "mixed blood child" for being half-American. The popular belief in China is that children who have "mixed blood" are cuter and smarter than ones with "pure" Chinese blood.

5 Wong's third Jindian Organic commercial was a Chinese New Year special for 2014. Wong is in a family gathering. She talked away from the dinner table and

stared at the family photos pensively. She thought about how she has been absent from family events in the past years and wished that she could repay her family with the gift of organic milk.

6 This relates to the hysterical structure of desire mentioned in Chapter 3 on green homes; the Chinese refuses to obey the Law whenever the authorities are not around. Consequently, only large corporations that are constantly under governmental or media surveillance behave more trustworthily than small businesses.

7 The appeal to elitism and the exclusion of farmers are not limited to advertisements for organic milk products. They can be widely recognized in other organic food advertising in China, from organic produce to sustainable seafood. The three advertisements for Zhenggu – Organic and Beyond (a company that sells sustainable seafood and organic produce) feature drawings of feasts or pictures of the company's CEO (PhD) and other higher officials. And so do the ads for Hona Organic / House of Natural Art (Figure 4.24–4.27).

8 This gaze is commonly used in the rhetoric of philanthropy and ethical consumerism. And now the "local" farmer joins the long list of the idealized others, i.e. the sad puppies in animal shelters or the smiling Africans on fair trade advertisements, as the big Other to issue moral injunctions to the consumer-subject.

9 Another example of an organic brand valorizing the farmers comes from the UK: it is a 2-minute commercial produced for the organic farm Yeo Valley released in 2010. It features four "rapping farmers" who sing and rap everywhere from the fields, the barn, to the tractor and the combine. This commercial became viral soon after its release and achieved wild success. On the one hand, the "rapping farmers" reinforced the ruggedness and crudeness of the farmers' traditional image; on the other hand, it combined the style of rap – an originally anti-hegemonic cultural form – with the traditional image and produced a new type of hybrid representation of the rural farm cultures.

10 The Organic Valley's "Who's Your Farmer" event was in fact inspired by the USDA program "Know Your Farmer, Know Your Food" (KYF2) launched in 2009. This program aims to "carry out President Obama's commitment to strengthening local and regional food systems." (http://www.usda.gov/wps/portal/usda/usdahome? navid=KYF_MISSION). Its website features a "compass map" to help loca-vores connect with the nearest farmers and farmers' markets in their region.

11 Horizon Organic, owned by Dean Foods, is the largest organic milk distributer of North America. Stonyfield Farm, mainly owned by the French diary giant Danone, is the number one selling organic yogurt in the US. In 2003, they acquired Brown Cow, which produces organic "cream top" yogurt.

References

Berthrong, J. (2003). Confucian views of Nature. *Nature Across Cultures: Views of Nature and the Environment in Non-Western Cultures*. Ed. Selin, H. Kluwer Academic Publishers.

Bezlova, A. (2006, May 27). China: Going organic. *Inter Press Service*. Retrieved from: http://ipsnews.net/print.asp?idnews=33392

Brady, D. (2006, October 15). The organic myth. *BusinessWeek*. Retrieved from: http://www.bloomberg.com/bw/stories/2006-10-15/the-organic-myth

Branigan, T. (2008, December 2). Chinese figures show fivefold rise in babies sick from contaminated milk. *The Guardian*. Retrived from: http://web.archive.org/web/20081205093042/http://www.guardian.co.uk/world/2008/dec/02/china

China seizes 22 companies with contaminated baby milk powder. (2008, September 16). *Xinhua News Agency*. Retrieved from: http://web.archive.org/web/20121021182912/ http://news.xinhuanet.com/english/2008-09/17/content_10046949.htm

Cloud, J. (2007, March 2). Eating better than organic. *Times Magazine*. Retrieved from: http://content.time.com/time/magazine/article/0,9171,1595245,00.html

Demick, B. (2011, September 16). In China, what you eat tells who you are. *Los Angeles Times*. Retrieved from: http://articles.latimes.com/2011/sep/16/world/la-fg-china-elite-farm-20110917

Diamond, J. (1987). The worst mistake in the history of the human race. *Discover Magazine*, May, 64–66.

Diamond, J. (2013). *The World Until Yesterday: What Can We Learn from Traditional Societies?* Penguin Books.

Dintenfass, D. (2011, March 29). Going organic in China, *eChinacities.com*. Retrieved from: http://www.echinacities.com/expat-corner/going-organic-in-china.html

Drinkwater, L. E. (2009). Ecological knowledge: Foundation for sustainable organic agriculture". *Organic Farming: The Ecological System*. Ed. Francis, C. ASA-CSSA-SSA, 19–50.

Eckhardt, R. & Hagerman, D. (2010, February 11). Going organic in China. *Zester Daily*. Retrieved from: http://zesterdaily.com/world/going-organic-in-china/

Flynn, D. (2014, April 22). Report: Organic industry achieved 25 years of fast growth through fear and deception. *Food Safety News*. Retrieved from: http://www.foodsafety news.com/2014/04/report-fast-growing-organics-industry-is-intentionally-deceptive/#. VUg1T0KQzwy

Foer, J. S. (2009). *Eating Animals*. Back Bay Books.

Foster, P. (2011, May 29). China goes organic after years of "glow in the dark pork" and "exploding watermelons." *The Telegraph*. Retrieved from: http://www.telegraph. co.uk/news/worldnews/asia/china/8544851/China-goes-organic-after-years-of-glow-in-the-dark-pork-and-exploding-watermelons.html

Fuller, F., Huang, J., Ma, H. and Rozelle, S.D. (2006). Got milk? The rapid rise of China's dairy sector and its future prospects, *Food Policy*, 31, 201–215.

Gao, X. (2012, June 6). Nongfu shiji: yiqun chengshiren de canzhuo zijiu [Farmers market: A group of urbanites' self-saving on the dinner table]. *Fazhi Zhoumo [Week-end Law]*. Retrieved from: http://www.youjinongfu.com/luntan/thread-210-1-1.html

Gerth, K. (2010). *As China Goes, So Goes the World: How Chinese Consumers Are Transforming Everything*. Hill and Wang.

Greenpeace East Asia, The problems of agriculture in China. *Greenpeace.org*. Retrieved from: http://www.greenpeace.org/eastasia/campaigns/food-agriculture/ problems/Winders, B. (2011). The food crisis and the deregulation of agriculture. *Brown J. World Aff*, 18, 83.

Hicks, L. W. (2011, September 3). Chipotle's Farm Team grows customer loyalty. *Denver Business Journal*. Retrieved from: http://www.bizjournals.com/denver/print-edition/2011/09/02/chipotles-farm-team-grows-customer.html?page=all

Kenner, R. (2008). *Food, Inc.* [Documentary]. Magnolia Pictures, Participant Media, River Road Entertainment.

Kolbert, E. (2009, August 31). Green like me. *The New Yorker*. Retrieved from: http:// www.newyorker.com/arts/critics/atlarge/2009/08/31/090831crat_atlarge_kolbert?current Page=all#ixzz0i7JE7nfs

Kolbert, E (2014, July 28). How the Paleolithic diet got trendy. *The New Yorker*. Retrieved from: http://www.newyorker.com/magazine/2014/07/28/stone-soup

Kristiansen, P. & Taji, A. (2006). *Organic Agriculture: A Global Perspective*. Cabi Publishing.

Lappe, F. M. (1971). *Diet for a Small Planet*. Ballantine Books.

Lim, L. (2008, April 19). China's growing thirst for milk hits global market. *Npr.org*. Retrieved from: http://www.npr.org/templates/story/story.php?storyId=89766337

Lord Northbourne (1940). *Look to the Land*. Sophia Perennis.

McBeath, J. & McBeath, J. H. (2009). "Environmental stressors and food security in China." *Journal of Chinese Political Science*, 14, 49–80.

Milk Drinking Started 7,500 Years Ago in Central Europe. (2009, August 29). *Science Daily*. Retrieved from: http://www.sciencedaily.com/releases/2009/08/090827202513.htm

Park, M. & Xu, C. Y. (2012, December 25). Is migrant system China's apartheid? *CNN.com*. Retrieved from: http://www.cnn.com/2012/12/25/world/asia/china-migrant-family/

Pasick, A. & Timmons, H. (2013, August 5). Despite tainted baby formula, Chinese women still shun breastfeeding. *Quartz*. Retrieved from: http://qz.com/111662/despite-tainted-baby-formula-chinese-women-still-shun-breastfeeding/

Paster, K. (2012). *In Organic We Trust* [Documentary]. Pasture Pictures.

Pollan, M. (2006). *The Omnivore's Dilemma: A Natural History of Four Meals*. Penguin.

Pollan, M. (2009). *In Defense of Food: An Eater's Manifesto*. Penguin Books.

Severson, K. (2009, May 12). When "local" makes it big. *The New York Times*. Retrieved from: http://www.nytimes.com/2009/05/13/dining/13local.html?pagewanted=all&_r=1&

Rogers, S. (2010). *What's Organic About Organic?* [Documentary]. Little Bean Productions.

Rohrer, F. (2007, August 7). China drinks its milk. *BBC News Magazine*. Retrieved from: http://news.bbc.co.uk/2/hi/6934709.stm

Roth, R. (2012, August 27). Chipotle at the farmer's market? An open letter to Sustainable Economic Enterprises of Los Angeles (SEE-LA). *Facebook.com*. Retrieved from: https://www.facebook.com/notes/thats-why-we-dont-eat-animals/chipotle-at-the-farmers-market-an-open-letter-to-see-la/10150993222721436

Schultz, M. & Huntrods, D. (2013), Organic dairy profile. Agricultural Marketing Resource Center, Iowa State University. Retrieved from:http://www.agmrc.org/commodities_products/livestock/dairy/organic-dairy-profile/

Shapiro, J. (2001). Mao's War against Nature: Politics and the Environment in Revolutionary China. Cambridge University Press.

Shen, H. (2012, April 13). Yili yingxiao zhongquan: Wang Fei daiyan Jindian youji nai [Yili marketing heavy punch: Faye Wong as spokesperson for organic milk]. *Meijie 360 [Media 360]*. Retrieved from: http://www.chinamedia360.com/newspage/102311/11969C56BD29A167.html

Singer, P. (1975). *Animal Liberation: A New Ethics for Our Treatment of Animals*. HarperCollins.

Sir Howard, A. (1940). *An Agricultural Testament*. Rodale Press.

Squires, S. (2004, September 21). Overfed, Undernourished. *The Washington Post*. Retrieved from: http://www.washingtonpost.com/wp-dyn/articles/A36955-2004Sep20.html

Tan, Y. (2007, September 3). In China, going organic is nothing new. *China Daily*. Retrieved from: http://www.china.org.cn/english/China/222951.htm

Wan, W. (2010, November 10). Young Chinese farmers sowing seeds for organic revolution. *Washington Post*. Retrieved from: http://www.washingtonpost.com/wp-dyn/content/article/2010/11/01/AR2010110106322.html

Warning: Your food, nutritious and delicious may be hazardous to your health. (1989, March 29). *Newsweek*.

Willer, H., Yussefi, M. & Sorenson, N. (2008). *The World of Organic Agriculture: Statistics and Emerging Trends 2008*. London: Earthscan.

Yao, X. (2003). *RoutledgeCurzon Encyclopedia of Confucianism*. London: RoutledgeCurzon.

Youji shipin, lvse shipin, wugonghai shipin de chabie [The difference between Organic Food, Green Food, and Non-public Harm Eatables]. (2010, December 2). *Shipin Chanye Wang* [*Food Industry Net*]. Retrieved from: http://www.foodqs.cn/news/sprz01/2010122111228293.htm

Yu putong caishichang buyiyang de Beijing youji nongfu shiji [Bejing organic farmers market different from average farmers market]. (2012, February 7). *iFeng.com*. Retrieved from: http://phtv.ifeng.com/program/ymxtx/detail_2012_02/07/12344184_0.shtml

Žižek, S. (2009, May 4). Ego ideal and the Superego: Lacan as a viewer of Casablanca. *Lacan.com*. Retrieved from: http://www.lacan.com/essays/?p=182#_ftn2

5 The "Useless" Sustainability
Discourse of Eco-Fashion and the Utilitarian Fantasy

On March 22, 2013, China's first lady Peng Liyuan accompanied her husband, President Xi Jinping, on his first state visit to Russia. As soon as their plane landed in Moscow, Peng captured international media attention with her choice of outfit: a trench coat custom-made by Exception de Mixmind (*Li Wai*), a domestic fashion label located near Guangzhou. Unlike most Chinese elites who prefer foreign luxury brands to domestic ones, the first lady supported a homegrown Chinese brand that not only showed an attachment to traditional Chinese culture but also shared a strong environmental ethic (Wang, Z. 2013). "The core value of oriental aesthetic is the theory of unity of man and nature," said CEO and co-founder of Exception, Mao Jihong. The brand focuses on incorporating traditional Chinese aesthetics with organic fabrics and targets clients "domestic and international alike, who appreciate Eastern beauty" (Lin 2013).

The first lady's patronage brought unprecedented publicity to this eco-fashion brand. From March 21 to March 23, Internet searches for Exception climbed from 290 to 31,626 (Gu 2013). Its stores, over 90 spreading all over China, also saw a soaring number of visitors. Along with Exception, the name of its designer came into the spotlight: Ma Ke, the other co-founder of the brand and the rumored designer for Peng's four-country tour. Ma Ke's first fame began in the international design community. In 2006, she created her own haute couture label *Wu Yong* (Useless) and exhibited two of its collections – "The Earth" (*Tudi*) and "Simplicity" (*Qingpin*) – at Paris Fashion Week in 2007 and Paris Haute Couture Week in 2008. Both exhibits featured her eco-conscious design philosophy and the revival of ancient Chinese clothes-manufacturing methods (Wang, D. 2013). They received widespread accolades. Didier Grumbach, president of the Chambre Syndicale de la Haute Couture, said of Ma Ke: "[she] burst on to the international market with something so creative it can only be Chinese […] The way she works, the place in which she works, her attitude, it can only come from China" (Leong 2008).

"It can only come from China." This phrase probably also explains why Ma Ke has become the first lady's fashion choice. As stated in *China Daily*, "Exception and Wu Yong are being singled out because of their use of Chinese culture and ethnic elements in their designs, based on the philosophy of simplicity" (Wang, Z. 2013). Simplicity and "Chinese-ness" are closely aligned with President Xi's policy changes of 2013. A few months after he took office, Xi launched the austerity drive to curb the society's rampant consumerism. He not only cracked down on corruption, but also banned luxurious banquets, extravagant funerals, and even TV ads promoting gift giving (Deng 2013). Party members were told to adopt a "frugal working spirit" and the public was called on to consume in more sustainable ways. The talk of anti-consumerism was coupled with the discourse of the "Chinese dream." Heavily promoted in media through TV shows and popular ballads, this concept called for national rejuvenation and personal fulfillment and became a defining slogan for Xi's administration ("Chasing the Chinese dream," 2013).

Xi's campaign represented China's top-down attempt to resist the problematic trend of globalization. Since the new millenium, the government has promoted the resurgence of "national studies" (through establishing Confucius temples, institutes, books, and talk shows), the reinstatement of traditional holidays (such as Tomb Sweeping, Dragon Boat, and Mid-Autumn festivals), and the revival of traditional art forms (such as Kung Fu and Beijing Opera). In many parts of the country, worship of Mao also returned as people became repulsed by the corruption brought by the economic reform and sought escape from the spiritual vacuum of consumerism. In consumer culture, this push for traditions takes the form of turning away from ostentatious luxury and toward a life of simplicity, intransience, and spirituality. Ma Ke's eco-fashion is representative of this bourgeoning trend in the realm of fashion. Her work expresses social and environmental concerns as well as the spiritual pursuit of inner harmony. Following her, other brands such as Tangy (*Tianyi*, "will of heaven", designed by Liang Zi) or Zuczug (*Suran*, "simple being", designed by Wang Yiyang) also received wide recognition by articulating Chinese elements with the themes of simplicity, nature, and harmony.

To a Western observer, however, "Made in China" eco-fashion may seem to be an oxymoron. First of all, fashion is one of the least sustainable industries in the contemporary marketplace. Designed for quick expiration, it is notorious for intense resource use, environmental pollution, and waste generation. Meanwhile, China's contribution to the global fashion system is far from sustainable: on the one hand, it is the land of large factories that churn out massive amounts of cheap clothing; on the other hand, it is home to a rising middle class that voraciously seeks high-priced luxuries and foreign brands. Both place China on the opposite end to eco-fashion, which is predominantly a Western concept. According to Sandy Black, the author of *Eco-Chic* (2011), eco-fashion can be traced back to the American hippie revolution in the 1970s. Since the 1990s, designers and fashion companies such as Esprit, Patagonia, and J Crew spread it to Euro-America as a way to answer the widespread criticism against the fashion industry (21). The term usually refers to the use of recycled materials, organic fabrics, and handicraft in the manufacturing of clothing. Since the new millennium, eco-fashion emerged in China through the works of designers such as Ma Ke. Their designs adopted similar methods such as recycling, organics, and handicraft, but articulated the "environmentally friendly" theme in very different ways. What, then, can China bring to the international dialog of eco-fashion? How can Chinese designers and their imagination of the "ecological" teach us new ways to think about the relationship between fashion, ethics, and environment?

This chapter answers these questions by comparing the American and Chinese discourses on eco-fashion. Due to the disparity in their market sizes, a strict "apples to apples" comparison is unlikely. In the US, eco-fashion has infiltrated into mainstream consumer culture, but its counterpart in China is still secluded in high-end designer studios and withdrawn from mass markets. Thanks to the endorsements of the first lady and the international and domestic awards the designers have collected, eco-fashion is gaining more media exposure in China and gathering a growing fan base. Nevertheless, it is still far from entering into the ready-to-wear market as it has in the US. For this reason, I focus on two most influential texts in their respective national contexts: major fashion companies' mass market advertising in the US and the leading eco-fashion designer in China, Ma Ke's press and promotional materials. My analysis identifies two dominant themes of American (Western) eco-fashion: garment recycling and eco-footprint assessment. Both reflect an ideology of utilitarianism that aims to maximize resource usage and minimize pollution and waste. Ma Ke's work, meanwhile, stands in opposition to utilitarianism. In one of her most famous lines, Wu Yong ("useless"), she proposes that we conceive our relationship with the material world not in terms of utility, but in terms of memory and history. Her work portrays textiles as a humble medium that records the past, while the traces left from past use constitute the most seductive part of our clothes. Ma Ke's work, I argue, provides an alternative perspective for us to reflect on the dominant ideologies in Western eco-fashion culture as well as the ethics of consumption in general.

The Psychic Mechanism of Fashion

"Fashion is obsolescence. Fashion is change," says Elizabeth Cline in *Overdressed: The Shocking High Cost of Cheap Fashion* (2012). Designed for quick expiration, modern clothing culture diverges from the traditional ones that had a more enduring relationship with the human body. Historically, according to Cline (2012), clothing was an "expensive, hard to come by, and highly valued" consumer item (4). Often handmade, they were usually "mended and cared for and reimagined countless times" until they fell apart (4). This deep attachment to clothes as singular and significant items, however, is mostly lost today. Consumers often purchase clothing at will, wear them once or twice, and leave them in the closet to collect dust. This wanton abuse, as Cline (2012) points out, is enabled by a global fashion industry that churns out massive amounts of cheap clothing and rapidly distributes them to consumers around the world. Often manufactured with cheap labor, these clothes are made to expire on a seasonal basis to make way for the new styles constantly emerging. This system of obsolescence culminates in fast fashion, a business model that "has broken away from seasonal selling and puts out new inventory constantly throughout the year" (96). As the sartorial equivalent to fast food, contemporary fast fashion – represented by companies such as Zara, H&M, and Forever 21 – turn chasing trends from an elite privilege into a mass activity (99).

Fashion's obsolescence, however, leads to severe social and environmental problems. In developing nations, low-wage laborers work long hours in poor conditions to produce the clothes that affluent nations consume (Claudio 2007). Some suffer health problems from first-hand exposure to toxins and others die in deadly factory explosions or building collapses. Also, fashion manufacturing consumes massive amounts of natural resources and heavily pollutes the public water, soil, and air. According to Redress, a fashion-centered environmental NGO located in Hong Kong clothing and textile production is second only to agriculture in terms of water consumption ("Environmentally-friendly fashion takes centre stage," 2009). The growth of cotton alone is responsible for using 25 percent of the world's chemical pesticide (ibid). In the hands of the consumers, fashion continues to wreak havoc on the environment. According to the US Environmental Protection Agency, Americans throw away more than 68 pounds of clothing and textiles per person per year and textiles represent about 4 percent of the municipal solid waste (and the figure is quickly growing) (Claudio 2007). These clothes either get incinerated, or decompose in landfills and unleash the toxins infused into them back into the environment. In addition, Americans donate more and more barely worn clothes to charities who sell most of them to secondhand vendors around the world – mainly in sub-Saharan Africa. But, according to Cline (2012), the US can no longer "use African countries as their own dumping ground:" since Africans are developing a more refined taste as their income rises, Western countries must find other ways to deal with their overconsumption (136).

To unravel fashion's social and environmental crisis, many critics attribute it to an issue of economics: Since the fashion industry profits from planned obsolescence, they strive to speed up the turnover of styles and trends, and thereby churns up the product flow and resource consumption. Our interest, however, takes a step further and inquires into the consumer desire that drives this obsolescence and the role media play in constructing such desire. These questions direct our attention toward the psychic significance of fashion. In sociological and cultural studies, fashion has always been closely associated with identity and the notion of the Self. In *The Presentation of Self in Every Life* (1959), Erving Goffman points out that dress is an important part of the "personal front" we put up in the presence of others to acquire social acceptance. Roland Barthes' *The Fashion System* (1990) and Alison Lurie's *The Language of Clothes* (1981) view dress as a "sign system" which the wearer uses to signify multiple aspects about the Self, such as social status, group belongings, political views, etc. Since clothing has always been a key manifestation of one's identity, the incessant need to change the former suggests certain instability in the latter. In *Fashion, Culture, and Identity* (1992), Fred Davis observes that fashion is marked by a collective "restlessness, an openness to new experience, and fascination with the new, viz., a rather generalized cultural predisposition to 'keep abreast' of the times" (117). This "restlessness," in large part, is a product of living in the mass society. Through "consumer affluence, democratization, and a loosening of class boundaries," urbanized mass societies uproot more and more people from their traditional communities and cast them into the hustling and bustling scenes of the city environment. This process deprives many of the relational networks that used to provide identity and belonging and throw them into a state of anxiety (Davis 107).

Fashion, therefore, remediates the anxiety and the loss of belonging by staging a new fantasy – a fantasy of an independent and unified Self. Fashion media such as runway shows, celebrity journalism, or fashion advertisements, strive to construct the subject as one that is not only glamorous, but also well-informed and in control. In *Fashion and Psychoanalysis* (2012), Alison Bancroft analyzes this psychic mechanism of fashion by applying Lacan's notion of the mirror stage (12). In the mirror stage theory, the young child, who can barely coordinate his motor activity, identifies with his reflection in the mirror and obtains an imaginary unity that helps organize his fragmented corporal experience. The glamorous bodies in fashion media (e.g. supermodels, movie stars, musicians, and socialites) can be said to perform this function. They provide consumers, who experience increasing fragmentation and transience in the mass society, a fantasy of a unified Self to cope with their situation. But this mirror image has a catch: while it seems to unify the subject's corporal experience, it also alienates her from it. This is manifested, for example, in fashion consumers' often cruelty towards their own bodies. In order to achieve certain desired looks, many undergo plastic surgery or drastic weight loss measures to conform to the socially constructed beauty standards. Bancroft (2012) quotes Lacan, who calls it the "Procrustean arbitrariness" of fashion:

> Procrustes is a robber from Greek legend who forced his victims to lie on a bed that he made them fit by cutting off or stretching parts of their body. By evoking him in the context of fashion, Lacan seems to suggest that dress does not act as it is often assumed to – demonstrating the body's limits and presenting a unified and contained self – but on the contrary invokes the violence and mutilation that characterize the subjects' sense of their relationship with themselves. (25)

In other words, the "unified and contained self" is also what motivates the subject to inflict violence and mutilation upon herself. By identifying with a fiction concocted from outside of her body, the fashion subject submits her corporal existence to the control of the Other. In the globalized fashion media, this Other that commands the Self is often a distant and disembodied figure rather than an intimate and nearby person. As teenagers in developing countries chase after the hottest "new" look in the *Glamour* magazine or Justin Bieber music videos, they subscribe to a massive global industrial machine that systematically dislocates people, things, and ideas from their origins and make obsolete of their own bodies, cultural traditions, and the natural environment.

Cry of the "Fashion Victims"

What fashion tries to forget, however, never simply disappears. In the last two decades, the environmental consequence of fashion has entered public consciousness – thanks largely to the effort of activist groups. WWF, for instance, issued the "Thirsty Crops" report in 2003 and exposed the high water usage of cotton farming around the globe. In 2011, Greenpeace released two "Dirty Laundry" reports and accused the world's top brands (e.g. Nike, Adidas, Puma, and H&M) for releasing toxic waste into China's waterways. In 2012, the subsequent "Toxic Threads" report revealed brands such as Levi's for dumping industrial wastewater into Mexico's rivers. These NGO campaigns generated a storm of critique against the billion-dollar industry and motivated the corporations to modify their practices. Take the Greenpeace Detox challenge as an example. Launched in 2011 as a follow-up to the "Dirty Laundry" and "Toxic Threads" reports, this campaign invited the "blacklisted" brands to commit to zero discharge of hazards substances through their supply chains by 2020. Within two months of its initiation, Puma, Adidas, and Nike responded publically to accept the challenge; by 2014, twenty major companies (ranging from luxury labels like Burberry and Valentino to high-street giants such as Zara, H&M, and Levi's) jumped on board.

Why was the Greenpeace Detox campaign so successful? According to the MobLab team (2014), Greenpeace's media strategy group, its success lies largely in its attempt to target at fashion consumers – i.e. the "'Now People', who are trendy and conscious of what's new, and the 'Transcenders,' who are culture shapers" – and mobilize them to urge companies into action. The campaign bases many of its advertisements on "high-quality fashion shoots with professional models," which are "friendly for fashion media and magazines to use;" it also uses innovative message platforms, such as viral videos, online petitions, stickers, and even stripteases, to capture the fans around the world. But the key to the success of Greenpeace Detox, MobLab (2014) emphasizes, is its central figure – the "fashion victim." The campaign widely distributes images of fashion models looking sick, sad, and silenced, and places them next to industrial contamination sites or textile factory workshops. The "Toxic Glamour" series released in 2012, for instance, portray sick-looking models, all wearing dark eye makeup, standing or lying next to foamy water on an ocean bank or empty cans of dyestuff in a textile factory (see Figure 5.1–5.3 on the author's blog "Environmental Advertising in China and the

USA"; same goes with all the following figures). These photos were shot on location in a manufacturing facility in Xiaoshan district, Hangzhou, the heart of China's textile industry. The toxic background besieges the models' glamorous bodies and generates a sense of disgust in the viewer. Yet their clothes bear the same color scheme as the background, implying certain complicity between the clothes and the pollution. Since the model's body used to represent the *ideal ego* that fashion consumers try to emulate, these ads, therefore, rupture the boundary of the ego and let the surrounding pollution seep in. It brings back the "toxic remainders" of fashion – which are traditionally excluded from fashion advertisements – and shatters the fantasy of the unified Self.

This "fashion victim" theme takes a more disturbing form in the Detox Zara series in 2012 (Murray 2012). Addressed specifically to the Spanish fast fashion giant, Zara, these ads portray the models themselves, rather than the environment, to be the primary victims to fashion. One of the print ads, "Toxic IV," pictures a young female model in a bright pink top holding an intravenous therapy package with the pink dye being injected into her veins (Figure 5.5–5.7). She is crying and her black eye makeup melts all over her face. Also, she is directly looking into the camera. Her gaze is weak, desperate, and pleading for help. The idea of injecting chemical dye into one's veins conjures up the imaginary of inner bodily contamination. Moreover, the model's pleading gaze turns her from an *ideal ego* into an *ego ideal* (see distinction explained in Chapter 4) – a moralized Other that issues demands to the subject by impinging guilt. Her despondent eyes address the consumer as a potential savior who is able to extricate her from her misery. This "fashion victim" figure epitomizes the rhetorical power of this activist campaign: it reminds consumers that outside their tiny fitting room lies a vulnerable world (e.g. sick workers, consumers, ecosystem) that is being injured by the very glamorous clothes that they are trying on.

Eco-Fashion Advertising in the US

As a response to the widespread criticism, the fashion industry starts to promote the discourse of ethics and social responsibility. Eco-fashion, as part of this trend (with others including "ethical," "sustainable," or "slow" fashion), proclaims to minimize fashion's impact on the environment. Black (2011) traces the rise of eco-fashion in the West to the hippie revolution in the mid-1970s. This stage embraced "fabrics such as hemp and natural dyeing" and adopted "homemade, ethnic and handcrafted fabrics and clothes" as the norm (19). The second stage was the 1990s, when American companies such as Esprit, Patagonia, and J Crew – the last two of which have eco-activism roots in California – revived the hippie idea and later spread to other major companies such as H&M, Levi's, and American Apparel (21). In the new millennium, eco-fashion grew increasingly pervasive in the US and the UK with "more small, ethical and ecologically-motivated fashion companies" joining the movement (21). Today, eco-fashion has a wide variety of participants, ranging from designers, manufacturers, retailers, NGOs, trade unions, consumer academics, to fashion academia. Generally speaking, the term refers to six types of practices: first, the use of recycled materials in the manufacture of clothing (e.g. leaf- or garbage-made clothes); second, clothing made from reclaimed or reused fabric, or, vintage clothing (e.g. a repurposed wedding dress, or the "I-am-not-a-plastic bag" bag by British designer Anya Hindmarch); third, organic fabrics (e.g. cotton grown without synthetic chemicals); fourth, handicraft (e.g. handmade jewelry); fifth, cause-related design (e.g. PETA's celebrities-go-naked campaign, or cruelty-free fashion designer); and sixth, NGOs and trade unions establishing manufacturing standards for the industry (e.g. the aforementioned Greenpeac Detox campaign, or the Sustainable Apparel Coalition, made of more than 60 companies and NGOs that launched the Higg Index to measure sustainability across their supply chains, Wang, J. 2013).

Among the various voices in eco-fashion culture, in US marketing, the most prominent ones come from major fashion corporations. This chapter will center on their mass-market advertising. These campaigns no longer dwell on the fantasy of the glamorous and autonomous Self, but instead focus on the wellbeing of the social and ecological collective. The first company that I will analyze is Levi's. Having long been criticized for its negative environmental impact, Levi's became a forerunner for its sustainability initiatives. In 2007, it conducted a "lifecycle assessment" of its major products that examined their ecological impact from "cotton seed to the landfill" (Wang, J. 2013). The data collected helped them "quantify – with precision – how new designs impact the environment" in order to "create the most fashionable styles with a smaller carbon footprint, using less water, and minimizing the environmental impact." The assessment found that "farming the cotton for a pair of its signature 501 jeans used up to 49 percent of the water associated it during its lifetime" (ibid). As a result, Levi's joined the Better Cotton Initiative, which works with farmers around the world to "reduce the amount of water and chemicals used to grown cotton and improve social and economic benefits for cotton farmers worldwide" (ibid). In 2010, Levi's released a range of Water<Less jeans, which purportedly only used 4 liters rather than 42 liters per pair to achieve a distressed look.

"Life Cycle of Levi's Jeans" is an ad from Levi's official page for the Water<Less jeans (Figure 5.8). Released in 2010, it is composed of a comic strip describing the eight steps of the jean's lifetime: "1. Cotton Production," "2. Fabric Production," "3. Garment Manufacturing," and "4. Water<Less Jeans" to "5. Transportation & Distribution," "6. Consumer Use," "7. Recycling" and "8. End of Life & Rebirth." Each of the eight frames contains small-font texts that explicate the details of Levi's efforts, such as "joining the Better Cotton Initiative," "participating in the NRDC's Responsible Sourcing Initiative," "using 1.5 liters rather than 42 liters of water to get a worn-in look," "saving more than 500 liters of water a year," etc. Cartoon icons are used to illustrate the statements. They are drawn with a childlike humor to

animate the drab subject of industrial manufacturing. For example, the first frame depicts a smiling sun shining on a cotton field, captioned as "Very thirsty!" The fourth frame pictures some jeans soaked in a bathtub that reads "Levi's Communal Bath (No diving)." The overarching comic format ties the eight frames together into a central imagery – a "life cycle." In the last panel, three pairs of jeans form a chasing arrow sign, and the text reads: "we used 25,500 pairs of jeans to create recycled denim insulation for [their] SF head-quarters." A caption points at the jeans and says: "Strongest, most reliable fabric on earth."

The first striking feature of this ad is its divergence from the traditional Levi's advertisements. While the traditional ads often featured models wearing scanty clothes, making sexual poses, and casting suggestive looks at the viewer, this ad does not represent the human body at all. Instead it adopts an infographic format to explain the procedure of clothing manufacture, dis-tribution, and disposal. Shorthand for "informational graphic," infographic is known for its ability to communicate complex information to a lay audience by converting them into digestible visual format. This medium commonly appears in corporate social responsibility (CSR) campaigns, which use it to commu-nicate professional information to the public. This infographic takes the viewer to the "backstage" of the fashion industry and presents a vintage point from which all of the "insider" practices can be seen. Considering the new type of eco-subjectivity that these ads are responding to, such a rhetorical choice would not be hard to understand. Since the environmentalists ruptured the fantasy of the unified and contained Self by introducing the desire of the Other (i.e. the "fashion victims"), this ad erases the Self – an image that has since then been associated with guilt and horror – from the purview of the Other. The Other, no longer being a disenfranchised "victim" (a feature in hysteric rhetoric), now becomes an omniscient, sustainability "god" that criti-cally oversees every detail in the jeans' lifetime (a feature in obsessive rhetoric). To pass the Other's scrutiny and avoid the punishment of guilt, a new fantasy of a "unified and contained" corporate industrial system is constructed. Here, it takes the form of a "closed loop" lifecycle: on the one hand, it draws minimum resources from the outside environment and emits minimum pollu-tion; on the other, it maximizes the utility of all resources and materials within by subjecting them to infinite reuse, reduce, and recycle. This system sees to be completely self-contained: it entails no "fashion victims" as it should have no "leakage" – e.g. excessive resource and energy use, pollution emission, and waste production – into the external world.

However, if one looks at this Levi's ad closely, an incongruity can be observed in the so-called "closed loop" lifecycle. The last of the eight frames ("8. End of Life & Rebirth") does not connect to the first frame ("1. Cotton Production"), as the former focuses on recycling old jeans as insulation materials and the latter is about growing cotton from the ground up. In other words, the "closed loop" is not really closed; it is only *imagined* to be "closed." And the critical step that patches up this broken loop is – recycling.

Recycling, in this sense, gives the jeans immortality: it suggests that they will never "die" and that material they are made of could be infinitely reused and remanufactured without wasting away. Thanks to this critical step, their life story turns from a linear process of one-directional wear-out into a cyclical process of destruction and renewal. However, this imaginary is far from reality. In *Gone Tomorrow* (2006), Heather Rogers points out that recycling is a far less effective method of garbage disposal than commonly imagined. In actual practice, it is plagued by numerous problems such as down-cycling (reduction in quality after each round of reproduction), contamination (misplacement of recyclables in a wrong category could ruin the entire batch), transportation (intense energy consumption during the transportation of recyclables), and market competition (rivalry from the cheap virgin material market and the heavily subsidized garbage industry). Yet the rhetoric of recycling, Rogers emphasizes, performs an important function for the industry: it convinces consumers that "their trash was now benign" and helps reduce guilt associated with overconsumption; moreover, it serves to "target individual behavior as the key to the garbage problem" and "steer public debate away from regulations on production" (176). Rogers' critique points out the economic agenda behind the recycling hype: that it is often favored by CSR campaigns not because it is the most eco-friendly choice to eliminate waste, but because it allows for minimum interference with the production-consumption cycle that drives corporate profit.

In 2012, Levi's followed up the Water<Less jeans with a new series – the Waste<Less jeans – which relied exclusively on the notion of recycling. Made from post-consumer recycled plastic, these jeans purportedly contain eight 12–20 ounce PET bottles per pair (Webb 2013). "8 Bottles, 1 Jean" is a 60-second commercial for the Waste<Less jeans (Figure 5.9). It opens with a plastic bottle being blasted into pieces and emitting a loud bang. The camera then cuts into various everyday life scenes: college students drinking soda at a house party, boy kicking around a cafeteria plate, police winding up a role of "caution" tape, man cutting up a credit card, girl jumping on bubble wrap, hand ripping open the lid of a coffee cup, etc. Soon the commonality between these scenes is revealed: all are stories of plastic objects being used in everyday life and turned into waste. The camera then follows these damaged objects to the garbage truck and the junkyard, and finally it enters a waste processing plant, where gigantic machines roll the plastics in, mold them, and turn them into new threads and fabrics. At the end, with another loud bang, we see fabric pieces implode – rendered by a computer reverse playback technique – and turn into a pair of jeans. Large fonts appear on top: "These jeans are made of garbage." "8 Bottles. 1 Jean. Waste<Less. Levi's."

This commercial constructs recycling as a magic time-reverser that could undo the effects of consumption. Its visual dimension is composed of many everyday life clips, which are quickly edited together to construct a transcendental, "all-seeing" position (i.e. the Other, the *supereco*) that tracks the destinies of different plastic objects. Its sound consists of diegetic noises from each scene (e.g. plastic bottle exploding, cafeteria plate scraping the ground, girl bursting bubble wraps, garbage truck crushing waste plastic, etc.) to form a consistent rhythm that ties the storyline together. The most interesting part of this commercial is the last scene. It returns a pair of exploded jeans into its original form and forms symmetry with the opening scene where a plastic bottle was exploded into pieces. This symmetry creates an illusion as if the process of consumption can be reversed; it suggests that even explosions – the fastest way of wasting away an object – can be rewound like a tape. Since recycling can always turn waste into new products, there is no reason for consumers to feel guilt.

The theme of recycling received worldwide publicity in H&M's 2013 garment collecting initiative, "Don't Let Fashion Go to Waste." As a prominent fast fashion brand, the Swedish retail giant has been subject to intense scrutiny for its business model (Lanyon 2013). In spite of, or, because of its precarious reputation, the company is also known for its sustainability endeavors. In 2007, it introduced an organic cotton line – as one of the earliest in the industry – and subsequently released the eco-fiber Garden Collection in 2010 and the annual Conscious Collection from 2011 (Marati 2012). In 2013, the company dabbled into recycling and launched purportedly the largest garment collection program worldwide. It involves the corporation's 48 markets and over 1,500 stores worldwide. The program asked shoppers to bring unwanted clothes (of any brand and in any condition) to its stores to receive a discount on their next purchases. When asked if giving consumers discounts encourages more consumption and contradicts sustainability, Anna Eriksson, spokeswoman of H&M's Communications and Press department said:

> The [discount] vouchers have a strong impact and are motivating to our customers. Today, there is only a small amount of clothing being reused for charity or for recycling. We want to offer an easy solution for the customer that today throws their old clothes in the garbage (Hundhammer 2013).

Eriksson's comment, however, exaggerates the benefit of garment recycling. In *Overdressed* (2012), Cline states that most Americans who donate their unused clothes to charity imagine that "there were some poor, shivering person in need of it or a thrifty woman out there thrilled to give it a second life" (128). However, this "clothing deficit myth" is largely untrue. According to Cline, American charities have long passed the point of being able to sell all their donations. Today, "of all the clothing that we dump on charities' door-steps […] less than 20 percent gets sold through thrift stores;" about half go straight to the waste stream or to textile recyclers and rag graders who turn them into wiping rags or car seat stuffing (128). That is to say, most of the clothes handed over to Salvation Army or Goodwill will not be worn by another human being, but will be torn into pieces or shredded into slices for industrial use. But this dire prospect for our abandoned clothes, according to the following commercial, is perfectly okay.

One of the most prominent advertisements for the H&M recycling campaign was a two-minute video titled "The Break Up" ("Don't Let Fashion Go To Waste," 2014). Released in 2014, the film uses a puppet theatre technique – inspired by the Japanese Bunraku tradition[1] – to create an animated world of garments (Figure 5.10). It begins with a monologue of a "shirt," which speaks as an abandoned lover of its ex-owner and begs him to donate itself to H&M.[2] The art of puppetry anthropomorphizes the shirt. It turns it from a passive object to be bought, worn, and disposed of, into an active subject that feels, loves, and remembers. Speaking to the viewer as a second person, the shirt first blames the viewer for changing heart: "Of course I understand if you've moved on, and need space;" "even that you've changed, while I remained exactly the same." After a long sigh, however, the shirt starts to adopt a "rational" voice: "Well, love is not forever." Then it promises to redeem the viewers' guilt if he takes up the "responsibility" and donates itself to H&M:

All I ask is, if part we must, we do so in a responsible way [...] You simply come to an H&M store, drop your old clothes in a collecting box, and leave the rest entirely to them. While the very best of us will find new homes after being resold as secondhand, others will be turned into different products, finding new work as cleaning cloths or rags. Garments in the worst condition can be transformed into insolation material, or textile fibers, woven into cloth, reborn into fashionable clothes in every conceivable kind, so every one of us will be reused, repurposed, or recycled.

In other words, the shirt asks the owner to send itself to a global industrial center, where it would be sorted, sold, torn into pieces, or shredded into threads. But this place sounds much more like a concentration camp, than a "good home" that the personified shirt would want to go to. This absurdity suggests that the voice of the shirt has, in fact, been hijacked by the disembodied Other: that it no longer speaks as an abandoned lover, but as a higher utilitarian "god" that deems itself as nothing but an object of human use. Much like the Starkist tuna fish that cheerfully invites the consumers to eat it own meat (see Chapter 4), the shirt sees in itself no intrinsic value other than its ability to serve for some external human purpose. Its personified form, ironically, asserts its precise lack of personality – as a complete tool that serves the *supereco*.

Aside from recycling, another theme frequently appears in corporate eco-fashion ads: eco-footprint assessment. In 2007, Timberland, an American company that manufactures outdoor boots and apparels, launched the Green Index. Similar to Levi's "lifecycle" assessment, the Green Index measures the all-around environmental impact of Timberland products on a scale from 0 to 10 and places the numerical charts on the shoebox. Titled "What kind of footprint will you leave?" a shoebox label for its Earthkeepers line presents the three dimensions of the rating – climate impact, chemicals used, resourced consumed – in suspiciously neat and tidy data-statistical forms (Figure 5.11). Adopting a "Nutrition Ingredients" layout, the label contains smaller fonts under each of three subcategory:

"Use of renewable energy – solar, wind and water energy that powers our facil-ities, 6.6%;" "PVC-free – footwear that uses alternative to PVC plastic, 74.4%;" "Eco-conscious materials – our total use of reviewable, organic and recycled materials, 3.4%" and "Recycled content of shoebox – your trash is our box, 100%." But when carefully examined, these percentages actually do not add up to one hundred (6.6+74.4+3.4=/=100%): this is a pseudo function. It could be read as a logical fallacy, but it in fact fits the "logic" of the unconscious. This eco-label is, again, the big Other speaking: it represents the sustainability "god" that watches from above, calculating down to every decimal point the value of all the eco-friendly deeds the company does, and summing up everything into a neat-looking report card. It pretends as if *all* of the product's ecological impact has been accounted for; however, it cannot hide the fact that the numbers actually do not add up to the imaginary *unity* (the "100 percent") that it promises.

The rhetoric of environmental impact assessment takes on a more radical form in Patagonia. Similar to Timberland, Patagonia is also an outdoor apparel company, but a veteran in environmental marketing. Since 1985, the company started to commit one percent of their total sales or 10 percent of their profit (whichever is more) to environmental groups. This practice is reminiscent of the Judeo-Christian religious tax that requires the believer to devote their 10 percent of income to God (i.e. the sustainability "god"). Similar to Levi's and Tim-berland, Patagonia also has their own recycling drive, the Common Threads Initiative, which invites consumers to bring back their clothes and sends them to refurbishment centers around the world to make new products. Yet what is more noteworthy is their impact calculation program – the Footprint Chronicles. Launched in 2012, the program uses an interactive website that adopts the GPS technology to let consumers follow a piece of clothing through its "journey" around the world. On the GPS map, "every factory is clickable, allowing the user to view even more information such as the proportion of male to female workers, average age, what items are produced at the facility, languages spoken, and the address" (Tohill 2012). A screenshot of a webpage shows the traveling path of a blue down sweater that goes from Eastern Europe, North America, to Japan and China, and back to North America (Figure 5.12). The world map pinpoints all of the company's factories and textile mills. On the bottom, there is a summary of the sweater's overall impact: "The Good: We use high-quality goose down [which] comes from humanely raised geese and is minimally processed" and "the light shell is made of recycled polyester;" "The Bad: We had to increase the weight of the shell fabric when we switched to recycled polyester, and the product is not yet recyclable;" and "What We Think: We're still looking for ways to recycle down garments."

Compared to the aforementioned infographics and eco-labels, this interactive website extends the surveillance vision of the *supereco* to a new depth, width, and precision. The GPS technology, which positions the viewer above and beyond the earth, promotes a type of technological rationality to scrutinize, manage, and control the ecosystem as a whole. Rather than treating the natural environment and the workers as disposable casualties outside of the system, this new vision tries to reincorporate them back into the system by turning them into objects of scientific and rational management (for example, by policing the workers' gender, age, wage statistics to ensure their assumed "happiness" and continued productivity). Timothy Luke (1998) calls this "astropanopticism," a type of totalizing gaze that pervades today's geo-economic planning of corporations and governments. The notion could be traced back to the 1960s, according to Luke, when Apollo 10's picture of the earth became widely circulated in the American society and generated the technocrats' desire to "manage" the entire ecosystem. Compared to the earlier forms of industrialization, this "astropanoptic" gaze aims to obtain a more profound control over nature. "Earth [was] redefined as 'the global environmental and developmental system' and what was once God's wild Nature becomes technoscientific managerialists' tame ecosystems" (9). Yet what underlies this vision, Luke points out, is a principle of commodification and utilitarianism: it reimagines the earth "as a rational responsive household in which economic action commodifies everything, utilizes anything, wastes nothing, blending the natural and the social into a single but vast set of household accounts" (10). In other words, measuring and quantifying the earth constitutes the first step toward subsuming it under the rationale of utility and profitability.

While Luke's critique was very incisive, his adoption of the Foucauldian notion of the gaze – a totalizing field of vision that the subject is supposed to docilely adopt – leaves no room to account for desire. An additional theory, therefore, is needed to explain the motivation for the subject to identify with the corporate utilitarian view. For this, we resort, again, to psychoanalysis. As mentioned at the end of Chapter 2, the notion of "utility" or "use value" is an ideological fantasy; it refers to the ability of an object (or a person) to satisfy a presumably "objective" need and predicates on the belief that "complete satisfaction is attainable by anyone who sets about realizing a rational plan" (Copjec 2004, 168). Utilitarianism, the English school of philosophy exemplified by Jeremy Bentham, proposes that the individual "convert his self-interest into dutiful commitment to the common good" (Copjec 1989, 73); it assumes that the individual cannot be trusted and assumes that a wise Other will amasses all our satisfaction and uses it for completely "rational" purposes.[3] This fantasy, however, misrecognizes the structure of human enjoyment. Psychoanalysis proposes that human enjoyment is fundamentally irrational and sometimes self-destructive. Due to the irrational nature of enjoyment, we derive more pleasure from rebelling against the superego (who proclaim to safeguard all our happiness) than from obeying it. While we consciously entrust our interests to it, we unconsciously imagine a "despotic superego" that would squander our enjoyment for "useless" purposes and, therefore, try to steal some enjoyment back for our own sake. In the utilitarian fantasy, this means that what drives the subject to identify is not what the superego sees (all that saving and economizing), but precisely what it does not see: the waste, the excess, and the surplus that escapes its purview. Žižek (1989) calls it the "surplus-enjoyment;" "if we subtract the surplus we lose enjoyment itself" (53). However, the fact that waste and excess are the true source of enjoyment must not be consciously recognized; it must be *repressed* or erased from the overt commercial fantasy.

If we assume that the superego is a critical agency for us to hide our wasteful enjoyment from, then this Patagonia ad seems strange. Its impact summary exposes both "The Good" and "The Bad" and, more particularly, does not erase the "bad," i.e. wasteful, aspects of the product. In other words, it does not try to "hide" anything from the critical superego. This apparent "honesty" sets it apart from the obsessive, perfectionist claims by Levi's and Timberland and presents Patagonia as a "down-to-earth" company that "dares" to acknowledge its imperfection. However, when considering the structure of desire, we realize that such "honesty" does not represent any true liberation from the superego: it does not attenuate its gaze, as it still imposes the meticulous standards of industrial manufacturing onto the fashion subject, yet it does change the subject's relationship with the gaze from *repression* to *disavowal*. Rather than hiding its imperfections from the superego, the subject is now encouraged to expose its own flaws and be okay with it. Put into the perverse formula of disavowal, the Patagonia consumer is expected to say: "I know very well (that manufacturing this shirt leaves a big environmental impact), and nevertheless (I will still buy it because the company is not hiding anything)." According to Fink (1997), disavowal manifests the splitting of the ego, where "contradictory ideas [...] are maintained side by side in the same agency" (171). Here, the juxtaposition of "The Good" and "The Bad" perfectly exemplifies this split (Note: it is the split *within* the ego, and not the split *between* ego *and* id). Although one might argue that such a "dialectic" format is common in performance evaluations, it is not common in corporate advertising, which almost never voluntarily exposes the product's shortcomings. This is a perfect symptom of perversion. As Fink (1997) puts it, the pervert submits himself to be a tool of the Other's enjoyment and strives to be the "sinner," or, the "bad" guy, that the "despotic superego" loves to hate. He feels no guilt because he officially has "nothing to hide" and has the license, granted by the superego, to continue its existing behavior.

Patagonia's perverse advertising helps it reap big dollars. Since 2011, the company launched aggressive "Buy Less" campaigns during every Black Friday to tell its consumers to buy less of everything, including its own products. Its 2011 full-page *The New York Times* ad (Figure 5.13) displays a gigantic image of its R2 coat in the center; and on top of it runs the big headline: "DON'T BUY THIS JACKET." The copy makes a heartfelt confession that everything Patagonia makes is bad for the environment, including this R2 coat: "To make it required 135 liters of water [...] its journey from its origin as 60% recycled polyester to our Reno warehouse generated nearly 20 pounds of carbon dioxide [...] the jacket left behind, on its way to Reno, two thirds its weight in waste." But the self-bashing was followed by benefits: "this is a 60% recycled polyester jacket [...] it is exceptionally durable [...] we'll take it back to recycle into a product of equal value." This ad again displays a similar structure of desire. In its fastidious numeration of the jacket's "eco-sins," we can detect an urge to turn the Self in to the superego, who is supposed to savor the cruel punishment of wrongdoings, and maximize its enjoyment. By aligning itself with the superego, the pervert acquires the license to "sin" and the permission to buy. No wonder this "Buy Less" campaign spurred more buying. Kyle Stock (2013) from *Businessweek* writes, "The corporate plea didn't work, which is to say it worked perfectly for a burgeoning company in the business of selling $700 parkas. [...] From 2011 to 2013, the 'buy less' marketing had helped increased Patagonia sales by $158 million [...] Consumers both signed the pledge to 'wrest the full life out of every Patagonia product by buying used when I can,' and bought the jacket en mass." It seems that, either obsessive or perverse, corporations' eco-friendly marketing eventually leads to more, not less, consumption.

To summarize this section, my analysis has identified two major themes in Western eco-fashion advertising: recycling and eco-footprint assessment. Underneath both imaginaries, there lies the ideology of utilitarianism, which aims to maximize the usage of all human and natural resources for the benefit of a social or ecological collective (a disembodied Other). In the name of altruism, the utilitarian subject sees the world through the lens of the *supereco* that quantifies, commodifies, and utilizes everything. But the obsessive ads (such as Levi's or Timberland) present a utopian vision and hides its wastefulness from the *supereco*, while the perverse ads (such as Patagonia) voluntarily exposes its own environmental flaws to the gaze of the latter. Despite their divergences, both serve to perpetuate consumers' existing lifestyles and contradict the claims of saving and economizing. This sad reality raises the question about the meaning of eco-fashion. If the ideological pursuit of utility always leads to counterintuitive results, then what is a more ethical way to connect to the natural environment? Can we see any value in people and ecosystems that is not utilitarian? The next section turns to Ma Ke, one of China's most prominent eco-fashion designers, for an answer.

***

China's Encounter with Modern Fashion

To understand Ma Ke's conceptualization of eco-fashion, it is necessary to first investigate China's fashion history. First of all, China's encounter with modern fashion is a textbook example of social, cultural, and environmental obsolescence. Its process spanned across several centuries through the country's gradual exposure to Westernizing and modernizing forces, as well as the vicissitudes of national politics. In *Changing Clothes in China* (2008), Antonia Finnane traced China's modern clothing history to the late imperial times. During the late nineteenth century, writes Finnane, foreign observers saw China as the "land of blue gowns" (1). Within the "simple and monotonous" clothing culture, however, sartorial codes varied along class and gender lines. Men and women of higher social standing wore "colored and embroidered silks and satins" that reflected beauty and artistry; wealthy women were heavily embellished and accessorized, with their hair braided, ear pieced, and feet bound. During the Republican Era (1912–1937), China was thrown open to Westernization and modernization. Women abandoned foot binding and heavy costumes and adopted simplified dresses (such as the *qipao*, a long one-piece gown which tried to resemble the male gown). Men also gave up traditional robes and slowly donned on Westernized clothing such as suits or leather shoes. By the 1920s, a modern fashion industry emerged in the urban centers and, Shanghai, as a major portal city, became home to a prospering textile industry and a thriving fashion scene. Cosmopolitan men and women started to pursue the latest styles on advertising billboards and fashion pictorials. Similar to the West, fashion in China marked the rise of an urbanized mass society where "capitalism, industrial production, advertising, fashion magazines and department stores" converged to form a hectic scene of social emulation and conspicuous consumption (15).

China's quick taste of fashion, nevertheless, was interrupted during the Sino-Japanese War and the Civil War (1937–1949). The war times interrupted commerce and industry and simple clothing prevailed due to resource scarcity. The outfit of the times, according to Finnane (2008), included "the trousers worn by soldiers of various armies, by the peasantry that supplied the manpower, and by the cadres that managed them" (200). The simplified and militarized clothing styles persisted after the establishment of PRC and throughout the reign of Mao (1949–1976). During the Cultural Revolution (1966–1976), the national dress was marked by a "feverish pursuit of frugality, simplicity, and sobriety" (Wu 2009, 3). Dominant trends were the "Three old styles:" *zhongshan zhuang* (Mao suit), *qingnian zhuang* (youth jacket) and *jun bianzhuang* (casual army jacket). The sartorial uniformity reflected the proletarian ideology, which proclaimed to unite the "revolutionary masses" against the corrupting forces of bourgeois culture. Fashion, in its pursuit of individual beauty, was deemed as a part of the corrupting forces. But this strict restriction on sartorial codes, as Wu (2009) states, staged a paradox:

> On the one hand, one was not supposed to concern oneself with superficial, outward appearances because of the association of fashion with a bourgeois lifestyle. On the other hand, any deviation from the rigid dress code could result in life-threatening consequences [...] ironically, one had to be fully aware of dress and appearance to an unprecedented degree (2).

In other words, the seeming anti-fashion attitudes prevalent during Mao's time actually promoted a key characteristic of fashion: social emulation. Individuals still strived to adapt their appearances to the changing times in order to preserve their identity and belonging (and perhaps, survival) in an alienated, centrally planned mass society.

The repression over the Chinese desire for fashion was finally lifted during the era of market liberalization (1978-Now). When foreign TV shows, movies, and other parts of popular culture flooded in, China was reopened to the dazzling world of changing personal appearances. "Almost every imported TV series in the early 1980s, no matter the country of origin," Juanjuan Wu (2009) writes, "caused a sensation and inspired millions to imitate and emulate" (25). Fashion trends from Hong Kong, Taiwai, Japan and the US especially captured the fancy of the consumers. Urban youths sought to adopt a plethora of new styles, such as bell-bottom pants, sunglasses, or polyester shirts. Women started to perm their hair, use make-up, and wear form-fitting dresses in public. The desire for a Western look escalated in the new millennium, when more adopted plastic surgery to get bigger eyes, taller noses, and longer legs (Wen 2013). Meanwhile, consumers developed a taste for foreign fashion brands. In Paris and New York, Chinese tourists are scrambling for luxurious handbags in department stores and factory outlets; in Shanghai and Beijing, designer stores such as LV, Dior, Gucci, and Chanel are shooting up in high-end shopping avenues; even in the fast fashion market, foreign companies are taking hold (although many of their products are manufactured in China), with Inditex, Zara's parent company, opening 75 stores in China during 2010 alone (Cline 2012, 172). According to the Boston Consulting Group (Zhou, et al. 2012), China is set to become the world's second largest fashion market by 2020 and will count for about 30 percent of the global market's growth over the next five years.

What ran alongside the bourgeoning Chinese fashion market was its massive, domestic fashion industry. Since the late 1970s, the government began to promote the textile-manufacturing sector and, by 1995, China had become the largest textile and garment exporter of the world. Known for its unbeatable power in mass-producing cheap apparel, China's fashion industry attracts pessimism: it has mastered the "art of copying" but lacks originality in creating its own brand. In the eyes of foreigners, the "Made in China" label often triggers the imagination of low-quality manufacturing and uninventive replication. Chinese fashion companies, in this sense, displays the same desire as Chinese consumers – to copy the styles of Westerners (or its more Westernized Asian neighbors) and reproduce them en mass. However, this cheap fashion model is economically unsustainable as it is environmentally unsustainable. As labor cost goes up, this industry will lose its competitive edge. Moreover, its environmental impact has become hard to ignore. According to Jeanette Wang (2013), China consumes the highest amount of textile chemicals of the world, using 42 percent of the global total. The World Bank reports that 17 to 20 percent of the country's industrial water pollution comes from textile dyeing and treatment; every year, polluted water causes 75 percent of diseases and over 100,000 deaths ("The Environmental Cost of Clothes" 2011). Cheap production also leads to frivolous consumption: about 217 tons of textiles were dumped in Hong Kong's landfills everyday in 2011 (Wang, J. 2013). This dire future shows that obsolescence creates both social and environmental crises: as we break away from our cultural and communal past, we also break away from the material and environmental past that fostered the interactions with our cultures and communities.

Restoring "History" in Contemporary Chinese Fashion

Facing cultural amnesia and foreign worship, contemporary Chinese designers aim to build domestic brands to revive the national heritage. Since the 1990s, it has been the dream of the design community to be known for the high-cachet label "Designed in China," but not "Made in China." In 2001, under President Jiang Zemin's directive, "to establish the national character and create a world brand name," a national association was founded to promote Chinese brands internationally (Finnane, 280). Chinese designers started to make frequent appearances in international design contests and fashion festivals. Seeking to make an impression in the world context, they often "spent a lot of time studying historical Chinese culture and artifacts" and strove to "distinguish their styles from those in the West" (Tsui 2010, 135). Their work often incorporated traditional cultural icons and gained much publicity from Western media. One designer, for example, infused her parades in Paris and New York with red lanterns, long tunics, and embroidery of chrysanthemums (281). Another combined elements of the Mao suit and army uniforms with *qipao* and created "a sartorial pastiche of references to the Chinese past" (292).

Such a "revival" of history and traditions, however, seldom matches the taste of the domestic market. Finnane (2008) points out that "Chinese customers find it difficult to recognize local retro as fashion" (292). One of the prominent reasons is that these designs cater to the taste of foreigners. They often consist of "predictable assembly of elements [to] satisfy established expectations of China" and revolve around very rigid interpretations of history and culture (282). In fact, this rigid interpretation not only reflects foreigners' exotic fantasy of China, but also has become how China's official rhetoric chooses to remember the nation's own "history:" red lanterns, Mao's suits, *qipao*, chopsticks, Great Wall, and so on – a collage of cultural symbols and narratives put together to trigger a patriotic sentiment when they image "the world is watching" (the opening ceremony for the 2008 Beijing Olympics is a good example of this). Still structured around the Western gaze, this imaginary "history" is often decontextualized and fragmented and represents no true reconciliation with one's cultural roots.

Yet younger generation of designers is slowly changing the situation. Still drawing inspiration from their cultural traditions, their work revives "history" in more intricate ways and is achieving longer-lasting success in the domestic market. Some of the representatives, highlighted in Christine Tsui's (2010) interviews with contemporary Chinese designers, include Liang Zi, Wang Yiyang, and Ma Ke. In their work, "the obvious Chinese icons such as *qi pao* or dragons are hardly seen," and "what is mostly seen are the spiritual and philosophical facets – harmony, peace, quiet, natural – originating from traditional Chinese values" (Tsui 2010, 211). More importantly, this group shows a strong environmental bent and shares some common practices with Western eco-fashion such as handicraft, use of natural and organic materials, recycling and repurposing. For example, Liang Zi, the founder of Tangy (which means "heaven's will"), makes all her clothes from natural fibers such as cotton, silk, and linen to diverge from the market trend of cheap synthetic fabrics. Known as "the environmental protector in the fashion world," she also helped rejuvenate a near-extinct ancient fabric – *Shu Liang* silk (ibid). Wang Yiyang, another well-known designer, is recognized for the simplicity and austerity in his aesthetic. His brands Zuczug (*Suran*, "simplicity") and Cha Gang ("tea mug") consist of clothes mostly in plain colors to express an anti-consumerist sentiment and nostalgia for a "simpler and friendlier life" in China's pre-reform period (189). Compared to the earlier "Designed in China" attempts with the stereotypical motifs, this generation of designers offers a more intricate conceptualization of domestic fashion by articulating ecological and spiritual values with cultural traditions.

Within this group, the most prestigious and explicitly eco-conscious designer is Ma Ke. As the rumored fashionista of the first lady Peng Liyuan, Ma Ke explicitly addresses social and environmental problems in her designs and media rhetoric. In 1993, she established Exception de Mixmind, a ready-to-wear line for women, with her partner Mao Jihong. The brand is characterized by "oriental minimalism, naturalism and romanticism" (Shao 2013) and features themes of simplicity, spirituality, and nature (e.g. "A spotless object to a spotless mind," "Simple Life Bazzar," "Earth is our Home," "Everything has a spirit, cohabitation"). All its clothes are made of organic and locally sourced materials and are manufactured through traditional techniques. In 2006, Ma Ke created her second brand, Wu Yong, an haute couture line that is "more suitable for museum exhibition and artistic display than the commercial market" (Tsui 169). Established on April 22nd, the "World Earth Day," the label aims to express the founders' "infinite respect to the earth that human beings depends on." (Wuyong.org). Housed in a small workshop in Zhuhai, Guangdong, Ma Ke and her colleagues did all stages of production in-house, including spinning, weaving, dyeing, and sewing, and even operated with a Chinese loom dating from the 19th century (Leong 2008). Some of its clothes are made out of recycled materials and found objects, such as "an old paint covered sheet transformed into a dress, the cracked paint creating a beautiful pattern on the garment, and an old tarpaulin constructed into a coat" ("Fashion in Motion," 2008).

The following analysis will focus on Wu Yong. Since its inception in 2006, the brand quickly gathered international fame and made frequent appearances at high-end fashion venues such as the Paris Fashion Week, London's Victoria and Albert Museum, and China's National Art Museum in Beijing. Compared to Western eco-fashion, Wu Yong combats similar evils – rampant consumerism, high product turnover, and disrespect for the clothing itself – and yet it differs in one significant way: its opposition to utilitarianism.

Explicitly spelled out in the brand name "Useless," Ma Ke explains the rationale on her official website:

> In the highly developed society, everyone is out to do useful things; even things with no immediate results are regarded useless. [...] I want to create things which, though they may appear quite useless today, are the bearers of values for the future; I want to change the point of view of people, who consider as useless some things that may be most useful in future; I *hope people will free themselves of the opposition between the useful and the useless* in order to find out the root of their desire. [emphasis added] (Wuyong.org)

This "manifesto" draws our attention to two sets of relationships. First, the distinction between *utility* and value: Ma Ke insists that objects, skills, and traditions that are deemed "useless" in the present will become "valuable" in the future. Second, the transcendence beyond the realm of *utility* into the realm of *desire* : she suggests that we look not to utility measurements, but to "the root of desire" as the ethical foundation for our actions. As her work will show, "value," in the way she defines it, is rooted in desire—as an object's worth fundamentally rises from its position in the psychic-symbolic economy. Moreover, an object only becomes "valuable" (or desirable) to us through our intimate engagement with it over time. These ideas allow us to rethink the meaning of "ecological" in the context of eco-fashion. By articulating ecology with desire and history, Ma Ke voices a powerful critique of utilitarianism— one that dominates the modern fashion world and wipes out the memory of our enduring contact with the environment. The following section will examine Ma Ke's most publicized exhibit, "The Earth," and its reception by popular media. I argue that mainstream media did not fairly represent her critical message and turn to the namesake documentary created by Jia Zhangke—an art house film about Ma Ke's design philosophy and practice—to shed more light on her artful critique.

Wu Yong/The Earth

Paris. February 25, 2007. A group of designers and journalists entered a darkened gymnasium. At the center, human figures stood motionless on illuminated pedestals. They wore heavy, rumpled, and dusty clothes, reminiscent of terracotta soldiers recently unearthed from the ground. The audience walked amongst the pedestals to examine the clothes up-close. This was not a museum; it was a fashion exhibit for Wu Yong in the Paris Fashion Week. There were no runways or scurrying models. The clothes were handcrafted and buried in sand for a few months to achieve an ancient, earthy feel. Meanwhile, the venue, a one-hundred-year old French middle school playground, was covered with dirt that Ma Ke brought from China (Figure 5.14). This exhibit "the Earth" (*Tudi*) became an instant sensation in the international fashion world. The French *Elle* magazine called it "brilliant... one of the great moments of the season" (le Fort 2007). In 2008, Victoria & Albert Museum in London invited her to reprise the show, as part of its "Fashion in Motion" events. Her work joined V&A's "comprehensive and important collections of Chinese art dating from 3000BC to the present time" and again received rave reviews.

To understand why this exhibit attracted so much Western media attention, we shall begin by examining a few elements that set it apart from conventional fashion. First of all, the spatial setup of "the Earth" differs from a common fashion show: the traditional runway, where models are set in motion, is gone; the peripheral seats, where the audience sits passively to observe the clothing, are nowhere to be found. In their place, a dozen pedestals are erected in open space and the audience walks around them to engage in active observation. The pedestals create a vertical distance between the audience and the figures standing on top, and also cultivate a "vertical" psychological distance—a sense of reverence and awe—toward the latter. Moreover, the immobility of the pedestals injects certain timelessness into the figures and coaxes the audience into slow and meditative thought. The lighting – white stage lights against the dark background – also creates a sense of mystery; it obscures the actual location of the event and transports the audience into a different time and space – perhaps an archaic cave, or an ancient Chinese tomb. Overall, the venue stands in opposition to a brightly lit, eye-catching, and fast-beat fashion show; it creates both spatial and temporal distance to the clothing artifacts on display and restores the aura of art that has been lost in the age of mass production.

When we lay eyes on the clothes, another set of differences becomes apparent. All the clothes are voluminous, heavy, and loosely hung onto the body. One model, for example, wears an oversized poncho shaped as a cone (Figure 5.15); another dons on a giant oval-shaped coat that looks like a pineapple (Figure 5.16); yet another has the entire top of her body (including the eyes and the face) wrapped by a thickly layered scarf (Figure 5.17). These large clothes diverge from the common Western fashion styles, which are more form-fitting, light-weight, and revealing of the body. More importantly, they differ from Western eco-fashion (as demonstrated above in the ads for garment recycling, closed-loop fashion cycle, and eco-footprint measurement), which displays the desire to economize resource usage and minimize waste. Judged by the latter's demand to save, Ma Ke's clothes seem almost "wasteful:" Made from excessive amounts of fabric, they are folded and stitched together to create a variety of large shapes that cover the entire human body. But if we probe into China's sartorial history, we realized that these designs are in fact reminiscent of pre-modern clothing styles. According to Finnane (2008), traditional clothing in China used to be "loose, wrapper-style garments:" "At the beginning o the [twentieth] century, clothing was hung on the body; people carried their commodious gowns and jackets around gracefully; the fabric was allowed rich play." During the process of modernization, however, the old styles gradually gave in to the more Western "close-cut, fitted" forms: "By the 1911 Revolution, this had already changed; clothing was fitted onto the body, and moved in sympathy with it" (296).

Yet to dig a little deeper, the transition from "loosely wrapper-style garments" to "close-cut, fitted" styles is not a marker of Chinese vs. Western distinction, but a pre-modern vs. modern distinction. Traditional sartorial cultures around the world, especially the non-tropical ones (e.g. Native American, European, Indian, Japanese, etc.) often appreciate the aesthetics of larger outfits, made from copious amounts of fabric, and composed of decorative layers and ornamental folds. The shift, nevertheless, started with modernity—an era that also saw the rise of utilitarianism. In *The Psychology of Clothing* (1971), Joseph Flügel documents the sartorial revolution in the eighteenth century Europe that greatly simplified and homogenized men's dress. Called the "Great Masculine Renunciation," the event witnessed men giving up "their right to all the brighter, gayer, more elaborate, and more varied forms of ornamentation, leaving these entirely to the use of women" (111)" A concurrent event, Flügel argues, was the French Revolution, which brought forth the modern ideologies of *equality* (must erase men's class differences) and *utility* (must maximize men's functionality and productivity at work). These ideals led to the increasing simplicity and uniformity of men's attire. While women's dresses were seemingly spared from this revolution, they also became progressively simpler, lighter, and fitting along the years. Modern dressmaking, for both women and men, had transitioned from the techniques of wrapping, folding, and draping, to measuring, cutting, and fitting. The term *tailor*, which emerged in the seventeenth century, can be traced back to the Latin word *taliare* – to cut; it refers to the professionals who make individually fitted clothes and arguably serve to maximize the mobility, expediency, and productivity of the human body.

From a psychoanalytic perspective, the notion of *cutting* is more than a sartorial technique; it is a psychic-symbolic function that gives birth to the modern Self. In Lacan's mirror stage theory as described earlier in this chapter, the fashion subject identifies with a neatly cut-out image of the Self in the mirror, which also alienates—or cuts—her away from her own body and inflicts self-cruelty (such as cosmetic surgery or eating disorders). Copjec describes a similar effect in her essay "Cutting Up" (1989). For her, the cut not only "*carves out* (or defines) a body image through which the subject will assume its being" but also "*carves up* (divides) the body image and thus drives the subject to seek its being beyond that which the image presents to it" (235). In other words, the cut at once constitutes identity and leads to the failure of it, as it initiates the subject's desire for the part of itself that is "cut off" from the self-image and lures him into the consistent pursuit of it. This missing part is called, in Lacanian terms, the object-cause of desire, or the *surplus object*, which generates desire through pure absence. In fashion, the notion of tailoring carves out not just a precise image of the Self, but also a precise image of the fabric or garment. Just like the modern bodies, modern clothing is also subject to the logic of measuring, calculating, and economizing. But due to the double-edged sword of the symbolic cut, this economizing mission often fails. Since our source of enjoyment does not lie in the already "saved" object, but in the *surplus object* that is not yet and could be "saved," we render more waste to bring the absent, fantasmic *object* into existence. Yet as soon as the fantasized "saving" is brought into existence, it loses its lure and gives way to the new imagined "savings" that has yet to happen.

More savings, more waste: such a paradox can be found in many aspects of modern consumerism. Žižek (2004) writes about capitalism's "sin of thrift" – the miserly disposition to accumulate wealth and avoid expenditure – and how marketers are exploiting this anti-consumerist desire to generate overconsumption:

> "[I]s the ultimate message of the publicity clips not 'Buy this, spend more, and you will economize, you will get a surplus for free!'? [...] The embodiment of this surplus is the toothpaste tube whose last third is differently colored, with the large letters: "YOU GET 30% FREE!" – I am always tempted to say in such a situation: "OK, then give me only this free 30% of the paste!"

Of course Žižek's request will never be granted, because the "free 30%" does not really exist; it is the *surplus object*, which is created by the symbolic cut to trigger our desire for the toothpaste that we do not need. The same hoax goes with green marketing: from water bottles made of 33% less plastic and hybrid vehicles with 50% higher MPGs, to LED light bulbs that consumes 84% less electricity, resource- and energy-saving claims often incur more consumption rather than curbing it. In economics, this effect has long been known as the "Javons Paradox," which holds that increased energy or resource efficiency tends to increase (rather than decrease) the rate of consumption.

Back to Ma Ke's exhibit: if modern fashion (especially eco-fashion) is plagued by the "sin of thrift," then Ma Ke's clothes are a radical diversion. She uses copious amounts of fabric, folding, layering, and sewing them together to form intricate patterns and budging shapes. The garments loosely hang over the bodies and hiding their curves. Together with the dim lighting, they blur the individual features of the models and emphasize their collective, bloated presence. These figures, quite uncannily, remind one of the French psychiatrist G. G. de Clérambault's photos of Moroccan drapery. In "The Sartorial Superego," Copjec (1989) writes about Clérambault's study of drapery in a range of cultures such as "Asyrian tunics, Greek chalamys, Roman togas, Arab cloth" (66). Considering "the flowing folds of clothes as the signature of a race, a tribe," the French colonial man focused on Moroccan drapery, of which he took over 40,000 photographs, and meticulously analyzed the utilitarian functions the cloths perform in covering the body, such as "protection against the sun or against the weight of various burdens" (69). Copjec, however, argues that Clérambault's attempt to classify Moroccan drapery with the modern taxonomy of utility only disguised his true passion: the colonial Other's sole enjoyment of the fabric – in their tucks, creases, sweeps, folds, and pleats – that does not seem to perform any use. As the photos showed, the cloth neither served to decorate, protect, nor to enhance attraction to the body. "What was capital in this fantasy was the surplus pleasure, the useless *jouissance* which the voluminous cloth was supposed to veil and the colonial subject, thus hidden, was supposed to enjoy" (87). According to Copjec, Clérambault has also observed a similar type of "useless *jouissance*" in some of his women patients with a cloth fetish. Like 'a solitary gourmet savoring a delicate wine," these women seemed to only enjoy the cloth "for itself" without using them to enhance their own desirability in the male gaze (87). Such a surplus enjoyment, Copjec argues, creates a special fascination in the male/ colonial/utilitarian subject (i.e. Clérambault) and generates his desire for the radical Other who stands outside the utilitarian system. She diagnoses Clérambault's attraction to these Moroccan figures as perversion: the subject that disavows the Other's lack (pretends that the colonial Other is complete and autonomous) and offers itself to be a tool of the Other's *jouissance* (by fetishistically photographing their superfluous fabric and eccentric pleasure).

Ma Ke's work parallels these Moroccan figures on multiple levels. On the one hand, she "wastes" materials and demonstrates that *jouissance* is useless; that is, human enjoyment is based upon the "wasting away" of materials.[4] On the other hand, Clérambault's fascination with these photos can be used to explain Ma Ke's fame in the West: by fetishizing her work and her "useless *jouissance*," Western media overlook her intention to send a critical message to the fashion world. Shrouded in a cloud of ancient and exotic mystery, media representations of Ma Ke present her as an eccentric artist that stands outside the utilitarian universe of Western fashion. As the rave reviews represent it, she does not need the approval of the colonial, utilitarian superego and can achieve autonomous enjoyment on her own. To her audience, she has in fact become the embodiment of the superego that derives surplus *jouissance* from the wasting of materials. This positive publicity of her work does not challenge utilitarianism. Instead, it feeds into the pathological desires of the media that seek to tame any outsiders by fetishizing their differences—in other words, by orientalizing her. If anything, the pervert is too ready to put the Other on the pedestal while refusing to entering into a truly communicative and desiring relationship with the Other.

I, however, suggest that we read Ma Ke not through this perverse framework (as an eccentric outsider that harbors mysterious enjoyment and remains uninterested in her uptake by society) but through a hysterical framework (as an engaged, critical thinker that seeks to address the pressing problems in contemporary fashion and to effect social change). To bring out the most radical part of her message, I turn to her central theme of "the Earth" – and its symbolic significance that popular media often ignore. Already present in the Paris Fashion Exhibit, Ma Ke's creative engagement introduces a new perspective to conceive "the ecological" in eco-fashion – not through utility but through memory and history. This perspective is more clearly laid out in the namesake documentary *Wu Yong* (2007), which features a restaging of "the Earth" exhibit at the Paris Fashion Week and an in-depth interview with Ma Ke.

"Wu Yong:" The Documentary

Released in 2007, *Wu Yong: The Documentary* is an art house film created by the director Jia Zhangke, who became internationally known for his films exploring the consequence of modernization on the Chinese society. *The New York Film Festival Review* sees the film as "less a typical documentary than a ruminative essay on the meaning and function of clothing in Chinese society" (Bourne 2007). *Wu Yong* features a tripartite structure: the first on the life of workers in Guangzhou's massive garment factories, the second on the designer Ma Ke and her practice and philosophies, and the last on the traditional seamstress and sartorial culture in rural Shanxi Province. This setup contrasts China's current state of modernization with the traditional rural culture and situates Ma Ke in the middle, as an intermediary that calls on the audience to reflect on the meaning and cost of this transition. Indeed, the revival of rural aesthetics is a main element of Ma Ke's designs. As she has stated in several interviews, the rural land, people, and culture had served as her main source of inspiration. During the creation of Wu Yong/The Earth, she travelled several times to the remote villages in China to study handicrafts: "Every time when I [...] was far away from the urban life and in the remote countryside, the majestic grand snowy mountain and the vast luscious landscape, which where there centuries ago, it evoked a memory of our ancestors' philosophy" (Tsui 2010, 182). Ma Ke holds that rural life not only offers a passageway to connect to the traditional ways of life, but also contains the ecological wisdom about how to properly coexist with nature. Such wisdoms are being symmetrically wiped out by urbanization and modernization. For her, thus, preserving traditions and protecting the environment are one and the same: as traditions are forsaken and history forgotten, ecological degradation follows; as traditions are preserved and history remembered, ecology thrives.

The linkage between ecology and tradition/history allows us to better understand Ma Ke's choice of *tudi* (the earth) as the central theme of her design. As stated in Chapter 4, the notion of *tu* (earth), in modern China, has always been unfavorably associated with rural populations. Urbanites often describe farmers as "*tu*" or "*tuqi*" (earth or earthy) to disparage them for lacking civilization and class. Unlike the English term "earth," *tu* is devoid of the connotation of direct heartiness and instead carries the stigma of poverty and backwardness (it perhaps bears more proximity with "dirt," a notion that modern American housewives cannot stand; see Chapter 3 on green home products). Ma Ke's work counters this modernist ideology in both the presentation and production of her clothes. In her Paris exhibit, this notion of "the earth" is explored in multiple dimensions. The documentary *Wu Yong* gave the viewer a backstage view of the elaborate stage show: in the dressing room, makeup artists cover the models' faces with mud to make them look like ancient, terracotta soldier-like figures; in the stadium, Ma Ke and her colleagues kneel on the ground to carefully scatter dirt across the entire venue; when the light comes up, the models are shown wearing the heavy, earth-toned clothing that have been buried in sand for months. The revival of the "earthy" aesthetics—through elements such as earth, dirt, mud, and sand—voices an implicit statement that China should perhaps reconsider its decision to modernize and reconnect with its agricultural roots.

Among Ma Ke's various means to engage "the earth," the most provocative act is the burial of the garments underground. At a glance, it seems to parallel clothes manufacturing with farming, as farming requires the seasonal, cyclical, ritual burial of seeds, and the harvesting of products from the ground. But unlike the seeds that are alive, the buried fabric is practically "dead" and can only decay with the passage of time. The "deadness" of the fabric, thus, turns it into a memory device, a recording medium. Its status of decay registers the changing conditions of its environment and its interaction with surrounding eco-systems over the course of time.[5] Ma Ke, later in the documentary, describes the rationale behind this unusual practice:

> Things with history are always full of attractions, because they have experiences. I had the idea a few years ago, to make a batch of clothes, bury them all underground, let time change their conditions. I've always been thinking if it is possible to create [clothes] by interacting with nature; that is to say, I am not the only controller of the outcome, but will leave some to nature; so I am just a basic creator, a source of the idea, but I leave the second part to nature to finish. Thus, when the clothes are unearthed, they will record the time and place where you buried them, all the impressions that the materials had made upon them. I always believe, objects have capacity for memory (*Wu Yong*: The Documentary 2007).

This dense paragraph reveals Ma Ke's design philosophy through several layers. First, "things with history are always full of attractions:" this suggests that humans are naturally drawn to things with a past as history is an important cause of desire. Second, "objects have capacity for memory:" it is not just humans that are capable of remembering history, as objects themselves can record the past. By burying clothes in earth, Ma Ke resorts to the inert medium of the fabric, rather than the malleable human mind, to record the history of its environment. She leaves the clothes underground to "let time change their conditions." This way, "when the clothes are unearthed, they will record the time and place where you buried them, all the impressions that the materials had made upon them." This material memory, exemplified by these wrinkled garments, differs from the fallible human memory. If human memory is subject to distortion and fades with time, material memory records history passively and impartially in the form of traces. Also, these traces are created through the medium's time-tested integration with the environment and are practically indelible. For Ma Ke, this type of memory creates the deepest intrigue and constitutes the root of desire.

This curious linkage between memory, environment, and desire makes Ma Ke a surprising conversation partner with psychoanalysis. For readers familiar with Freud, her notion of material memory have perhaps already reminded one of the notion of the unconscious. In his 1925 essay "A Note Upon the 'Mystic Writing Pad'," Freud compares the human mind to a writing device composed of two layers, with "a translucent sheet of wax paper" on top and "a slab of dark brown resin or wax" on the bottom. When written on, the wax paper comes into contact with the dark resin underneath and makes the writing visible. When the paper is lifted from the slab, the writing is erased. For Freud, the wax paper resembles consciousness: it stores short-lived memories, which must be erased to receive new stimulations; the resin slab represents the unconscious: it stores impressions in the form of "permanent memory-traces," which are only "legible in suitable lights" but are inerasable. These "permanent memory-traces," according to psychoanalysis, are the seats of desire. They are left from our historical encounter with the object—the cause of desire—which became internalized in us through our once intimate contact with the external world. In Freud's famous account of psychic formation, the infant forms the first bond with the mother (i.e. his first "environment"). During this process, parts of her body (such as the breast, voice, gaze, touch) are internalized in him and function as the pleasure centers that his drives encircle and derive enjoyment from. These objects later become lost—due to socialization or other trauma—but they leave permanent traces in the child's psyche. In search of these lost objects, the child steps into the world to find people and things that remind him of the "mother"—the initial "environment" that supported and nurtured him. The psychoanalytic notion of the lost object, when viewed in conjunction with Ma Ke's "material memory," thus teaches us an important lesson. It says that desire, in a sense, can be considered as a recording medium; it is spun from the "permanent memory-traces" left by the once-alien object, which became a part of us through our intimate contact with it over the course of time.

Returning to the subject of eco-fashion, Ma Ke's clothies feature these conspicuous "memory-traces"—i.e. wrinkles and creases—that set them apart from their Western counterparts. If we may recall, in the corporate recycling programs of H&M, Levi's or Patagonia, the remanufactured clothes are always represented as "new;" each round of recycling is supposed to give the fabric a "rebirth;" it is supposed to restore the materials to ground zero, a "tabula rasa," a clean slate onto which a new garment can be made. The popular pursuit of "tabula rasa," as Copjec (1989) points out, is a distinctively modern gesture:

> [...] to wipe the slate clean, all the way down to the material support itself, pure, pristine, and generalizable: humanity itself; Being as such; a neutral, Cartesian grid; the white walls of modern museums on which paintings of all historical periods could be equally well displayed; and so on (92).

In this gesture of "wiping away," "reboot," or "restored to factory condition," the traces of the past are killed, forgotten, and annihilated. Utilitarianism, in particular, aims to erase the traces of the past in order to build a new use, for a new person, in a new context. A utilitarian view of the "ecological," therefore, is fundamentally ahistorical. In the eyes of the *supereco*, the earth is nothing but a collection of resources to be utilized by humans. To be rendered an object of use, each component of the ecosystem needs to be stripped of its context (past and future) and its attachments (human and inhuman) to be made equally accessible on the universal grid. Ma Ke's conceptualization of the "ecological," by contrast, is precisely the opposite. Rather than raising the clothes from the "dead," she preserves their "corpses" and requires them to be haunted by the ghosts of their past lives. For her, the value of the earth (and the ecosystems it contains) resides within the historical imprint it leaves on the human psyche. Moreover, this history does not claim any positive essence but exists in pure negativity; it is manifested only through its absence – in the form of traces – and cannot be absorbed into the human symbolic grid. Viewed within the positivistic scheme of utility evaluation, history is literally "useless" because it practically does not "exist;" viewed within the psychic economy, however, history is the most intriguing, absent cause that generates desire.

At this point, the reader might wonder: What, then, sets Ma Ke apart from the Western eco-fashion ads that also claim to preserve "memory" and restore "history?" For instance, the H&M commercial tells the history of a pair of pants who were "dumped" by their owner; the Patagonia website tracks the journey of a jacket to factories that manufactured its parts; the Timberland label records the environmental footprint of its boots through their "life cycles." If we broaden the scope of eco-fashion a bit more, we see that, the appeal of "history" has already become a signature technique of "eco-hipster" fashion.[6] Brands such as American Apparel and Urban Outfitters often try to meet the popular demand for vintage by creating "retro" effects in their clothes. Many of the "worn-in" looks, including pre-made holes, frayed edges, and fading effects, are achieved through labor-intensive and environmentally damaging techniques such as acid-washing and sandblasting. This type of "memory," when examined closely, differs from Ma Ke's "material memory." Standardized and mass-produced, it is artificially concocted to fulfill human purposes; it flattens history into statistics, flow charts, and predictable "aging" effects and displaces the clothes' real interaction with the environment. Ma Ke's burial technique, on the contrary, involves minimum chemical or technical interference to accelerate the "aging" process. Her clothes bear the raw effects from their visceral integration with the earth and the sedimentation of time. Messy, random, and unique, their wrinkles and creases reveal a history that resists any standardization and mass production—a history that refuses to be factored into the utilitarian scheme.

History is "useless," or history makes things "useless:" this important argument has not just been made by Ma Ke alone. Heather Rogers (2006), in her aforementioned accounts of the difficulties of recycling, has already demonstrated the same point. In recycling, problems of downcycling (the quality of materials being downgraded after each remanufacture) and contamination (materials get tainted during the process of recycling) exist precisely because of the materials' ability to "remember" the past. Resulting from the clothes' *real* interaction with the environment, these "memory-traces" refuse to be wiped clean; they persist through each cycle of "rebirth" as added blemishes, impurities, and wrinkles (as all post-consumer goods tend to have), and reduce the quality of the "new" product each time. Sometimes these traces get fetishized and give manufacturers new reasons to boost up the price tag (as in many "eco-friendly" post-consumer goods), but they eventually render the product completely "useless"—that is, un-exchangeable as a commodity—and expose the utilitarian fiction of infinite reuse.

Conclusion

In summary, this chapter has demonstrated significant differences between the corporate eco-fashion advertisements in the US and the work of Ma Ke, China's leading eco-fashion designer. The American ads, as the analysis shows, often feature themes of garment recycling, closed-loop fashion cycle, and environmental impact calculation. Dominated by the ideology of utilitarianism, such rhetoric sees the "ecological" in eco-fashion as the wise use of resources and conceives material resources as "tabula rasa" that can be infinitely reused, repurposed, and recycled. Consistent with fashion's obsolescence, it aims to create an ultimate amnesia against consumers' historical connection with their material objects and provide a buffer between consumption and true ecological consequence. This ideology of utilitarianism is openly challenged in Ma Ke's work. She proposes that we conceive our relationship with the material world not through utility, but through memory and history. Her work portrays textiles as a humble medium that records the past and the traces left from the past reveals an intimate linkage between environment and desire. In the psychic economy of desire, the historical and the ecological can be said to coincide: On the one hand, our historical engagement with the environment leaves memory-traces in our unconscious and shapes our desire. On the other hand, history can only be an effective cause of desire if it arises from one's patient, time-tested engagement with the material environment. In a sense, Ma Ke's philosophy reveals an important point that desire, just like any other forces in the universe, follows the basic principle of evolution – the process through which the ecological and the historical becomes one.

The final task of the chapter is to trace the philosophical roots of Ma Ke's "useless" eco-fashion. Throughout her work, she emphasizes the idea of relinquishing control of her creative outcome and letting nature run its course. This idea bears the imprint of the Chinese philosophy of Daoism. In another interview with Tsui (2010), Ma Ke has expressed admiration for the Daoist notion of *wu wei* ("no action", "action without action," or "action along Nature's paths")—a term that has clearly inspired her brand name wu yong ("no use"). For her, *wu wei* means:

[...] natural action—as planets revolve around the sun, they 'do' this revolving, but without 'doing' it; or as trees grow, they 'do', but without 'doing.' Thus knowing when (and how) to act is not knowledge in the sense that one would think "now" is the right time to do "this," but rather just doing it, doing the natural thing (242).

One frequent misinterpretation of *wu wei* is "inaction," which is often associated with passivity or laziness. On the contrary, it is better translated as spontaneous action without artificial contrivance. Unlike Western enlightenment thought that tries to control the outcome of human actions through measurement and calculation, *wu wei* suggests that we act in accordance with the *dao* ("path," "way," "route") of nature, and leaves the consequence of our actions to larger environmental forces.

As this chapter has shown, this Daoist philosophy can be said to coincide with the psychoanalytic ethics of desire. In Ma Ke's work, whenever she opens her creative outcome to environmental influences, the marks left from this process generate desire and constitute the intrigue for her work. In a sense, we can say that desire follows the rules of *wu wei*; that is, the flame of desire can burn in the most enduring way if we let go of control and dwell in the empty space of the lost object that once was a part of our environment and has now become who we are. Viewed in an ecological context, the notion of the object applies to the entire material world surrounding us (e.g. a place in the woods, the smell of the morning air, the taste of a wild fruit, the melody of a birdsong). In consumer culture, the object also seizes hold of us: Be it a dress, an old bike, an ice cream flavor, or a television show, as time passes, we develop a similar attachment to the products we consume as to the places or people we love. Once this attachment happens, the item ceases to be a commodity and is no longer exchangeable. We fall in love with it. Our attachment to it ages like wine and we will never get tired of it. It is the same type of attachment, I believe, that Ma Ke has expressed for her earth-aged clothes. Her love with these traces points us toward an alternative ethics of consumption in face of global environmental crisis. Instead of the utilitarian ethics of resource conservation, she suggests that true ethical consumption lies in us falling in love with the lost object, and the traces that our personal, familial, communal, and ecological past has imprinted onto the consumer objects around us. It is through this object-love that we can find a more sustainable relationship to our desire, community, and ecology.

Notes

1   The Bunraku technique lies in the cooperation between different puppeteers to maneuver the limbs, eyelids, eyeballs, and mouths of the puppets; moreover, the black outfit of the puppeteers allow them to be taken as "invisible" while standing in full view of the audience. http://www.japan-guide.com/e/e2092.html

2   "Well... of course I understand if you've moved on, and need space. And even that you've changed, while I remained exactly the same. [Sigh]. Love is not forever. All I ask is, if part we must, we do so in a responsible way. [Two puppeteers carry the

shirt away from the camera and stick it onto a globe.] If you just throw me out, it damages the planet. The earth simply cannot bear so many clothes ending their lives as waste. [The camera pans right to show a group of puppeteers delivering different pieces of pants, dresses, coats from the globe to a recycling box.] H&M has a far better answer. They've started what they call their 'garment collecting program,' to welcome any of us, of any brand, size, age, or color, and in absolute in any state. [The camera zooms into the box and another stage appears; on it, more puppeteers hold up large pieces of cloth to form the shape of a T-shirt, which is then magically transformed into a piece of garment, and finally into many fabric pieces.] You simply come to an H&M store, drop your old clothes in a collecting box, and leave the rest entirely to them. While the very best of us will find new homes after being resold as secondhand, others will be turned into different products, finding new work as cleaning cloths or rags. Garments in the worst condition can be trans-formed into insolation material, or textile fibers, woven into cloth, reborn into fashionable clothes in every conceivable kind, so every one of us will be reused, repurposed, or recycled. This means natural resources are saved and together we can reduce our environmental footprint. [All lights come up and the camera zooms out to reveal the entire studio setting.] H&M caused a closed loop for textile fibers. This might not sound too exciting, but what H&M are doing is really jolly good for our planet, and for everyone. Though, perhaps you already know that."

3　Here I follow Copjec (1989) and refer to utilitarianism "not as a minor and somewhat quaint English theory concerned merely with the distribution of goods, but rather as the clearest articulation of the basic principle of the modern notion of ethics that, at the beginning of the nineteenth century, replaced the Aristotelian concept" (73).

4　According to Raymond Williams (1983), one of the oldest definitions of "con-sumption" is "to destroy, to use up, to waste, to exhaust" (78). This proves that the wasteful *jouissance* is already inscribed into the etymology of the term

5　An interesting anecdote has it that Michelangelo had buried a cupid statue he created in the style of the Greeks to make it look like an ancient artifact. He then sold it to a buyer at a higher price. But when the buyer learned that the statue was a fake, he promptly demanded a refund. Despite this "shameful" scam, Giorgio Vasari, his contemporary biographer, sides with Michelangelo: "The fact is that, other things being equal, modern works of art are just as fine as antiques; and there is no greater vanity than to value things for what they are called rather than for what they are." (See blog post "Forgery and Michelangelo" on August 16, 2006, accessed through: http://www.eeweems.com/michelangelo/) Ma Ke's practice is not far from that of Michelangelo's: her work has undergone authentic aging process that has become integral to the value of her art.

6　Hipsterism sells a disembodied relationship with history; it uses a few predictable cultural icons (e.g. stonewashed jeans, thick framed glasses, fixed gear bicycles) and historical narratives (e.g. Sylvia Plath, Buddy Holly, organic, gluten-free grains, sustainable living) to fetishize a "past" that never was there. In fact, despite its proclaimed interest in the past, the reconstructed "history" has its eyes more on the present: to turn a quick profit or to adopt a ready-made identity that requires no time-tested integration with the social and cultural environment that constituted the identity. As Matt Granfield (2011) puts it, for hipster culture, "old is the new 'new':" that is, the "old" is only desirable when its "oldness" is gutted out and converted into the form of the "new." This is again a resurgence of utilitarianism: the past is only desirable when it can be used for present purposes.

References

Bancroft, A. (2012). *Fashion and Psychoanalysis: Styling the Self.* I. B. Tauris.
Barthes, R. (1990). *The Fashion System.* University of California Press.

Black, S. (2011). *Eco-chic: The Fashion Paradox*. Black Dog Publishing.

Chasing the Chinese dream. (2013, May 4). *The Economist*. Retrieved from: http://www.economist.com/news/briefing/21577063-chinas-new-leader-has-been-quick-con solidate-his-power-what-does-he-now-want-his

Claudio, L. (2007). Waste couture: Environmental impact of the clothing industry. *Environmental Health Perspectives*, September, 115(9), A449-A454. Retrieved from: http://www.ncbi.nlm.nih.gov/pmc/articles/PMC1964887/

Cline, E. (2012). *Overdressed: The Shocking High Cost of Cheap Fashion*. Portfolio.

Copjec, J. (1989). The sartorial superego. *October*, 50 (Autumn), 56–95.

Copjec, J. (1989). Cutting up. *Between Feminism and Psychoanalysis*. Ed. Brennan T. Routledge.

Copjec, J. (2004). *Imagine There's No Woman: Ethics and Sublimation*. The MIT Press.

Davis, F. (1992). *Fashion, Culture, and Identity*. University of Chicago Press.

Deng, C. (2013, December 24). Austerity drive reflected in China's buzzwords of 2013. *The Wall Street Journal*. Retrieved from: http://blogs.wsj.com/chinarealtime/2013/12/24/austerity-reflected-in-chinas-buzzwords-of-2013/

Don't let fashion go to waste. (2014). *H&M Official Website*. Retrieved from: http://www.hm.com/us/longlivefashion

Environmentally-friendly fashion takes centre stage. (2009, January 9). *Redress.com.hk*. Retrieved from: http://redress.com.hk/2009/01/environmentally-friendly-fashion-takes-centre-stage/

Fashion in Motion: Ma Ke Wuyong. (2008, May). *Victoria & Albert Museum Official Website*. Retrieved from: http://www.vam.ac.uk/content/articles/f/fashion-in-motion-ma-ke-wuyong/

Fink, B. (1997). *A Clinical Introduction to Lacanian Psychoanalysis: Theory and Technique*. Cambridge, MA: Harvard University Press.

Finnane, A. (2008). *Changing Clothes in China: Fashion, History, Nation*. Columbia University Press.

Flügel, J. C. (1971). *The Psychology of Clothes*. International Universities Press.

Granfield, M. P. (2011). *HipsterMattic*. Crows Nest, New South Wales, Australia: Allen & Unwin.

Goffman, E. (1959). *The Presentation of Self in Everyday Life*. Anchor Books.

Gu, W. (2013, April 4). The first-lady effect on China's fashion labels. *The Wall Street Journal*. Retrieved from: http://www.wsj.com/news/articles/SB1000142412788732364 6604578401731453745400

Hundhammer, M. (2013, April 11). Don't let fashion go to waste: An interview with H&M. *Urban Times*. Retrieved from: https://urbantimes.co/2013/04/clothing-recycling-scheme-hm/

Jia, Z. (2007). *Wu Yong (Useless)*. [Documentary]. China Film Association, Mixmind Art and Design Company, Xstream Pictures.

Lanyon, C. (2013, October 1). Fashion-fashion brands launch eco-initiatives – but are they serious? *South China Morning Post*. Retrieved from: http://www.scmp.com/lifestyle/fashion-watches/article/1321447/fast-fashion-brands-launch-eco-initiatives-are-they

le Fort, M. (2007, March 6). Défilé Wu Yong, *Elle*. Retrieved from: http://www.elle.fr/Mode/Les-defiles-de-mode/Automne-Hiver-2007-2008/Femme/Paris/Wu-Yong/Defile-Wu-Yong-91703

Leong, K. (2008, August 9). Oriental haute couture. *Financial Times*. Retrieved from: http://www.ft.com/intl/cms/s/2/34e1c414-64dc-11dd-af61-0000779fd18c.html#axzz2m FuYHqjk

Lin, L. (2013, December 2). Chinese fashion label Exception de Mixmind looks abroad. *The Wall Street Journal*. Retrieved from: http://blogs.wsj.com/chinarealtime/2013/12/02/chinese-fashion-label-exception-de-mind-looks-abroad/?mod=WSJBlog

Liu, L-F. (2008, August 28). *Liang Zi, yong mingdai gongyi zaixian zui anggui de sichou* [Liang Zi – Refreshing the most expensive silk with the legacy techniques from Ming Dynasty], *Waitan Huabao* [Bund Picture], B36.

Lui, V., Zhou, Y.Hsu, H.Jap, W., Liao, C. & Lou, Y. (2011, July). Dressing up: Capturing the dynamic growth of China's fashion market. *BCG Perspectives*. Retrieved from: https://www.bcgperspectives.com/content/articles/retail_consumer_insight_dressing_up/

Luke, T. (1998). The (Un)Wise (Ab)use of Nature: Environmentalism as globalized consumerism. *Alternatives: A Journal of World Policy*, 23, 175–212.

Lurie, A. (1981). *The Language of Clothes*. Random House.

Ma Ke: China's first lady of fashion: The elusive fashion designer who dresses Peng Liyuan talks with Time Out. (2013, July 6). *Timeout Shanghai*. Retrieved from: http://www.timeoutshanghai.com/features/Shopping__Style-Shopping_features/12818/Ma-Ke-Chinas-First-Lady-of-Fashion.html

Marati, J. (2012, February 7). Behind the label: H&M's Conscious Collection. *Huff Post Green*. Retrieved from: http://www.huffingtonpost.com/jessica-marati/h-and-m-conscious-collection_b_1261082.html

MobLab Team (2014, June 12). Fashion victims speak up: How the Detox campaign is changing giant company supply chains. *The Mobilization Lab*. Retrieved from: http://www.mobilisationlab.org/fashion-victims-speak-up-how-the-detox-campaign-is-changing-giant-company-supply-chains/

Murray, J. (2012, November 30). Zara commits to detox after Greenpeace dressing down. *Greenbiz.com*. Retrieved from: http://www.greenbiz.com/blog/2012/11/30/zara-commits-detox-after-greenpeace-dressing-down

Rogers, H. (2006). *Gone Tomorrow: The Hidden Life of Garbage*. The New Press.

Shao, H. (2013, December 11). Making clothes for "Big Women" – The designer behind China's first lady effect. *Forbes.com*. Retrieved from: http://www.forbes.com/sites/hengshao/2013/12/11/making-clothes-for-big-women/

Stock, K. (2013, August 28). Patagonia's "Buy Less" plea spurs more buying. *Businessweek*. Retrieved from: http://www.bloomberg.com/bw/articles/2013-08-28/patagonias-buy-less-plea-spurs-more-buying

The environmental cost of clothes, (2011, April 18). *China Water Risk*. Retrieved from: http://chinawaterrisk.org/resources/analysis-reviews/the-environmental-cost-of-clothes/

Tohill, J. (2012, May 18). Patagonia maps out its supply chain with "the Footprint Chronicles." *The9billion.com*. Retrieved from: http://www.the9billion.com/2012/05/18/patagonia-maps-out-its-supply-chain-with-the-footprint-chronicles/

Toxic threads: Greenpeace puts fashion pollution on parade – in pictures. (2012, December 6). *The Guardian*. Retrieved from: http://www.theguardian.com/environment/gallery/2012/dec/06/toxic-threads-greenpeace-fashion-pollution-in-pictures

Tsui, C. (2010). *China Fashion: Conversations with Designers*. Bloomsbury Academic.

Wang, D. (2013, April 28). Ma Ke: Designing "Useless." *China Pictorial*. Retrieved from: http://www.chinapictorial.com.cn/en/people/txt/2013-04-28/content_538362.htm

Wang, J. (2013, July 1). Sustainable fashion. *South China Morning Post*. Retrieved from: http://www.scmp.com/lifestyle/fashion-watches/article/1271151/sustainable-fashion

Wang, Z. (2013, March 26). First lady sparks frenzy over domestic fashion brands. *China Daily*. Retrieved from: http://www.chinadaily.com.cn/bizchina/chinadata/2013-03/26/content_16344769.htm

Webb, F. (2013, April 18). Rubbish jeans: How Levi's is turning plastic into fashion. *The Guardian*. Retrieved from: http://www.theguardian.com/sustainable-business/rubbish-jeans-levis-plastic-fashion

Wu, J. (2009). *Chinese Fashion: From Mao to Now*. Bloomsbury Academic.

Wen, H. (2013). *Buying Beauty: Cosmetic Surgery in China*. Hong Kong University Press.

Žižek, S. (1989). *The Sublime Object of Ideology*. Verso.

Žižek, S (2004). Death's merciless love. *Lacan.com*. Retrieved from: http://www.lacan.com/zizek-love.htm

Conclusion

An Ecology of Desire

I started this book with a story about my family; I would like to conclude with one as well. My family has not only benefited from China's rising consumer economy, but has also suffered from the accompanying environmental degradation. My father, as a former textile worker, has been a victim of the toxic industry of fashion manufacturing, for instance. At the age of 18, he was assigned to work in a state-owned bed sheet factory in Shanghai. His job was to print colored patterns onto bed sheets. In the dyeing workshop, toxic solutions and sharp fumes pervaded the space and my father and his colleagues labored without any protective measures. For 34 years, he suffered from severe insomnia, neuralgia, and fatigue. To compensate for his hazardous work, the government issued him a "toxic and hazardous work certificate" and a bottle of milk per day. Milk, deemed the luxury of the time, was naturally given to me, the "little empress" of the household. Without understanding at the time, I grew up drinking milk at the expense of my father's health. In 2003, the bed sheet factory finally went bankrupt due to corruption and my father was laid off. The good news was, for the first time in 34 years, he was able to enjoy some sound sleep and improved stamina. And yet, it was not until then that he linked his chronic insomnia to the pungent chemical odor he had been inhaling all his life. "Do you regret not knowing this for so many years?" I asked him. "What's the point?" he replied, "Even if I had known, I wouldn't have had a choice. In fact, I think I'd rather not know."

The moral of the story is: our desire for a better environment is usually triggered by certain losses – a loss in health, a loss of clean air and clean water, a loss of community, a loss of tradition, a loss of an ecosystem – but such losses often remain unconscious to us because if they ever did become conscious, they would overwhelm us. It is not uncommon to see people living in the most dangerous environment being the least aware of their own risks. This dilemma helps explain what I observed in the beginning of the book: The Chinese have front row seats for the world's worst ecological disasters, but they cannot acknowledge what is unfolding in front of their eyes – probably because they cannot handle it. We are back at the question I raised in the introduction: Can an environmental apocalypse occur in a country that does not believe in apocalypses? The answer is yes and no: yes, because the catastrophe may happen regardless of whether we are aware of it or not; no, because it will never be perceived as such if we do not invent the language to talk about it and, more importantly, to take actions against it. This problem highlights the critical role that media and communication can play in the environmental movement. If a lack of environmental actions can be traced back to a certain loss, it is a loss not in "objective reality" but in psychic reality, which results from a failure of symbolic communication. And this psychic loss – "not only of loved ones, but also of a place, species, or favorite tree" – when not properly acknowledged, can trigger defense mechanisms such as "denial, projection, paranoia, grandiosity or an acute sense of inferiority" (Lertzman 2008, 16). In popular media, environmental rhetoric reflects such defense mechanisms, preventing us from confronting our psychic loss and perpetuating our environmentally destructive lifestyles.

Environmental advertising, as I have shown, is particularly "defensive" in this way. In both China and the US, advertisements for "eco-friendly" products – hybrid cars, green homes, organic food, and eco-fashion – provide ideological fantasies to protect consumers from the psychic trauma inflicted by the evolving, interconnected web of global environmental crises. Some of these environmental crises are reinforced and perpetuated by the very technologies these ads are trying to sell. As the chapters have demonstrated, the automobile, which epitomizes the notion of mobility, "in-car-cerates" the driver and severs him from his social and ecological environment; it in turn pollutes the common air and land with its exhaust and thirst for oil. Private housing, in promising a green and spotless "oasis," separates the home-dwellers from public and communal life and the open space of nature; and, during the process, it sickens the dwellers and their children with the toxic decorative and cleaning products. Farmed milk, incarnating security and privilege, undermines the intimidate bond between mother and child as well as the social bond between rural and urban, rich and poor; it also creates a general public health menace because of the chemical adulterants and growth stimulants used, not to mention the industry's egregious water consumption and methane production. Fashion, which feeds off of glamor and obsolescence, separates consumers from the natural form of their bodies, intimate memories of personal history, and communal roots and cultural traditions; meanwhile, it also contributes to the poisoning of public water and air, exploitation of developing-country workers, and the production of fabric and textile waste, among other harms.

Transportation, housing, food, and clothing: These four realms of consumer culture, though represented here in small samples of advertising, give us a glimpse into a global industrial machine matrix that so powerfully defines our contemporary situation. Each of these techno-symbolic divisions (e.g. body from environment, private from public, urban from rural, new from old) inflicts trauma on the human psyche by robbing us of enjoyment or *jouissance* derived from our connectivity to the world. Each one is a type of "castration" that severs us from our "holding environment" such as family, community, tradition, land, or earth, which provides "the feelings of being held, psychologically and emotionally as well as physically" (Winnicott 1987, quoted in Dodds 2011, 59) and generates our desire for the connectivity and intimacy that we have lost.

How do we relate to such "castrations" structuring our desire? Chinese consumer subjectivity, as implied in the ads, is mainly characterized by hysteria. The hysteric submits to the "castration," but refuses to surrender her enjoyment easily: rather than obeying the abstract Law that threatens to take her enjoyment, she confers power to the embodied authority that enforces the Law. This can be observed in China's family-centered, relationship-based social structure, where desire is often shaped through communal and interpersonal contact but not the sheer knowledge of laws, rules, or principles. In consumer culture, many Chinese pursue identity or social status through consumer products in order to seek approval from family and close friends. The traditional Chinese home, influenced by the ideologies of Confucianism, ensures the child's primary identification with the family's interests and emphasizes the filial piety to obey the parents' will. However, the centrality of family and interpersonal networks also create difficulty for China's environmental endeavors. From a legal perspective, it hinders the government's ability to implement environmental laws, or to regulate small-scale industries, due to the corruption from nepotism. In the face of environmental degradation, many affluent citizens choose to flee the country – i.e. emigrate abroad with their families – since China lacks a mature civil society and a sense of citizen solidarity to fight for public interests and engender collective actions from the bottom-up.

The American consumer subjectivity, by contrast, displays very different structures of desire. A common one, as reflected in the green advertisements, can be characterized as obsession. The obsessive is more likely to succumb to the power of the abstract Law rather than the specific authorities that enforce the Law. This tendency can be seen in the relatively weaker family structure in American mainstream society and the more "law-biding" appearance of the citizens. The American educational philosophy, in comparison to its Chinese counterpart, encourages the child to be independent from home and integrate with the world at a much earlier age. Probably influenced by the nation's Judeo-Christian background, mainstream American consumers can more easily identify with a morality based upon the disembodied Word rather than a morality based upon allegiance to the embodied "face" of authority figures (Jesus says, "Love your neighbor," but Confucius says, "Obey your parents"). Even in advertisements that express desire for authentic interpersonal connections (e.g. "local farmer," "happy cow," and "fashion victim"), such connectivity is often imagined based upon the abstract figure of a disembodied Other (e.g. the "Farmer," the "Cow," the "Victim") rather than a concrete other that the consumers know from personal experience. Confronting ecological crisis, the obsessive tends to respond with guilt and attempts to remediate the problem singlehandedly by following strict behavioral instructions. Yet this "law-binding" appearance does not mean that the obsessive willingly gives up his *jouissance* to the Other. In fact, his methodical obedience to the Law is only an attempt to minimize his culpability in the eyes of the Other and, therefore, allowing the Other no enjoyment from punishing him for his "unlawful" actions.

In American green advertising, there is a further type of subjectivity emerging – perversion. The pervert denies the symbolic division and pretends that no "castration" ever happens; he completely identifies with the position of the Law, especially in his enjoyment in exposing and censuring "unlawful" actions – including that of his own (e.g. the Patagonia ad spontaneously exposes its own large environmental impact, which ironically improves its sales). Facing environmental degradation, the pervert responds with neither disgust nor guilt, but exuberance and celebration – as all its "imperfections" now become reasons for self-congratulation (e.g. the Method commercial rejoices in a postmodern paradise where neither class, race, nor gender inequalities exist; the Patagonia ad congratulates the brand for "always trying to do better" despite its large eco-footprint). On a broader scale, the perverse subjectivity is increasingly popular in postmodern green con-sumerism, such as New Age marketing (yoga, meditation, "being one with nature," "loving your self"), hipster chic (thrift-shop fashion, vintage cloth-ing, fixed-gear bicycles, organic and vegan diets), multiculturalism (exotic food ingredients from indigenous and ancient cultures, Tibetan Buddhist spiritual practices and gift shops) and lifestyle journalism (recycled DIY fashion, "make your own… food, dress, art"). A commonality among such discourse is a proclaimed "openness" to differences and diversity. At a glance, this endless engagement with, and attempt to overcome difference seems to "free" the society from the symbolic divide (e.g. human and nature, ancient and modern, elite and masses, American and foreign), but in fact it does nothing to undo the "castration" except for confidently disavowing it. Žižek (1999) mentions that, in perversion, "what is repressed are […] pro-hibitions themselves;" that is, in the postmodern mantra of "anything goes," there is a faux tolerance that openly denies the "castration" of the system but forces its members to internalize the "castration" by removing their fundamental differences. It is only after gutting others of their radical otherness can this commercial "diversity" exist – as part of a homogenous system of global consumer capitalism.

Viewed from the Lacanian perspective, this perverse structure is even more problematic than hysteria and obsession. Since it constantly indulges con-sumers in nonstop and uninhibited enjoyment, it threatens to renounce the very limit that constitutes our desire – i.e. the "castration" that keeps us wanting – and rob us of the basic motivation to take meaningful actions. "Do not give up on your desire [*ne pas céder sur son desir*]," says Lacan (1997) when addressing the ethics of psychoanalysis. Indeed, as desiring subjects, we should persist in our division and stay lacking of the objects that we have lost and the *jouissance* that we have sacrificed. In a sense, it is this barrier to satisfaction that makes us continuously striving for a better community and environment, without ever becoming satiated or complacent.

Overall, this book has provided a critical framework for reading desire (and its manipulation by market interests) and drives (and their various representations) as they manifest in environmental advertising. What is the takeaway? This main lesson concerns the importance of developing a critical attitude towards the so-called "ethical" advertising. Due to the increasing privatization and commercialization of media worldwide, advertising is aggressively encroaching on private and public spaces and supplanting other discourses that do not directly promote commercial interests. Its pervasiveness, along with its mastery of the latest media technologies, makes it a powerful agent to shape our collective values, beliefs, and worldviews. Yet the stories that they consistently tell, as many critics point out, had primarily dealt with private, individual happiness rather than public, collective interests. As Jhally (2000) puts it,

> "[Advertising] addresses us not as members of society talking about collective issues, but as individuals. It talks about our individual needs and desires. It does not talk about those things we have to negotiate collective, such as poverty, healthcare, housing and the homeless, the environment, etc. The market appeals to the worst in us (greed, selfishness) and discourages what is the best about us (compassion, caring, and generosity)."

Yet Jhally's observation, as I observed in the book's introduction, seems to be negated by contemporary "ethical" advertising. Since the end of the 1980s, advertising – especially that in the West – starts to stray away from topics of private consumer affairs and tries to address larger, systematic issues such as environmental destruction, social inequality, public health problems, psychic and spiritual crisis, etc. Rather than appealing to the "worse in us (selfishness)", they seem to promote the "best about us (compassion, caring, and generosity)." So now let us return to this question: has Jhally been proven wrong?

The answer is a resounding "No." As this study has shown, advertising may have changed its superficial message, but its psychic and social structure remains the same. When it proclaims to embrace values such as ecological harmony, social equality, and communal solidarity, it is still mainly addressing the insecurities and anxieties in individual consumer lives and proposes private consumption as the main solution to these problems. Ironically, in the so-called "ethical" advertising, we often see what Jhally considers as the polar opposites of humanity – i.e. "the best about us" and "the worst in us" – coming together. For example, in claiming to save the planet, we engage in "conspicuous conservation" and turn our "altruism" into another item of egotistical exhibition. In attempting to economize energy and resource usage, we often commit the "sin of thrift," which is manipulated to lead to excessive consumption and more waste generation. In trying to promote social equality and communal bonding, we welcome the marginalized members (e.g. farmers, workers, minorities, and non-human members of the ecosystem) to join our globalized consumer capitalism and pretend that all their desires are thereby satisfied and that social inequality and ecological problems are solved once and for all.

There are a few ways to explain why "ethical" advertising is full of these contradictions and paradoxes. The political-economic answer is that the corporate for-profit agenda manipulates altruistic, and collective values into serving private, individualistic goals. Yet if we dig deeper, we see that the problem is in fact embedded in the alienated nature of advertising itself: that it tries to promote human bonding through disembodied forms of communication (such as mass and social media) and establish emotionally invested connections in the mass society without bringing the bodies together. In the absence of real bodies, new media and technology have been used to simulate such intimacy and bonding in the virtual world: for example, Organic Valley's "Who's Your Farmer?" website lets consumers "like" the Facebook page of farmers who live within 50 miles radius; Chipotle's "Farm Team" video game teams up players with virtual farmers to grow virtual crops "together"; Patagonia's GPS tracking tool allows visitors to "inspect" its factories around the world and "meet" the workers that "personally" handled their clothing. However, no matter how vivid and realistic these simulations are, the same emotional investment cannot be made in virtual interactions as in our daily face-to-face contact. Body and desire are profoundly intertwined: this is the most rudimentary lesson that psychoanalysis has taught us. From the moment of birth to the moment of death, we derive enjoyment from nesting and embedding our bodies in its "holding environment" and continue to search for such enjoyment after being separated from it (the way in which our drives encircle their lost objects). This principle seems to be better received among the Chinese than the Americans.

Where should we go from here? We should learn to recognize our separation anxieties from our "holding environment," which are the products of hundreds of years of modern industrialization and mass consumerism. We should especially acknowledge the denials and defensiveness that are still present in the very industries and institutions that claim to be part of our healing, green solutions. The final takeaway of this study, thus, boils down to the acknowledgement of our separation anxiety: the more we can see the profundity of loss underlying our environmental crises (and their psychosocial and physical elements), the more honest we can be about our so-called "environmental" solutions. This is a significant part of grappling with our changing and suffering ecosystems – interrogating how we connect to our environments, how we tune into the world, both in physical and psychosocial terms. Advertising plays a big role in that tuning, which is why it is important for us to focus on its evolving campaigns and strategies. We need to be attuned to the fictions we are fed by market interests in order to stay focused on an ethics of recovery (and also discovery) of our worldhood. Environmentalism, after all, is but a part of a broader ecology of desire and cannot be reduced to narrow and vain efforts to buy the correct items and consume our way into ecological harmony.

References

Dodds, J. (2011). *Psychoanalysis and ecology at the edge of chaos: Complexity theory, Deleuze|Guattari and psychoanalysis for a climate in crisis.* New York, NY: Routledge.

Jhally, S. (2000). Advertising at the edge of the Apocalypse. *Critical Studies in Media Commericalism.* Ed. Robin Anderson and Lance Strate. Oxford University Press, USA.

Lertzman, R. (2008, June 19). The myth of apathy. *The Ecologist.* Retrieved from http://www.theecologist.org/blogs_and_comments/commentators/other_comments/269433/the_myth_of_apathy.html

Lacan, J. (1997). *The Seminar of Jacques Lacan: The Ethics of Psychoanalysis (Vol. Book VII).* Ed. & Trans. Miller, J-A. W. W. Norton & Company.

Žižek, S. (1999, March 18). "You May!" *London Review of Books,* 21(6), 3–6. Retrieved from: http://www.lrb.co.uk/v21/n06/slavoj-zizek/you-may

Index

For Product Safety Concerns and Information please contact our EU
representative GPSR@taylorandfrancis.com
Taylor & Francis Verlag GmbH, Kaufingerstraße 24, 80331 München, Germany